Comics, Manga, and Graphic Novels

Comics, Manga, and Graphic Novels

A History of Graphic Narratives

ROBERT S. PETERSEN

 PRAEGER

AN IMPRINT OF ABC-CLIO, LLC
Santa Barbara, California • Denver, Colorado • Oxford, England

Library of Congress Cataloging-in-Publication Data

Petersen, Robert S., 1961–
   Comics, manga, and graphic novels : a history of graphic narratives / Robert S. Petersen.
      p. cm.
   Includes bibliographical references and index.
   ISBN 978-0-313-36330-6 (hard copy : alk. paper) — ISBN 978-0-313-36331-3 (ebook)
   1. Comic books, strips, etc. —History and criticism. 2. Graphic novels—History and criticism. I. Title.
   PN6710.P415   2011
   741.5′09—dc22   2010037608

ISBN: 978-0-313-36330-6
EISBN: 978-0-313-36331-3

15 14 13 12 11   1 2 3 4 5

This book is also available on the World Wide Web as an eBook.
Visit www.abc-clio.com for details.

Praeger
An Imprint of ABC-CLIO, LLC

ABC-CLIO, LLC
130 Cremona Drive, P.O. Box 1911
Santa Barbara, California 93116-1911

This book is printed on acid-free paper ∞

Manufactured in the United States of America

Contents

Illustrations

Preface

This book reflects my circuitous arrival to the subject of comics by way of the study of narrative art and theater. I read comics when I was young, but I was never an avid collector and had largely lost interest in reading comics years before I first picked up Art Spiegelman's *Maus* in 1992 and then three years later discovered Scott McCloud's *Understanding Comics*. Although these works rekindled my interest in comics, they were not as influential as Victor Mair's *Painting and Performance* (1988), which ultimately inspired me to take up the task of writing this book. Mair traced the outlines of an ancient picture recitation tradition in India through Southeast Asia, China, and Japan and across the Middle East to Europe. He demonstrated that there was a deeper and broader interconnected history of narrative art traditions in the ancient world that has been carried on into modern times. Picture recitation formed the foundation for the visual literacy that would gradually develop into modern graphic narratives. This development is generally not the history of a few innovators but a broad and gradual dissemination of a new way to construct narratives that incrementally came into being through the drive to create novelty in the intensely competitive markets of commercial publications.

In tracing this broad history of graphic narratives, I am indebted to a great many pioneering scholars besides Victor Mair who have contributed significantly to the understanding of narrative art and comics. Among them, I credit Vidya Dehejia for her scholarship on Buddhist narratives in India, David Kunzle for his extensive work on early popular prints in Europe, and John Lent on Asian comics. In undertaking this ambitious project, I was very fortunate to have excellent colleagues who are expert in a number critical subjects. I thank Stephen Canfield for his insights into all things francophone, Janet Marquardt in medieval art, and Stephen Eskilson in contemporary art and graphic design, who were willing to discuss my work and give me valuable guidance along the way. I am especially indebted to Dr. Eskilson for his patient reading of the first draft that helped clear up some of my more indulgent digressions and convoluted arguments. Needless to say, the errors that remain are all of my own doing. I also owe a great deal of thanks to Glenn Hildt, the chair of the art department at Eastern Illinois University, not only for sharing his own knowledge of underground and independent comics but also for his enthusiastic support for my class on the history of graphic narratives, from which I have had many valuable opportunities to discuss and debate with my students the ideas contained in this book. To my students, I am eternally grateful for showing me new ways of thinking about graphic narratives and for asking hard questions, among them, what has this to do with comics?

Introduction

"The future of comics is in the past."

—*Art Spiegelman*

Stories in Pictures

In John Furnival's *Semiotic Folk Poem* (1966), a field of 25 squares forms an abstract arrangement of circles and triangles that when read correctly suggests the amorous liaison between a boy and a girl. On one level, a viewer needs to understand the "lexical key" at the bottom of the picture, which identifies the elements of the composition as a "laddie," "lassie," and "rye." The words suggest other stories and songs that require more information to fully appreciate, but they are evocative enough that one does not need to know the Robert Burns poem turned into a folk song "Coming Through the Rye" to grasp the meaning behind the interplay of the shapes. Though the whole story is visible, the viewer also needs to see how the shapes can be understood over time and order the images into a logical sequence from top to bottom. Finally, the viewer needs to see how the unfolding actions in the pictures are causally linked images, that one image represents a moment in time that leads to another moment in an unfolding chain of events.

Over the centuries, artists have found many creative ways to tell stories with pictures, but often the pictures remain coded, relying on conventions and symbols that could be understood only by the original audience long since gone. Before the advent of writing pictures of forgotten stories scratched on cave walls do not easily yield up their mysteries. Seeing a figure throw a spear at an animal, we may deduce the figure is hunting, but we

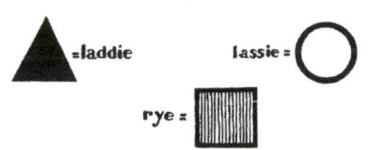

John Furnival, *Semiotic Folk Poem*, 1966. (Reproduced with permission from the artist)

may not know the reason for the hunt or if the hunt was successful because these aspects of the story occur before and after the actual moment being represented. Images do not easily tell stories because they are perceived more or less all at once, synchronically, whereas stories are naturally told or written diachronically, over time. Therefore, to understand a story from a single picture, it is necessary to have some inkling as to what the artist intended to communicate. Even when an artist adds more information about the story by describing earlier and later events, it is important that the audience knows how to follow the path of the story through the picture. These challenges that thwart our understanding of the story from a picture are what can reveal the great art of narrative images. For even as our eye synchronically sees the picture, the artist has also designed the composistion to lead our eyes to allow the story to unfold over time. The diachronic view allows the reader to understand the sequence of the actions and the synchronic view allows the reader to connect the moments together to see the larger themes and values that appear over time.

Furnival's *Semiotic Folk Poem* is a good example of a graphic narrative, which is a story told using nonmoving images. This term also describes comic books and graphic novels, but not film and animation. It is critical to distinguish the artistic qualities of graphic narratives from animated cartoons because even when they share a common visual style, they use different visual codes to tell the story and are different in the way the audience experiences them. With graphic narratives, the pace of reading the story is more like reading a book than watching a movie or a television show, where the narrative pace is dictated by the medium. But unlike the reader of a book, the reader of a graphic narrative does not always read the story in a linear fashion. Furnival's *Semiotic Folk Poem*, for example, does not unfold one picture at a time like words on a page; rather, by looking over the whole picture and seeing the relationships between the smaller individual pictures, with some empty and others filled with interlocking forms, the reader apprehends a sense of movement over time. From this example, it is clear that reading a graphic narrative involves distinctly different perceptual processes than do other genres of storytelling and looking at art.

Despite its long history and unique means of communication, the graphic narrative remains an elusive category between art and literature that has struggled to establish its own distinct terminology and theories about how it works. "Graphic narrative" is a relatively new expression first minted by David Kunzle,[1] but since picked up by many other scholars, among them Hillary L. Chute and Marianne DeKoven, as more content neutral than "comics" because it is not historically or culturally linked to a specific era or style. The term "graphic narrative" allows our focus to rest on two essential ideas: *graphic*, a composed and nonanimated visual form, and *narrative*, a crafted story. Another similar term that also eschews specific content is the French term "*bande dessinée*," which simply means "drawings in a row" and is often quite conveniently abbreviated simply as "BD," although the term BD does not specifically indicate that a story is being told. Graphic narrative is also better suited for the purposes of this book than "graphic literature," which unnecessarily emphasizes the idea of words. Although many people today are comfortable with the terms "comic art" and to a lesser degree "graphic novel," it seems inaccurate to talk of the wide range of popular narrative art from all parts of the globe merely as "comics" or, to use other specific terms, as "manga," "cergam," or "fumetti." Although graphic narrative is not as catchy or even memorable as some of these other terms, it serves as a valuable reminder of the broad range of works that define its current diversity and extensive history.

The Act of Reading Art

Wolfgang Kemp noted that "narratives—even narratives of beginnings—seldom come in isolation and are seldom original."[2] In this passage, Kemp is commenting on the way narrative is always situated between retellings and, like all language, is built upon shared structures for communication. Narrative fundamentally establishes a relationship between storyteller and audience, and for this reason, narratives are derivative in order to assure that all concerned understand each other.

Graphic narratives express ideas by transforming them into a story where the actions of characters become a way of describing experiences and sensations beyond one's own lived experience. Despite this common purpose across all storytelling forms, different means of communication are intrinsically linked to culturally formed modes of reading that convey different values and judgments. Lera Boroditsky has researched the linguistic structures of meaning in different cultures and how they change the way people perceive and recall phenomena. She observed that when people were given a set of pictures of a particular action, for example, a man growing old or a person eating a banana, they would invariably arrange the individual pictures into a narrative by placing them in the same direction they would read or write. For English speakers, this direction is left to right; for Hebrew speakers, this is right to left; but in the Aboriginal language Kuuk Thaayorre, which has no words for the idea of left or right, the pictures are always placed from east to west regardless of the direction the reader sits. By looking at the range of ways language influences perception, Boroditsky concluded, "These results show that linguistic processes are pervasive in most fundamental domains of thought, unconsciously shaping us from the nuts and bolts of cognition and perception to our loftiest abstract notions and major life decisions."[3]

By looking back into the history of graphic narratives, it is possible to see that as a mode of communication, graphic narratives often have a didactic quality in the way they seem to moralize about the actions they depict—either to extol some virtue or, through a negative example, to display some contemptible behavior. David Kunzle's authoritative history of early comic strips points out, "The moral quality of a [comic] strip is in direct proportion to the strength of the narrative element. To narrate is, first of all, to polarize a sequence of events into Before and After, Then and Now, Cause and Result, Crime and Punishment."[4] Kunzle notes the similarity of this kind of narrative strategy to many folktales that encapsulate the dualites of right and wrong, good and evil. Morality, or even immorality, is not essential to graphic narrative action, but it tends to put the narrative into sharper focus and heighten the drama.

The rise of the graphic narrative in Europe parallels the rise in popular melodrama, and it is in this direction that we find some important similarities. Melodramas, like most graphic narratives, are concerned with "the surface of the world—the surfaces of manners, the signifiers of the text," writes Peter Brooks, who observes that the objective of such artistic activity is ultimately to use the visible world to make sense of itself. In other words, melodrama is about "recognition and clarification, how to be clear what the stakes are and what their representative signs mean, and how to face them."[5]

In a similar fashion, graphic narratives rely on representing things in a way that is predicated on our cognition of how we make sense of our known world. In this respect, the visual elements in a graphic narrative are like objects on stage: they are animated with potential signification, adopting meanings beyond what they may simply represent in the everyday world. One important way graphic narratives differ from theater is that the drawings that make up the story are not at all dependent on being real objects in real space and real time to establish the story; rather, the images are compiled in the reader's mind, and inferences are drawn from the similarities and differences between the available visual forms and how that information correlates to real experience. As in Furnival's *Semiotic Folk Poem*, once we understand the code, we do not need to actually see bodies to perceive that we see bodies.

Graphic narratives not only describe the real world, after a fashion; they tend to be figurative, focusing especially on ways of describing a body in motion. The human figure provides the reader with a vehicle for emotional empathy. Bodies can also give a story a kind of spontaneity and allow the reader to see the action represented as if it is happening or unfolding before the reader's eyes. Bodies, and especially faces, communicate this spontaneity through the way they are intimately connected to our perceptions of body language. Readers naturally look to bodies and faces for clues to determine expression. It seems humans are predisposed to see faces and expressions, as the pioneer of modern comic art, Rodolphe Töpffer, pointed out in his study of physiognomy: "One must never forget that any human face, however poorly and childishly drawn, possesses necessarily, by the mere fact of existing, some perfectly definite expression."[6] More recently, Scott McCloud has also commented on this phenomenon, pointing out that the human capacity to see faces in suggestive abstract forms is an outgrowth of our ability to project our self-image onto those forms. McCloud concludes that because these projections onto the form are still connected to our self-identity, they become evocative images that have a compelling power over us.[7]

Reading a graphic narrative, such as a modern comic, requires some translation of coded images into real experience; by and large, however, the images are remarkably transparent in their meaning and do not need instructions or a lexicon for their comprehension. This is one reason why McCloud refers to comics as the "invisible art," for readers easily accept the visual conventions with almost no need for explanation. Ernie Bushmiller's long-lived comic strip *Nancy* is a good example of the essential conventions of comic strip narrative, which is so self-evident that it has been described as "easier to read than not read." Despite the economy of the information provided in the very simple drawing style, the *Nancy* strip has the studied grace of a classic joke with the setup (seeing the other kids getting squirted) and the payoff (the knowledge that Nancy is prepared for Sluggo's trick). The final event of Sluggo getting wet is self-evident because of the the way Bushmiller has set up the comic so that it does not even need to be shown for a reader to get the joke.

The most fundamental of all graphic narrative conventions is the fact that English readers can presume the order of events so that they form a meaningful sequence. Graphic narratives often help facilitate reading in one particular direction by being composed in such a manner that the eye of the reader moves easily from one action to another. The focus is initially drawn to Nancy because she is standing at the end of the fence, which makes her seem larger and closer to us in the picture. Our eye then moves to Sluggo, who is squirting the girl because he is the most active element in the picture, but he is secondary because he is smaller and over to the left of the picture. Last, we see a girl being hit in the face with the water; her gesture indicates that she is responding to what is happening to her, and her proximity to Nancy suggests that Nancy is also in danger of getting hit too. The eye then moves to the next, smaller panel where Sluggo is in the primary position because he is on the right and has the most active roll. But Sluggo is now smaller than before, and the horizon line has been raised a little, suggesting a different location and a later time. Although this moves us away from the threat to Nancy, it reinforces the primary theme and the expectation that Nancy is next. The smaller panel size makes us take in the action more quickly and thus renders it less significant than the final panel, where we see once again Nancy in the dominant position at the end of the fence. This time, however, a hose connected to the dripping faucet is our first order of significance and directly leads to Nancy, who is now facing off against Sluggo. Sluggo repeats his cowboy patter and, because of the earlier evidence, now appears to be on the verge of squirting her. Nancy, however, is now in the dominant position to the left and is almost assuredly going to get him before her gets her. The laugh comes not from actually seeing the final blast of water but from recognizing its visceral potential.

Bushmiller can assume his English readers will cast their eyes from left to right, but he has gone further in composing the elements to enhance our reading experience and our understanding of the joke. These compositional strategies form visual connections between elements that are called "paths."[8] Such paths often appear in all kinds of art and design. They may or may not convey a narrative, but graphic narratives are always dependent on paths to organize visual information into a meaningful sequence. Paths provide a means for the reader to sort the complex information of the composition into a meaningful hierarchy of relative importance. Artists use these strategies just as a magician uses sleight of hand to direct the eye of the viewer to create an illusion. An experienced craftsman such as Bushmiller can use paths to more economically tell the joke, confident that a reader will see just what he intends in just the right order.

Another important skill an artist must master is the use of visual conventions that allow the artist to employ a shorthand for describing ideas or phenomenon. Speech balloons or speech bubbles are one of the more obvious and nearly invisible conventions of comics. The loosely defined shape that holds the text does not actually represent a "balloon" or any real thing; it is, rather, a placeholder for a type of information that is understood as an indicator of sound or thought. We know, without conscious consideration, that by representing speech, the identical words in each of Sluggo's speech balloons do not represent some common object found in each scene but are words and sounds that stand apart from the scene itself, yet in the comic appear as opaque and visible as the characters themselves. This illusion can be ruined if the design of the speech balloon calls too much attention to itself by being improperly placed or by having a tail that is too long or goes too close to the figure speaking.

Speech balloons take on all kinds of shapes, or no shape at all, and by their design can change the way the text is read. The convention of speech balloons has a long history that can be traced back to medieval times, when they were called phylactery or banderole. Although phylactery looked nothing like today's speech balloons, they did have a similar function of representing the voice in a graphic manner. The idea of speech balloons is also related to all manner of visual codes that appear in graphic narratives to represent such invisible elements as music, noise, thought, and motion. These elements have been given any numer of different fanciful names, here they will be described collectively as emanata.[9]

E. B. White once wrote, "Analyzing humor is like dissecting a frog. Few people are interested and the frog dies of it." Indeed, there is nothing worse than having to explain a gag; a joke can never achieve its intended effect unless the basic elements of the humor are completely self-evident. Most critical to interpreting a gag is a sense of the context, that is, understanding why the characters are acting the way they do. Graphic narratives reward the viewer by showing something recognizable, but they produce novelty and humor by placing those known elements in a new arrangement. To an audience familiar with squirt guns, garden hoses, water faucets, and playing cowboys, the appeal of the comic strip *Nancy* is self-evident. The novel combination of these known elements creates a satisfying twist, which confirms our prior knowledge and proposes some new possibilities. In a lighthearted way, *Nancy* also plays with our sense of social justice—the expectation that Sluggo gets his just deserts—and it also demonstrates how innovation can overcome adversity, as well as the playful competition that exists between boys and girls. Without trying to read too much meaning into this gag, it is evident that the comic *Nancy* is a by-product of American culture in the 1950s and that its style of humor is aimed at American sensibilities from that time.[10]

Despite the cultural references in *Nancy*, almost any modern reader could decipher the basic narrative actions and have an understanding of what is most likely going to happen after the last picture. Psychologists who administer the Wechsler-Bellevue (WB) or Wechsler Adult Intelligence Scale (WAIS) have consistently proven that people of ordinary intelligence have the capacity to sort through a set of images and correctly arrange them so they make sense as a single developing action. Only when someone is unfamiliar with the content in the pictures will he or she have trouble discerning the proper sequence; for example, someone living in the country may not know how to hail a taxi, or someone from the city may not understand milking a cow. Apart from recognizing content, humans appear to have an innate capacity for recognizing signs that allow them to formulate a coherent narrative out of disparate pieces of information. That common intelligence can reconstruct a visual story just as the artist intended suggests that narrative art taps into our basic sense-making mechanisms in the brain, which allow us to predict, estimate, and anticipate.

Boris Breiger (1956) discovered an interesting corollary to the innate human ability for recognizing narrative patterns: though people will assemble picture narratives in the same way, their interpretations of the motivating actions represented in the pictures may vary considerably according to their cultural background. Identical arrangements of pictures on the intelligence test elicited different explanations between Americans, Germans, and Japanese.[11] Although this phenomenon has not been widely studied, it does reaffirm the idea that something fundamentally human is at work in the underlying process of reading narrative pictures, which must correlate to the way humans naturally process lived experiences and memories. Cultural ideas do not alter the shape of that interpretive process as much as they give it fuller meaning and significance. It is a valuable lesson for modern readers of ancient graphic narratives to remember that even if they recognize the plot of the story, they may not understand the significance of the actions.

Marking the course of the cultural ideas that have shaped graphic narrative form and interpretation is the objective of this book. Given that no one text can cover the entire breadth of this subject, this book will look specifically at three major conceptual developments that have guided its course: literacy, caricature, and the rendering of sequential action. Literacy was the first concept developed in human culture that established the idea that signs could be ordered into a deliberate sequence and formed around a grammar. Literacy allowed known stories to be told with greater sophistication, but it also was essential for helping to develop a structure of signs whereby original stories could be told in pictures. Caricature then helped to further specialize the visual language of narrative art. Unlike naturalism, where all surfaces and forms have a specific and consistant relationship to the visible world, caricature revealed that by selectively applying distortions to the rendering of a face or body the figure achieved an even greater capacity for expression and animation. Prior to this time, narrative art and nonnarrative art shared a common vocabulary; but with the invention of caricature in the 16th century, there began an exploration into a new means to simplify and amplify faces and figures that helped graphic narratives to become more expressive and appear more spontaneous as if the action were happening just as the viewer looked at the picture. The third and final aspect of graphic narrative development was the rendering of sequential action. Literacy and caricature pushed graphic narratives to evolve increasingly plastic means of communicating the flow of experience over time. With the use of sequential action in graphic narratives in the 18th century, stories could convey complex relationships between groups of images in what is called a montage, where the variation among a sequence of images creates for the reader a wholly new idea not seen in any one picture.

The history of graphic narratives also concerns the critical reception of these developments and how they were fostered or thwarted though censorship, copyright laws, publishing technology, and creator's rights. Altogether the history of graphic narratives represents the evolution of a special kind of visual literacy that has developed over thousands of years and has spread to every part of the globe. Unfortunately, the study of graphic narratives has often exclusively focused on modern, mass-produced comic books. The consequence of this narrow view is that it has limited the analysis of the form only to its modern manifestations. This limitation has distorted the nature of the medium of comics by exaggerating the significance of such modern genres as superheroes and obscuring the underlying and larger development of this visual language.

The common practice of focusing just on U.S. comics in the 20th century has established a kind of "comics exceptionalism," where the medium is regarded as if it were comparable to film or television, which simply did not exist prior to the invention of the movie camera or the cathode ray tube. Comics exceptionalism has also exaggerated the contributions of a few innovators and publications without acknowledging the broader changes that made such innovations possible. Comics certainly did not appear "whole cloth" as a direct result of a single technological advancement or artistic innovation; rather, they are the result of slow and broad shifts in visual literacy that occurred over centuries among hundreds of artists from many different parts of the world. For this reason, the study of contemporary graphic narratives (comics, comix, manga, manhua, *bande dessinée*, historitas, cergam, fumetti, etc.) must concern the broader history of narrative art; for without establishing the links to that history, the study of modern comics remains wholly disconnected from the deeper grammar of this visual language.

CHAPTER 1

The Language of Graphic Narratives

At its core, the history of graphic narratives concerns a series of conceptual developments that follow a similar trajectory to the invention of the alphabet. Each stage of the development of the alphabet, from the ancient Egyptian logographic hieroglyphs and Mesopotamian cuneiform to the Greek alphabet, was predicated on a previous era of communication where new strategies were slowly developed. Broader literacy eventually brought about new advances in writing with simpler letters and eventually punctuation allowing for even more efficient and complex communication. Thus, writing that began as a tool to aid in record keeping eventually developed the means to record a greater variety of experience through such forms as epic poetry and the novel.

Developments in graphic narratives have been expanded by new technologies, but more fundamentally on a widespread visual literacy that came from the broad dissemination of common images. For images to communicate more complex stories, they had to be based on a shared understanding of signs and their significance. Verbal literacy helped establish more complex visual literacy by lending it a concrete means for ordering events into a diachronic sequence. Once the idea of using a sequence of images was established, artists were able to structure their work into patterns that were gradually less dependent on an interlocutor or a text for their interpretation.

To understand the impact of literacy on graphic narratives, this chapter examines the various visual strategies for telling stories that developed in preliterate and early literate cultures across the globe and compare their means for communicating narrative action. Although this section by no means presents a complete history of early narrative art, it attempts to introduce the various distinctive forms of narrative art and describe their essential characteristics. By comparing these forms of narrative art, it is possible to discern the fundamental building blocks of this visual literacy.

Narrative Art before Writing

Though much of Paleolithic art is undecipherable to people today, a few ancient preliterate cultures have survived long enough so that some of their narrative art can now be partially understood. The most striking case is in the San rock paintings from South Africa, which were once falsely believed to be the work of a long-lost "Phoenician" civilization but were in the late 19th century actually discovered to be related to the mythology of the surviving San people of the Kalahari Desert. Because of the exposed desert conditions where most of the paintings have been found, it is difficult to date many of the paintings, but the oldest works have so far been carbon-dated at between 25,500 and 27,500 years old. Some of the mystery surrounding the paintings was caused by the fact that the San people had stopped painting with the encroachment of European settlers in the late 19th century. Furthermore, as a result of the subsequent impact of modern society, very little remains of this nomadic civilization. As researchers began to decipher the images on the rock and compare them to the San ethnographic record, it became evident that San rock art did not represent scenes from everyday life; instead, the paintings vividly represent a trance experience by a San healer or shaman. The San shaman comes out of trance at the end of a healing ceremony and relates to the others his trance experiences. Trance experiences among the San are not regarded as mere hallucinations but are considered real lived experiences, and the symbolic meaning of these experiences is taken seriously.

The connection with trance experience is evident in the Linton panel, which is a large rockface that was removed from its original location in the Drakensberg Mountains and is currently on display in the South African Museum in Cape Town. The panel has several large figures that are part human and part animal, representing the close affinity the San feel for animals while in trance. One prone figure with animal hooves has fish swimming around its head, indicating the notion that the trance experience has a floating, euphoric quality like swimming in deep water. Also near the figure's head is a snake flipped upside down with blood coming from its nose, suggesting feigning death or temporarily going into the world of the dead and the frequent nosebleeds that accompany trance experiences.

What makes this panel a fascinating example of narrative art is the way the various trance-experience symbols are interconnected by a fine red line marked with white dots. The line leaves the figure's mouth and branches off, connecting animals and people; in a way, it appears as a rope winding between the legs or as a track through the wilderness. The lines that irregularly criss-cross the surface of the rock represent an aspect of San mythology called *!gi*, which is natural power that runs through all things. The line defines specific relationships and possibly suggests some form of transformation over time. Whereas it is impossible to determine how the trance events described in the paintings unfolded, it is possible to see that there are multiple symbols which appear as a constellation around a loosely defined center. This particular kind of visual narrative strategy is called a simultaneous narrative because two or more different stories are overlapping each other and there is no fixed sequential order among the different narrative events.

Such preliterate, or oral, societies as the San have cultural features that are distinctive from those of literate societies because they have ways to store and retrieve important cultural information without the aid of writing. It has mistakenly been said that such oral societies lack history when, in truth, they often have very complex means for recording and remembering their past. Studies have shown that such societies tend to have elaborate rituals that allow them to memorize copious amounts of information organized in redundant systems, mnemonically supported by songs, dances, and visual culture. Oral cultures also tend to remain conservative about stylistic forms, since any individual changes might bring about a loss of their collective knowledge. Because oral cultures must function without writing, knowledge is imbedded in the living memories of the people themselves, so its recollection is dependent on the current needs of the society to know about the past.

Ritual knowledge is the central organizing principle for the way in which Aboriginal artists represent the stories, or "dreamings," from the spirit world known collectively as "dream time." The Papunya paintings by Aboriginal painters in central Australia represent separate mythic tracks across the landscape referred to as "countries," which reflect the segmentary religious character of their indigenous beliefs. Different local descent groups are responsible for maintaining the memory of particular countries, which cover vast distances across the harsh desert climate. By linking together with other groups' countries, disparate people can forge a relationship that helps sustain ritual organization. Children who inherit countries that are passed down through the father are called *kirda*, and children who have countries passed down through the mother are called *kurdungurlu*. The ownership of the ritual knowledge circumscribed by the country belongs to the *kirda* members, and the guardianship of the country is the responsibility of the *kurdungurlu*. Although guardians do not have the same claim to ownership, they are responsible for making sure the *kirda* maintain their ritual obligations to their countries. Most painters will only paint dreamings relating to their own *kirda* and will sometimes paint dreamings from their *kurdungurlu* rights, but artists will never paint another's country without being invited. *Kurdungurlu* will sometimes oversee the making of an acrylic painting to make sure the mythic events are properly represented. It is also common for several people to work together on one painting, pooling together their ritual knowledge and artistic skills.

The painted landscapes are full of abstract signs and patterns whose interpretation requires sacred knowledge of the dreaming and the landscape where the dreaming took place. Decoding a painting is circumscribed by certain conventional symbols: rock holes or campsites are represented by concentric circles, water or rain is represented by wavy lines, people seated are shown as small U-shaped designs, and utensils and tools are seen as straight lines. Very often, the view represents the land from above, cartographically, and symbols of footprints can be found marking the path of sacred ancestor beings. The characteristic dotting patterns that cover most surfaces of Western Desert acrylic painting derives from the decoration of traditional ritual objects and patterns derived from traditional body-paint designs. The patterns are described in three different ways: rows of parallel dots are called walking in a straight line (*yirrarni kanardi*), curved parallel lines of dots are called clusters of boomerangs (*wirlki wirlki yirrarni*), and a dotted spiral is called "to go from hole to hole" (*rdaku kari rdaku kari*), which describes the manner for hunting goannas.

The paintings often focus on one dreaming track through the *kirda*'s country; but depending on the status of the *kirda*, a country may be a location where several dreamings converge. Michael Jagamarra Nelson's acrylic painting *Five Dreamings* (1984) represents a meeting between the Flying Ants, the two Kangaroo ancestors at Yintarramuru, the Rain Dreaming near Mount Doreen, and the Rainbow Serpent Dreaming at Yilkirdi. Convergences of dreamings speak of social relationships, alliances, and common histories among various groups in the Western Desert region. In many ways, the paintings have become a way to reaffirm those connections at a time when many of the Aboriginal people are displaced from their ancestral lands.

A great deal of secrecy surrounds the meanings of the Aboriginal paintings, and depending on whom the artist is talking to, various levels of interpretation may be discussed. Christopher Anderson and Françoise Dussart relate several levels of interconnected meanings they discussed with the artist Japinjinpa regarding his work *Burrowing Skink Dreaming at Parrikirlangu* (1986). Japinjinpa openly discussed the public meaning of the painting that describes men hunting for Liwirringki (Burrowing Skink) by the use of controlled fires represented by the long straight lines. The concentric circles are conventional designs representing the camps where the men cooked the game they had captured. Other meanings are restricted according to the ritual status of the viewer, which was generally summed up by Anderson and Dussart (with Japinjinpa's permission) in this manner:

> In Japinjinpa's painting, the old men in the story are both subject and object: Liwirringki is both an old man at Yajarlu and the animal being hunted and eaten. The old men who are owners of the Dreaming today are also seen, in some ways, to *be* burrowing skinks themselves. Here the boundaries between the mythic past and the actual past and the actual present as non-Aborigines understand them are blurred. [emphasis in the original][1]

The simultaneous narrative of the painting enhances the dream-time mythology, where actions in the past are repeated again through rituals in the present. The painting does not privilege one time over another, and the meanings of the past are reflected in the present.

In response to the growing popularity of Aboriginal art, some observers have noted that the paintings are growing more visually complex in part as a result of the artist's greater control of the acrylic medium but also in what seems to be an effort to further obscure the ritual knowledge contained within the iconography so that it remains hidden to the uninitiated (see box 1.1).

Rock painting was the source of another long-lived oral narrative art tradition in North America. The Plains Indians had for centuries painted ceremonial images on rock; then, just prior to the arrival of the Europeans in the 17th century, the rock art began to record biographic events. It is not known how the biographic rock art began, but it seems to be historically related to the westward migration of Blackfoot, Gros Ventre, and Plains Cree Indians in the mid-17th century. By the 1800s, all the Plains Indians were engaged in producing rock art; the most prolific were the Blackfoot, Crow, Cheyenne, and Sioux Indians. Drawn from the symbols of the ceremonial rock art, biographic rock art depicts such expressive events as battles,

> **Box 1.1**   Aboriginal Artist Paddy Fordham Wainburranga
>
> Among contemporary aboriginal painters Paddy Fordham Wainburranga is a highly respected artist whose traditional depictions of the myths of his Mimi ancestors are bold and vigorous. His 1990 bark painting *How World War II Began* (*through the Eyes of the Rembarrnga*) is a poignant retelling of recent history when a dispute with Japanese pearl divers off the coast was soon followed by the bombing of the city of Darwin by the Japanese. These events are linked in the eyes of the Rembarrnga, who saw their harsh fate at the hands of the Japanese military as retribution for the earlier dispute. In the painting, the Japanese are depicted by the short trousers they are wearing. Beginning at the lower right, the story advances across the middle of the work to the upper-left corner, where the Japanese boats and planes advance onto Aboriginal territory, represented by the serpent. This particular composition does not follow the traditional system of simultaneous narrative form but seems to have been influenced by modern comics and uses frames to organize the story into specific events. Unlike in a modern comic, the individual panels are not arranged in a linear sequential order.

raids, and hunting scenes. Etched into the sandstone cliffs east of the Rockies, these pictures can be found in a wide swath cutting across the western prairie from southern Canada to northern Mexico. The largest concentration of rock artwork is located near the Milk River in Alberta, Canada, in an area Native Indians called Writing-on-Stone. More than 50 different sites with thousands of figures spanning the whole history of the Plains Indians can be found at Writing-on-Stone.

The biographic rock-art tradition is distinctly different from ceremonial images on rock because it uses more schematic and less detailed images with a deliberate emphasis on describing specific events happening over time. As in the Australian Aboriginal art, symbols that represent footprints or hoof prints are commonly used to describe the movement of people and animals. In later images from the historical period, dotted lines represent the path of a bullet. Another very common feature in biographic rock art is the use of multiple representations as a way of recording the number of horses stolen or warriors killed. These tally images are typically represented separate from the action and are arranged in neat rows in order to provide a synchronic count of the results of the raid or war party.

There are several narrative innovations that create a pictographic shorthand, making the action easier to read. An opponent may be represented only by a gun, or a horse by its tracks, and sometimes the repetition of a figure is a way of describing two different events happening to the same person over time. The simultaneous narrative style in rock art emphasizes the superlative moment for describing the relationship between the principle figures, at the same time indicating the total number of actions that occurred over the entire time of the event. One of the largest and most complex compositions is a battle scene drawn at Writing-on-Stone that represents the "Retreat up the Hill Battle" fought along the Milk River in 1866 between the Piegan Blackfeet and a war party made up of Gros Ventre, Plains Cree, and Crow warriors. This event was later described by a Piegan elder named Bird Rattle, who described the heroic advance of Chief Many Horses's wife, Lone Coupe. The chief and his wife both died in the battle, but the Piegan were ultimately victorious and soundly defeated the attacking war party. Hugh Dempsey, who researched the origins of the "Retreat up the Hill Battle" rock art, points out that in Bird Rattle's account, the rock art was a supernatural warning discovered by the Piegan elders *before* the battle. The elders, according to Bird Rattle, successfully interpreted the painting, allowing the people to prepare for the attack and ultimately be victorious in their battle. Dempsey speculates that the pictographs were obviously placed after the event. Over the years, however, through the retelling of the story, the purpose of the rock art assumed a mythic stature and no longer merely recorded an event but also foretold the future and was a living warning of potential battles to come. The unspecific time cues in simultaneous graphic narratives make the rock art susceptible to shifting interpretations depending on the needs of the context. This shifting is a detriment for documenting the historic past, but it is a strength when asserting new meanings that allow the past to be made relevant in the present.

Interpreting biographic rock art was largely made possible by interest in more contemporary Native American works on paper and hides. Collectively called robe and ledger art, these works were traded and sold to tourists, but they also appeared as one of the last ways the Native Americans had to communicate their stories after they had been driven from their ancestral homelands. The range of topics found in robe and ledger art is a little more diverse than that in biographic rock art; besides the common subjects of war records and hunting stories, there are also vision images, winter counts (calendars), and depictions of everyday life. Robe and ledger art was also practiced by a slightly larger range of Native American people than the rock art, with identifiable stylistic differences that were specific to the Crow, Blackfoot, Sioux, Cheyenne, and Pawnee Indians.

"Medicine robes," along with shields made from hides, were used as cere-monial dress that confirmed and enhanced the status of the wearer by dis-playing the spirit powers and associated ritual visionary symbolism. Animal and part-animal human figures representing guardian spirits play a promi-nent role in these works, alongside biographical symbolism that depicts such status-building events as horse stealing, leading a war party, and counting coupe, where warriors would better an opponent without killing him.

Ledger artworks were strongly influenced by contact with white settlers, missionaries, and the U.S. military, who traded or gave used paper ledgers to the Indian artists as a means to record their stories. The earliest ledger-drawn works were created by the Native American prisoners at Fort Marion in Florida, where the internees were encouraged to participate in the market economy by learning to produce commercial goods for tourists. Despite the commercial interests, ledger art remains a fascinating record of commonplace experiences in the lives of Native Americans. In ledger art, there is greater attention to natural details, especially in the clothing of the figures and the physical gestures of the horses. The wider range of subjects drawn by the Fort Marion artists in part resulted from the fact that they were prohibited from drawing Anglo-Indian battles, as well as from a fascination with the new soci-ety that surrounded them and their memories of their everyday lives before their imprisonment.

A careful study of the compositions of Cheyenne ledger art reveals remark-able consistency in the orientation of the narrative elements. Candace Greene observed that in scenes of warfare, a full 84 percent of the time the figure on the right is the Cheyenne.[2] In other compositions, including the subjects of hunting, horse raiding, and courting, the dominant male figure is also most often on the right side, setting up the understanding that the right and left spaces on the page display an unequal power relationship. Greene describes how male status is the common theme that runs through these representa-tions. Compositions where the Cheyenne male appears on the left usually indicate that the dominant male has been overthrown, as seen in the depic-tion of the hunting scene where the dying buffalo gores the hunter's horse. (For more on ledger art, see box 1.2.)

Oral narrative art compresses time to simultaneously express abstract rela-tionships connoting cultural notions of power, spiritual order, and social influence. Often for oral artists, mnemonic necessity dictates that they remember interconnections between actions rather than the precise sequence of individual events. The lack of specific time markers allows for a freer chronology of events and makes it possible for a past event to be reshaped to

Box 1.2   Ledger Art Tradition in the Work of Silver Horn

One of the preeminent artists among the Kiowa was a painter by the name of Silver Horn (Haubgooah 1861–1940) whose career spans the transition from traditional painter to contemporary artist. Silver Horn's brother was one of the interned Native Americans at Fort Marion, and he may have influenced Silver Horn's understanding of Western art. While employed at Fort Sill, Oklahoma, Silver Horn began to experiment with keeping a daily visual journal of his life recorded in a recycled record book for target practice. One hundred and nineteen pages were drawn in a continuous narrative style utilizing a line that folded back and forth from one page to the next indicating days, weeks, special events, and both Kiowa and Western months from the years 1893 to 1897. His Target Record Book is a unique diary adapted from the Kiowa Winter Count tradition of painting where an owl indicates a death; but unlike traditional winter count drawings which simultaneously represent all the year's events, Silver Horn invented a linear narrative design representing his daily life. Much of the diary today, unfortunately, has become cryptic due to a lack of understanding of the unique signs and symbols that Silver Horn invented. The calendar does record an interesting transformation in Silver Horn's sense of time. As he became more accustomed to the military regimen at Fort Sill, there is a gradual shift in Silver Horn's reckoning from Kiowa time markers to exclusively Western time markers. By 1895, Silver Horn stopped recording Kiowa names of the months altogether, and the daily record becomes dominated by markers indicating paydays and other ordinary routines of camp life at Fort Still. Later in life, with his eyesight failing, Silver Horn took up painting on leather hides, reverting to a medium that, less than a generation before, had been given up for the use of paper. His distinct style of art, with its elongated figures with colorfully rendered clothing, would provide inspiration to the first generation of Native American studio artists in the 1930s who were searching for a means to represent the traditional past.

fit the needs of each new context. Oral narrative art tends to be honed down to its essentials, with extraneous details removed so that the key players take focus in a heightened moment of contact, which reverberates with meanings on multiple levels. Abstract elements—the red lines across the surface of the Linton panel, the concentric circles for campsites in the Aboriginal art, or the dotted line representing the path of a bullet in Native American art—represent simultaneously a moment in time or a direction across time. Regardless of the culture, it is evident that simultaneous narratives represent, not an absence of time or history, but rather a heightened awareness of a moment caught in time, echoing from the past toward future retellings.

Literacy and Narrative Art

Much of the surviving early narrative art from literate societies memorialized significant political events. Both the Egyptian pallet of Narmer (3200 BCE) and the Assyrian Stele of Vultures (2525 BCE) have images of brutally vanquished armies, which served to demonstrate the military superiority of the ruling power that commissioned the works. Although both narratives have common visual elements, more is known about the specific function and context of the Assyrian Stele of Vultures that was created to honor the victory of the state of Lagash over Umma. The Assyrian stele is different than the Egyptian pallet in that it has narrow lines that divide one side of the stele into two sections and the other side into four, showing the oldest example of narrative register lines, which were used to organize the images on the stele into a readable order. The stele was read much like an early Sumerian text from bottom to top, with the preparations for war along the lower edge, leading to the battle formation in the middle, which concludes on the topmost register with vultures feasting on the carcasses of the fallen enemy. Scholars have noted that the stele actually has two distinct modes of communication on either side of the stele: one side represents the authority of the city god, Ningirsu, and the other the narrative of the battle as just described. It is the combination of the mythic and the historic modes of communication that attempts to give lasting religious significance to the singular historic event. Religious teachings and political propaganda, such as found in the Stele of Vultures, were originally formulated in written works that were largely inaccessible to most people until the visual power of the graphic narrative was used to introduce them into the broader public by putting the story on display.

Register lines provide visual organization much like the lines on a page. They can also be found in ancient Egyptian art and as far away as the Mayan culture in Central America and the Southeast Asian Khmer culture in Ankor Wat. What all these civilizations had in common was the development of a written literature. Ancient texts usually came either rolled up as a scroll on a spindle or as a codex with pages of wood, parchment, or bark bound on one side or folded in a fanlike fashion. The ancient Egyptian *Book of the Dead* was a scroll commonly placed in the tombs of high officials and pharaohs as a guide to the path from death to the afterlife. Because of the preservative qualities found in the sands of the Sahara, these texts are some of the oldest surviving texts in the world. Written on the woven and pressed pith of a common marsh plant, papyrus, Egyptian scrolls have survived from as far back as 1980 BCE. The word "papyrus" literally means "that which belongs in the house," referring back to its common bureaucratic use in ancient Egypt for cataloging inventories in warehouses. Its durability and easy manufacture made papyrus the writing material of choice for several thousand years in the ancient world surrounding the Mediterranean. All along a papyrus scroll, which could be up to 30 feet in length, narrow columns between two and four inches wide defined the organization of the text and images. In what is now called the papyrus style, the illustrations were framed by the column registers, placing the emphasis on the figures and objects without detailed backgrounds.

With the slow advance of literacy through the classical world, a variety of more complex strategies for telling stories were devised. Though the examples here follow more or less a chronological order, there is no evolutionary pattern to these various forms of early narrative art. Once a society developed a certain degree of literacy, its members tended to gravitate toward certain forms; but the mode of visual narrative used was a choice among a range of possibilities.

Single-Frame Narrative Art

One of the early masters of narrative art was a black-figure-vase painter in ancient Greece by the name of Exekias (sixth century BCE), who was renown for his exceptional skill in selecting a single poignant scene that evoked the tragedy of the whole story. The design on the amphora by Exekias depicts the tragic moment when in the heat of battle Achilles meets the Amazon Penthesilea and kills her. This much is clearly evident in the design with the warrior queen at the mercy of Achilles, but a more nuanced look at the figures shows Penthesilea turning back to look at him. A fateful gesture, as Achilles falls in love with her; but it is too late for him to check his battle fury, and she dies by his hand. Exekias's choice of this particular moment would not have been lost on the ancient Greeks, who were well versed in this story from the Trojan War.

In the example of the amphora by Exekias, a single scene describes the narrative action; it is through the careful choice of the moment depicted

Achilles killing Penthesilea, queen of the Amazons. Black-figured amphora (wine-jar) signed by Exekias as potter and attributed to him as painter, sixth century BCE, Vulci, Italy. According to the Greek myth, Achilles fell in love with Penthesilea at the moment she died. (British Museum, London, Great Britain © The Trustees of The British Museum / Art Resource, NY)

that prior and future events are implied but not represented. Such visual narrative representations are called monoscenic because the painting represents a single event and there is no repetition of characters or later scenes to suggest the passage of time. Monoscenic narratives require the reader to know the story well because there are few intrinsic visual clues to signify actions beyond the specific moment shown.

In discussing the way stories are represented, it is valuable to make a distinction between a story and a narrative. The particular choice of scene, the way events are ordered, the way the actions appear, all represent the narrative, which is how a story is shown or told at a particular time. The story is a larger and more amorphous category that includes all the related various narrative renditions of a tale that not only lets viewers understand what they are seeing but also allows them to compare this depiction with their memory of other representations and retellings. Artists create narratives out of our memories of stories. It is through their creative selection that the new narrative becomes a different, unique retelling that will, if memorable, shape future representations of the story.

Related to monoscenic representations are conflated monoscenic narratives, where more than one event is taking place though there is no repetition of characters or scenes. This type of narrative is demonstrated in the Attic black-figure kylix by the painter of the Boston Polyphemos, ca. 550 BCE. Across the outside of the kylix are represented several events from the part of *The Odyssey* (10.203–335) where the crew of Odysseus are given a potion that changes them into animals. This particular painting not only shows the transformation of the sailors but also depicts the escape of Eurylochos who warns Odysseus, and on the other side of the painting, the return of Odysseus armed and ready to confront the sorceress Circe. The use of conflation is a way of expanding the immediate narrative action to convey broader narrative meanings. By conflating the action to include Odysseus, the story is not just about the fate of the indulgent sailors but also conveys the sober intervention of their quick-thinking captain.

The painting does not have formal boundaries that demarcate one event from another, but the viewer's prior knowledge of the story makes it possible to sort out the various actions and to recognize the overall sequence of events. Single-frame narrative art often arranges the figures into smaller groups, creating what is called visual nuclei that help define distinct moments in the story. Greek narrative art developed this compositional strategy to a high degree, allowing for longer and more complex narrative arrangements along an unbroken frieze, as in the Siphnian Treasury (Dephi, 525 BCE) and the Parthenon (Acropolis, Athens, 435 BCE). Although both of these works are unbroken visually with actual frames, their sheer size and location—high up on top of large buildings—make it impossible to take in the whole narrative all at once. The north Siphnian Treasury frieze represents the mythic battle between the gods and titans over control of Mount Olympus called the Gigantomachy. The action does not represent a series of sequential events; rather, it depicts a number of thematically related scenes that are occurring more or less at the same time and thus represent a panoramic narrative. The groupings of figures define different nuclei in the composition, thereby allowing for more complex interaction between the figures locked in the battle and providing areas where the viewer's eye can rest as it takes in one portion of the frieze at a time.

The Parthenon frieze that appears inside the colonnade of the temple to Athena also takes into account the progress of the viewer moving across the

160 meter (525 feet) length of the relief carving. As a viewer moves around the colonnade to see the inner frieze, distinct nuclei appear in the composition that help define specific units of the narrative, which depicts the Panathenaic procession in honor of Athena. The frieze does not tell a sequential narrative but instead shows what has been called a progressive narrative, where there is no repetition of characters as the action unfolds like a parade. In this case, it is the viewer who moves to take in the event rather than the procession moving before the viewer.

In monoscenic, panoramic, and progressive narratives, the emphasis of the narrative is on the individual characters who are acting, not on the particular the actions the characters are making. In each of these forms of narrative art, there is no repetition of characters; therefore, the art focuses the viewer's attention to what Meyer Schapiro called "being in state," which he contrasted with narratives that have multiple character representations as "being in action."[3] With single-frame narratives where there are multiple representations of a character, the emphasis shifts toward the action itself as the viewer is shown what is happening. Narrative art with multiple representations of a character within a scene is called a synoptic narrative.[4] This is beautifully realized in Sandro Botticelli's (ca. 1446–1497) illustrations of Dante's *Divine Comedy*

"Inferno XVIII, 8th Circle of Hell: Punishment of Panderers, Seducers." Illustration to Dante's *Divine Comedy*, ca. 1480. (Bildarchiv Preussischer Kulturbesitz / Art Resource, NY)

commissioned by Lorenzo de' Medici (1482–1490), where Virgil and Dante make their way alongside the damned in hell. Dante and his guide are repeatedly represented as they make their way through the levels of hell, whereas those souls in torment are fixed in their eternal condition. The colors, composition, and synoptic narrative style all vividly portray the different epistemological conditions between the living and the damned.

The term "continuous narrative" has been broadly applied to a number of different kinds of narrative art, from Tommaso Masaccio's *Tribute Money* (1427) to Trajan's Column (113 CE). In both cases, multiple representations of characters exist, but the length and size of the frame vary considerably. *Tribute Money* is a single work within a longer series of frescos at the Brancacci Chapel that have a very clear frame that defines the action within a single scene. Christ and his apostles appear center, stopped by the Roman tax collector, and the story unfolds first to the left, where Saint Peter takes money from a fish's mouth, and then to the right, where he hands it to the tax collector. Although the painting has three compositional nuclei that shape the narrative action, the overall fresco is not so large that it cannot be taken in all at once and be read and reread quickly. In contrast, Trajan's Column is a 200 meter (656 feet) frieze that wraps 23 times around a column 38 meters (125 feet) tall. Emperor Trajan appears 59 times along the whole of the narrative marshaling his forces to repeated victory against the Dacians. Needless to say, it is impossible to take in the whole composition at once, and the height and location of the column outdoors make it difficult to read much beyond what can be seen from the ground. As in the Parthenon frieze, the long composition contains clear visual nuclei that define units of action that make it possible to identify distinct narrative scenes, but the overall effect is of the unstoppable march of Roman armies toward victory.

Because Trajan's Column requires the viewer to move about the column, it is compositionally similar to Chinese scrolls that require the reader to view the work one section at a time though there is no visual frame that breaks up the overall composition. Therefore, it is best to consider these longer compositions continuous narratives in order to distinguish them from the single-scene variety, like the *Tribute Money* mentioned earlier, which are more accurately described as synoptic narratives. The distinction is important because a synoptic narrative allows for quick reading and rereading of the entire frame; hence the moral of the action is more apparent because the figures tend to represent attitudes and conditions, like an aphorism, that can be summed up in a few words. Continuous narratives, on the other hand, emphasize the unfolding continuity of the scenes. Just as beads strung together cumulatively create a necklace, each scene in the unfolding continuous narrative is designed to impress on the viewer the complex progression of the whole journey.

The most famous continuous narrative in Europe is the Bayeux Tapestry, which commemorates the Norman and English Battle of Hastings (1066 CE). The impressive embroidery, done in eight different colors, spans more than 70 meters (230 feet) in length and contains as many as 50 different interconnected scenes. The Bayeux Tapestry relates the political motivations, battle preparations, and ultimately the humiliating defeat of the English. As in Trajan's Column, there are symbolic references to the mythic past, which are intended to lend greater urgency and significance to the battle. Unlike the column in Rome, however, the reasons for the creation of the Bayeux Tapestry remain something of an enigma; the images stitched into the story sometimes reveal contradictory messages, which complicates the idea that the tapestry was commissioned merely to celebrate the Norman victory. The victorious Norman king, William, is depicted similarly to villainous Herod in the New Testament, whereas the eventually defeated king of England, Harold, is shown in a more tragic and sympathetic manner. The peculiarities of these mixed messages are perhaps a result of the origins of the Bayeux Tapestry, which was most likely made in Canterbury by the vanquished English monks and nuns. Although the work was commissioned by the Normans as a memorial to their victory, it also subtly encoded the memories of those defeated.

The most common varieties of single-frame narrative art are monoscenic and synoptic. Both use a relatively small frame that allows the viewer to take in a few characters in a limited number of actions, and both are predominantly found in codex illustrations. Continuous, panoramic, and progressive narratives are all longer works that adapt well to scrolls that are unfurled one section at a time, or around a monument where the viewer moves from one scene to another (see box 1.3). The chief difference between the smaller and larger works is how they choose to represent the passage of time. The number of different actions represented is typically greater in synoptic and continuous narratives, where the convention of using multiple representations of single characters allows for more specific actions being narrated over time.

Multiple-Frame Narrative Art

The earliest and most common type of multiple-frame narratives are called cyclic narratives, where each picture in the sequence represents a unique scene and each subsequent picture is related through a common story or related story. The individual frames do not have a causal relationship—one

> **Box 1.3** Single-Frame Narrative Types: A Comparison
>
> | Single-Frame Narrative Type | Multiple Images of Characters | Multiple Events | Can Be Seen All at Once |
> | --- | --- | --- | --- |
> | Monoscenic | No | No | Yes |
> | Progressive | No | No | No |
> | Panoramic | No | Yes | No |
> | Continuous | Yes | Yes | No |
> | Synoptic | Yes | Yes | Yes |

action does not lead directly to another as it would in a comic book. Instead, each frame represents an autonomous moment in the overall narrative much like a series of monoscenic pictures. The Temple of Zeus at Olympia (470–456 BCE) depicts the 12 labors of Herakles in the metopes. Each scene represents one of the labors, and all the scenes taken together represent the complete heroic accomplishments of Herakles, which will eventually lead to his apotheosis. Jocelyn Penny Small has pointed out that it was more important to classical artists and audiences to see the gist of what occurred rather than to see sequential accuracy.[5] Aristotle said as much in his *Poetics*, where he preferred the general truths of poetry to the specific facts of history. Cyclic narratives emphasize those general themes rather than the specific events of a story. They are more effective in summing up the idea behind the story than in telling the whole story from beginning to end. For this reason, they are often used as a didactic tool to reinforce the morals found in a story.

Cyclic narratives assume a temporal progression, where one picture is understood to precede another, but the meanings that can be derived from cyclic narratives are not limited to those linear temporal orientations. At the Abbey Church of Saint Michael from the 10th century CE, the Hildesheim bronze doors are designed in 16 scenes from the Bible in two columns. The first column tells the Old Testament story of the fall of humankind and the expulsion from Eden, and the second column tells the New Testament story of Christ's crucifixion and resurrection. Each story is arranged in such a way that by reading downward on the left and then upward on the right, the events follow a chronological order; but by looking across to the event in the other column, the viewer can make thematic associations between the Old and New Testaments, for across from Eve's temptation is shown Christ's crucifixion. Given that people viewing the doors were accustomed to reading horizontally from right to left, the organization on the Hildesheim bronze doors emphasizes the medieval notion of prefiguration over the actual temporal order in the narratives.

Cyclic narratives are more dependent on words for comprehension than are linear narratives and are often used in book illustration alongside the text of the story, where they provide clarity and focus to the story. When a cyclic narrative appears by itself, as in the metope reliefs of Herakles, the story must be well known, or in the case of some traditions, the pictures become a tool for storytellers who provide the narrative details. Picture recitation, as it is commonly called, has existed for centuries in many parts of the world and has been chiefly responsible for the dissemination of some stories across the globe. According to the research of Victor Mair, picture recitation most likely developed first in India, as far back as the fourth century BCE, where a smattering of references inside Hindu, Buddhist, and Jain texts suggests a thriving subculture in picture recitation. In the Hindu text of the *Arthashastra*, for example, in a list of low-status entertainers, there is the name for a picture showman (*patua, manka*, or *saubhika*). The common traits found in all these early references are that the players were itinerant, low-status people who essentially begged for alms by spreading out a painting on cloth and reciting stories as they sang and danced. Victor Mair has built up an extensive case that these itinerant performers spread outward from India and by adapting their stories to the local culture established themselves as far away as Sweden, Spain, Japan, and Indonesia. Their moralistic and educational stories provided both topical commentary on current events and religious themes dealing with punishments and rewards.[6]

The Pabuji *bhopo* of Gujarat, in eastern India, is among the few surviving picture recitation traditions in India. The performer, called a *bhopo*, is performing a story of the legendary hero Pabuji. He is accompanied by his wife, who sings and collects money during the performance, which lasts all night long. *Bhopo* are more than just street entertainers; they also function as folk-priests or shamans serving poor rural communities with their small, portable shrines. The performance is part of a low-caste religious practice, which blesses the audience and the sponsors for their participation. *Bhopos* seldom survive on their performances alone and typically need to supplement their meager income with farming or some other trade such as animal trainer or village veterinarian.

The picture reciters of Bengal in western India perform a tradition called *patuan* and belong to one of the lowest castes in India, Chitrakars. With the rise of Islam in the 16th century, many Chitrakars converted to Islam to escape the plight of their lowly Hindu status. Despite their conversion, Chitrakars continue to perform Hindu stories and demonstrate extensive knowledge of Hindu customs in their recitations of stories from the *Ramayana* and the *Mahabharata*. Other stories represented in *patuan* picture recitation include the *Sahib pat*, of the Santhal Revolution (June 30, 1855), an account of the historical event that has been passed down orally among the Chitrakars. New stories have also been commissioned, including a rendition of the French Revolution,[7] an adaptation based on the movie about the sinking of the *Titanic*, and the terrorist attack on the World Trade Center.[8]

Picture recitation provided an important link for communicating ideas from the world of literate society to that of preliterate society. Buddhist monks in many parts of Asia commonly employed picture recitation to carry moral messages to their followers, which helped disseminate Buddhist teachings across much of Asia. Buddhism was especially influential in developing narrative strategies because of the pedagogical character of its stories (jataka) that often spoke of the process of becoming enlightened. In Julia K. Murray's analysis of ancient Chinese scroll paintings she observes that it was not the technology of the scroll that brought extended narratives to China rather it was the arrival of Buddhism that inspired longer narrative works painted on scrolls.[9] Buddhism's influence on narrative art is an important example of a recurring motif in the history of graphic narratives: the need to communicate an idea often predicates the technology used to communicate that idea. This is why the history of graphic narrative is essentially a conceptual history of a visual language because as the ideas for communicating narratives advanced, they in turn spurred technical innovations to help further those aims.

Many of the narrative strategies that Buddhism inspired carried over into the Buddhist monuments themselves and provided a ritual framework for the recitation inside the sanctified space. The largest cyclic narrative ever devised is the Buddhist monument Borobudur (Central Java, 760–830 CE). Nearly two miles of relief carvings depicting the many lives of Buddha wrap 10 times about the mountainlike monument. The common theme in each picture emerges from the many virtues the Buddha conveys in his spiritual journey toward enlightenment. Walking through the long corridors lined with relief carvings, the pilgrim would have been led by a monk narrating the story and the morals according to what is represented in each picture. At the base of the monument, the carvings begin with the simple moral tales found in the Buddhist parables called the Jataka. These stories along the lower level are appropriate for lay practitioners with a minimum of Buddhist knowledge. The stories gradually become more and more complex and reflect higher levels of Buddhist learning as pilgrims approach the top of the monument.

Borobudur represents the fullest embodiment of a whole library's worth of texts into art, and yet all by itself it cannot by tell the stories of the lives of Buddha. Literacy had allowed for new concepts in story organization and created the notion of ordered sequences of images; but for pictures to become an autonomous means for telling stories, the pictures needed to have a visual means to describe phenomena over time. Doing this required not just images ordered sequentially but also a way of conveying gesture and expression unfolding one moment to the next. This next advance in the visual language of graphic narratives would come about only with the invention of caricature and the development of a popular press. With these innovations in visual communication, artists would seek to capture the imagination of literate audiences by rendering urgent and outrageous stories that reenact the drama of a moment as if it were unfolding before their eyes.

Chapter 2

Popular Prints and Caricature

Popular prints provided an important medium for the development of graphic narratives by encouraging greater diversity and complexity in the way stories could be told with pictures. Audiences of popular prints sought to be entertained, and so artists were pressed to create work that continually provided novelty at the same time as they remained accessible. The need for novelty encouraged artists to explore stories that were wholly original or drawn from current events, thereby expanding the range of topics in the popular press to more than was possible under religious patronage alone. Popular prints also encouraged the development of a visual language that would be self-evident and reward an audience's continued engagement. The visual language of popular prints assumed many of the conventions for representing authority and depravity from the fine art world, but it also expanded that vocabulary to include new visual representations of voice, sound, and movement, as well as the graphic means to communicate asides, thoughts, and dreams.

Popular Prints in China

A woodblock print of the Chinese Buddhist Diamond Sutra (dated 868 CE) is the earliest surviving print publication, and yet the intricate lines that reproduce the brushwork quality of the Chinese characters suggest that this was already a fully developed technology that had been in use for several centuries. Despite the huge advantage China had in adopting print technology early in its history, the printing press was not intended to make information widely available; rather, it was used as a means to accurately reproduce long documents for official use. Early ambitious print productions included the entire

Buddhist canon with more than 6,000 volumes. The total number of copies made of each volume remained relatively small because the publication was not intended for the general populace. Popular-print books in China remained a rare commodity for many centuries because the best quality ink, paper, and wood used for printing was under direct government control.

Such individual popular prints as posters and home decorations were designed for mass consumption and thus were of inferior quality and seldom preserved. Early records describe woodblock prints being used as New Year's prints (*nianhua*), which were posted on the New Year with the hope that they would inspire protection, prosperity, and virtue in the coming year. Such Chinese Taoist and Buddhist deities as door and kitchen gods were the frequent subject of these prints, but also depicted were historic events, legends, theatrical scenes, and pious Confucian morals. Images of the demon queller Zhong Kuei date back to the Northern Song Dynasty (960–1127 CE) and have remained a popular staple of *nianhua* publications ever since. The legend states that Zhong Kuei was a brilliant scholar who had a hideous countenance that kept him from receiving his just recognition. He appears as the magistrate of the underworld, brandishing a staff in order to keep at bay other unseen demons, and he becomes the archetype for the avenging magistrate, a role that would be explored in later popular literature.

One of the earliest popular-print stories was the *Twelve Confucian Tales of Filial Piety*, which first appeared in written form in the Yuan Dynasty (1279–1369 CE). All 12 tales appear on a single page, with each story represented by a single medallion that sums up the moral message. In each case, a devoted son goes to great lengths to honor and care for his parents: in one instance, the son sells himself into slavery to pay for his parent's funeral; in another tale, he carries his mother on his back to escape war and famine. The pictures describe only a few choice details and, like most cyclic narratives, rely on a reader's prior knowledge of the action to make sense as a story.

Moveable type first appeared in China as early as 1041 CE, but it never caught on because of the difficulty of using thousands of separate characters to reproduce the Chinese calligraphic writing. Moveable type was more widely used in 13th century Korea, where the language needed fewer individual characters to form words; it would eventually be developed in Europe by Johann Gutenberg in 1440 with cast-metal type. Individual pages composed and carved on woodblocks continued to be a more pragmatic solution to replicating the handwritten character of the Chinese and later Japanese languages.

The wide gap between the literate elite and the unlettered general populace persisted until late in the Yuan Dynasty. Popular publications were eventually able to flourish in the southern region of Jianyang, where materials used in publishing were considered too inferior for official government purposes. Publishers in Jianyang at this time worked in relative obscurity from official concerns and devoted their energies to appealing to as wide a popular audience as possible. A few of the extant Jianyang works from the 1320s bear the description "Newly printed, fully illustrated popular stories" (*xinkan quanxiang pinghua*); these stories were published in a format called *shangtu xiawen*, where the upper third of each page was dedicated to illustration. A new genre published in this *shangtu xiawen* form comprised historic fictions based on the legendary exploits of such exemplary magistrates as Judge Bao, which have been described as the first murder mysteries ever written. Other kinds of texts—Buddhist prayers, divination manuals, dramas, and classic texts, for example—also used this *shangtu xiawen* format, and from among these various kinds of texts emerged creative ways of mixing words and pictures.

A number of early Ming Dynasty Judge Bao texts in the *shangtu xiawen* style demonstrate novel ways in which the words and pictures support, confirm, and negate each other according to established conventions. *Shangtu xiawen* illustration was organized to be viewed in the same manner as the Chinese text below it, from the upper right down to the lower left. Most figures look and move in this leftward direction, with only a few exceptions, as when characters are returning home or when an evil character enters to perform some deviant behavior. In a similar manner, the right-left axis is used to reflect social standing, with the upper right reserved for persons of status and power and the lower left, by contrast, for figures of lower rank. The stories used these conventions to thematically link narrative actions and highlight moral and immoral actions. In one instance, Judge Bao attempts to dislodge a demon snake in a temple and the snake maintains the upper-right position in each illustration, a position normally held by Judge Bao. This reversal may reflect some sympathy the illustrator felt for the demon snake, but a more likely answer is that the illustrator wanted Judge Bao to battle a formidable opponent and so created the impression that this was no ordinary snake by placing it in the upper-right portion of the image.

Other conventions established at this time were the use of square patterns on the floor to give the impression that the viewer was looking down on the scene with a portion of the roof removed, a hierarchic scale where more important characters were rendered slightly larger, and balloonlike shapes that emerge from characters to represent dreams, magic spells, and the human soul. Many of these conventions, along with the print technology itself, found their way to Korea and Japan, where they would influence the development of narrative art in those regions for many centuries to come.

European Medieval and Renaissance Popular Press

One of the oldest-surviving European woodblock fragments is dated between 1370 and 1380. The French "Bois Protat" block, as it is called, represents a small portion of a scene of Christ on the Crucifix and was most likely used for printing portable fabric altars rather than printing on paper. The fragment shows a group of three men below the right side of the crucifix, and emanating from the mouth of the frontmost figure is a phylactery, or scroll used to represent speech.[1] The beginning of the scroll touches the mouth of the figure, and the sentence in Latin flows outward and eventually upside down toward Christ, visually linking the patron with the Crucifixion. The visual link the scroll creates between the speaking patron and Christ was an effort to convey the power of human speech to assert relationships even when it compromised the legibility of the words.

The representation of scrolls in paintings first appears as an adaptation of Greek and Roman "Honor Cloths," which were draped behind authors as a sign of their eminence and later were understood as a visual sign for someone being an author. Such later depictions of scrolls as at the eighth century Coptic Church mural in the monastery of Saint Apollo at Bawit, Cairo, shows the Christ child holding a scroll while seated in the lap of Mary and surrounded by the elderly apostles, who all carry books. The scroll, in contrast to the books, represents the original prophetic voice of Christ, which would only later be recorded in the different Gospels of the New Testament. Thus, the idea of the scroll is not a record of past events but a vehicle for an original expression, a way of conveying the first utterance.

Laura Kendrick persuasively argues that the motivation behind textual illumination in the medieval era was an effort to embody the "text within the text," that the words on the page were indeed the voice and body of God through his apostles.[2] There were many political, cultural, and spiritual reasons for embodying the text within itself, but one was the need to distinguish it from the classical and pagan way of seeing the texts as disembodied, in a sense lacking a voice that needed to be contained within a reciter. By illuminating their texts, medieval Christians hoped to convey greater authority in the text and to represent through illustrating a body—the body of Christ—an image that would act metaphorically as its speaker. By making the book a work of art, medieval illuminators hoped the reader would accept the book as the ultimate source of knowledge, one that was authenticated beyond the interpretation of a speaker.

The earliest popular printed materials (broadsheet) followed the biblical illustrative traditions and were designed to appeal to Christian pilgrims who wanted a modest means to remember a particular saint or Christ's Passion. The Swabian print from the mid-15th century depicting *The Tortures of St. Erasmus* is an early example of a broadsheet commemorating the penitent suffering of a saint. The print organized the episodes as a series of 12 images, arranged in a grid, which focus on the nine different brutal tortures enacted before the saint's final beheading. The cyclic narrative–style pictures, like the 12 labors of Herakles from the classical world, describe a well-known story in a formulaic manner; thus 12 sufferings were often attached to a saint's story regardless of his or her actual biography.

When secular original stories appeared, they were based on similar religious themes and followed similar religious designs. The wood-cut print *My Heart Doth Smart* (ca. 1485), by Caspar of Regensburg, mimics the themes of a saint's tortures and applies them to the trials of being in love. In a panoramic fashion, a series of thematically related images of hearts being tortured surround the central picture of a man kneeling before a naked woman, lamenting, "Oh maiden pretty and tender, free me from the suffering and close me in your arms."[3] Panoramic narratives were a fairly common narrative strategy for religious icons that allowed for large thematically unified compositions, but without an unfolding series of actions,

Synoptic narratives, where a story unfolds in several directions across a unified background, often employed letters or numbers to help the reader link portions of the picture to an accompanying text. This strategy is seen in the Bavarian print *Origin and Character of the Swine Who Call Themselves Jesuits* (1569), which is read back and forth from the top to the bottom according to the accompanying letters. Curiously, the artist left out the letter *J* in this sequence, perhaps as a further reminder of his aversion for Jesuits. Print propaganda flourished from this time forward, catering to one side or another of the ongoing religious wars between Catholics and Protestants or indulging either side in their mutual obsession with anti-Semitism. Depictions of one creed or another as animals or as possessed by demons constitute the bulk of early popular prints. Their widespread proliferation across Europe is evidence that these prints were able to stir up powerful passions.

Early prints in Europe were fairly expensive; in England, the cost was anywhere between threepence to a whole shilling.[4] Even among the lower-middle classes, the price of a broadsheet might constitute a month's wages. They were more like moderately priced art books rather than newspapers and would not be widely accessible for lower-class audiences until the advent of the chapbook in the early 19th century. Broadsheets were available through booksellers, but they were also sold in the streets by traveling performers of picture recitation. This development can be seen in an illustration from 1830 of an Italian picture-recitation performance, where broadsheets for sale can be seen in the woman's hand and in the performer's hat. Although the stories were different, the European picture recitation bore many similar features to the Asian tradition originating in India. In both continents, the tradition was maintained by low-class itinerant performers who used passages of music and song to help tell a story. Though the origins of picture recitation in Europe are relatively obscure, performers called *cantabanco* (bench singer) first appeared in Italy in the first half of the 16th century. Today, such performers are referred to as *cantastoria* (story singers). From Italy, the practice of picture recitation spread throughout Europe and died out only with the advent of radio and television. As in the broadsides, the narrative content of the *cantastoria* consisted of religious and political propaganda, as well as tales of horror and heinous crimes. This content can be seen in a German print from 1626 that has the descriptive title "True and Horrible News of what happened and took place in the town of Limburg with daughter of a rich baker called Catherine, who bore seven illegitimate children and murdered and killed them all."[5] This broadsheet also includes a note on how the story should be presented, "to the tune *Come up to me bids the Son of God.*" Thus the two mediums complemented each other, supporting and enlivening the artistic form and narrative content of each.

By the 15th century, secular stories of adventure and moral allegories were among the most popular books published. These included the *Travels of Marco Polo*, Giovanni Boccaccio's *Decameron*, and Sebastian Brant's *The Ship of Fools*. The illustration of these tales was a critical selling point, and publishers overcame challenging technical hurdles to find ways to bring words and pictures together. The chief obstacle was the combination of cast-metal type for the words and woodblock cuts for the illustrations. The different temperament of the materials under the pressure of the printing press meant that most books had their words printed first and illustrations inserted later. Another persistent problem was the division of labor wherein the separate guilds of printers, writers, and illustrators fostered many inconsistencies and contradictions in the way printed books were illustrated. Often, pictures bore only a casual relationship to the text because the publishers regularly reused illustrations from one publication and inserted them into another. In 1473, Günther Zanier helped spread that practice by instructing his illustrators to make their pictures type-measure wide so that they could be more easily inserted and reused among various publications and even within the same book. A decade later in an edition of the *Seelenwurzgarten* from Ulm, one woodcut was reused 37 times; and though the publication boasted 134 illustrations, that was accomplished with only 19 different woodcuts.[6]

Brant's *The Ship of Fools* in 1494 was illustrated by the young Albrecht Dürer (1471–1528) and became one of the most widely published secular books of the time, with translations in Latin, French, and English. Dürer did almost all the 114 drawings for the publication, adding his astute observations of daily life and a kind of playful immediacy to the allegorical depictions of foolish characters. The character of these early designs influenced many later popular publications, which also followed the example of depicting various social ills in the guise of people with foolscaps.

Dürer had the good fortune of being born in Nüremberg at a time of tremendous expansion of print culture. His own godfather, Anton Koberger, became one of the leading printers in Germany and was famous for his 1493 publication of the *Nüremberg Chronicles*, which was one of the most copiously illustrated books of the day. Dürer, like most artists who worked in woodblock prints, did not cut the design into woodblocks himself but, rather, drew on the wood directly or had his drawing pasted to the wood so that a master carver could cut the design for publication. During the 1490s, Dürer would learn the new art of engraving and would produce his own designs. Engraving was more durable than woodblocks; because it was done in metal, like the type, it did not warp or crack under pressure from the press.

Engraving was also a more direct means of rendering the image for reproduction because the groove that was cut in the metal was filled with ink to become the actual line reproduced in the image. The process allowed for more gradations of black through the use of cross-hatching and further encouraging artists to employ more intricate and nuanced linework in print reproduction. The delicate work of rendering words within illustrations was also made easier, and so words began to appear with greater frequency inside pictures, where they could bend and curve to create very elaborate phylacteries. Hans Sebald Beham's vivacious and vulgar etching *Peasant Dance* (1537) displays some of the virtuoso flowing lines found in etchings. The figures dancing to the musicians in the first frame grow evermore frolicsome in their dancing until—as seen in the last row of pictures—the dance descends into retching and sexual foreplay. The elegant phylactery in the last frame aptly sums up the action when the man says to his vomiting friend, "You really are too vulgar."[7]

Just as phylacteries became more commonplace in prints in the 17th century, there was a growing aversion for the use of phylacteries in paintings. Art critic and historian Giorgio Vasari belittled the practice by declaring, "This thing pleased Bruno [di Giovanni] and other foolish men of the time, just as today it pleases certain clumsy fellows who have thus employed vulgar devices worthy of themselves."[8] From Vasari's comment, it is evident that phylacteries were not simply convenient devices for representing a voice but were also laden with class associations and possibly with even darker connotations. Many cartoons from the period often follow the aphorism that silence is a virtue. Devils and corrupt politicians were more likely seen to speak using phylacteries, whereas virtuous characters were more often depicted as silent. When virtuous characters speak, they tend to use text without the fancy scroll-like boarders of the phylactery. Underlying this distinction in the use of phylacteries was a broader cultural aversion for things emanating from the mouth. In medieval art, exorcisms were often depicted as demons flying from the mouth—an image that can also be found in many prints from the period. An early British cartoon from the 17th century employs a phylactery held in the hand of the Pope as demons fly from his mouth to the mouths of other accomplices nearby.

A phylactery held in the hand often had a slightly different signification than a phylactery emanating from the mouth. As seen in the aforementioned 17th century cartoon, the Pope is not speaking to those present, whom he is infecting with demons, but actually revealing his true motive to the viewer. Here and elsewhere, a phylactery held in the hand serves the same purpose as a theatrical aside or soliloquy, where the character on stage directly addresses the audience and explains his or her motives. The hand phylactery suggests greater sincerity and a way for characters to express thoughts not spoken aloud, much the same way a cloudlike speech bubble functions in comics today.

Fancy scroll-like phylacteries were in evidence until the mid-18th century, when they were replaced with simpler and less convoluted shapes. The simpler shapes allowed for more text to appear in the print, but they also point to changing ideas about speech and texts. Interpreting the meaning of these changes is difficult because they constitute hundreds of years of artistic and cultural change, but it may be safe to say that they reflect the loss of medieval associations of voice and authorship with the scroll and the development of new allegorical associations. A seminal moment in that shift took place in 1720, when wild financial speculation brought about the catastrophic economic failure of the South Seas Bubble in Britain, which became a major subject for political and social commentary in satirical prints. In one print called "The Bubblers Medley," there appears what might be the first instance of a

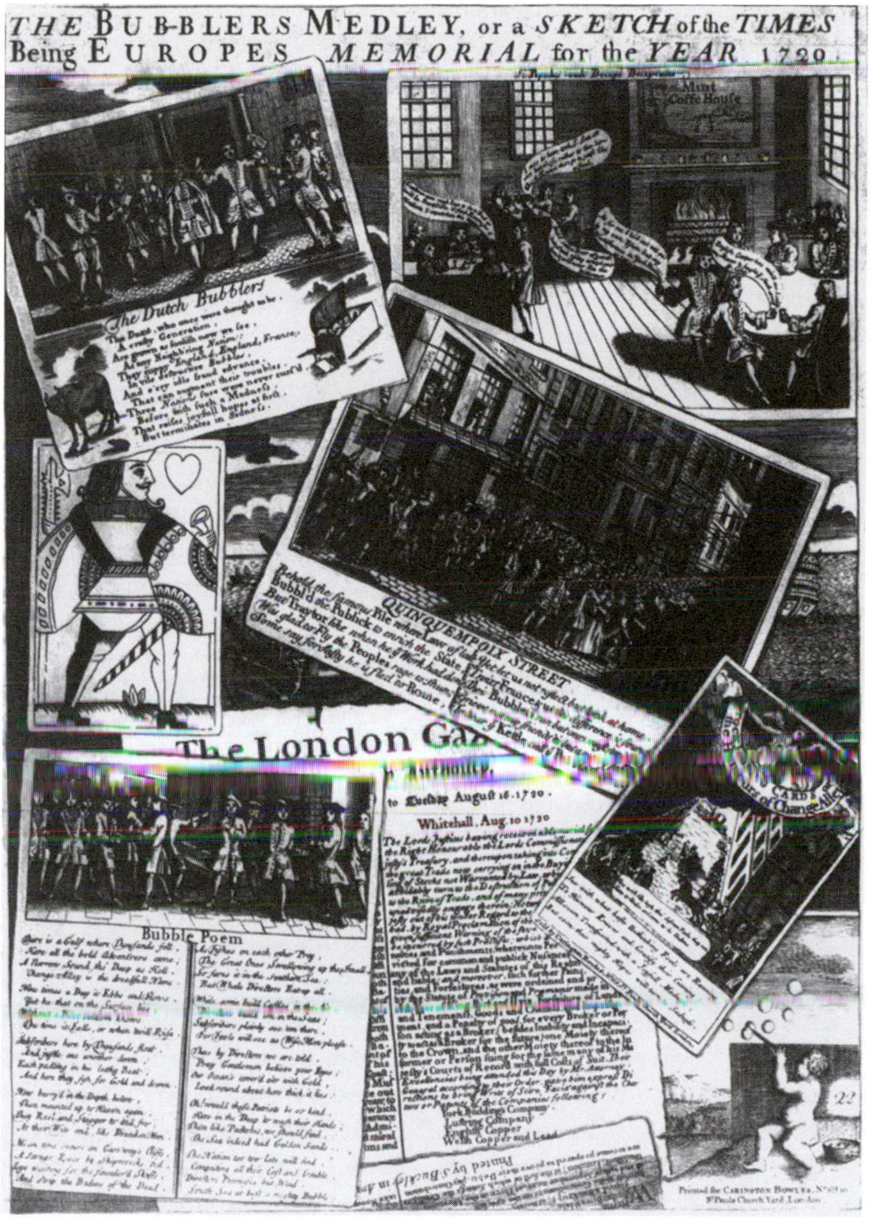
THE BUBBLERS MEDLEY, or a SKETCH of the TIMES
Being EUROPES MEMORIAL for the YEAR 1720.
The Dutch Bubblers
QUINQUEMPOIX STREET
Bubble Poem

"The Bubblers Medley, or a Sketch of the Times Being Europes Memorial for the Year 1720." Printed for Tho. Bowles, Print & Map Seller, London. (British Cartoon Prints Collection, Library of Congress)

round-ended, bubblelike emanata. The artist's intent was to make a satirical comment on the fanciful speculation that men indulged in at coffee shops by representing their speech in the shape of ephemeral bubbles. Another change in the shape of speech was evident a decade later with the advent of the fashion of pipe smoking. Some instances of speech now had a wispy, smokelike quality as they mocked the decadent fashion. One final shift away from the medieval phylactery was the way speech resembled less an unfurling scroll than a waving banner or flag. Such emanata are often aptly named banderoles and signify yet another way in which speech was now turning away from religious iconography and becoming more commonly represented as a secular and political means of expression.

The Invention of Caricature

Evidence of satirical drawings, especially animals foolishly acting like people, have appeared from at least the time of the ancient Egyptians; but the wide popular enjoyment of grotesque and distorted portraits, exemplified by the term "caricature," is a uniquely modern phenomenon. Caricatures first emerged in the Italian Renaissance and flourished thereafter mostly as a consequence of changing attitudes about the nature of art and the role of the artist in society. A caricature drawing represents a fundamental change in the relationship between the artist and the subject being represented. No longer are artists duty bound to represent their patrons in flattering terms by maintaining the continuity between their subjects with what is established under social decorum; instead, the unique vision of the artist is an essential component of the work. In this manner, caricatures embody an artist's vision; but it is not just the uniqueness of the creator's vision that matters as much as how the drawing reveals some inner truth of the subject. The distortions the artist applies are not arbitrary or merely humorously added features—a big nose, for example—but to work as caricature must possess a sense of unmasking the true or real subject.

An older variety of caricature, the grotesque, parodied social classes or occupations such as peasants, apprentices, and lawyers, and commonly conflated these roles with less noble animals like pigs, foxes, and sheep. Or, as in the case of Dürer's illustrations for *The Ship of Fools*, foolscaps applied to anyone was a sure marker for being an idiot. Another strategy was to introduce demonic features, horns, bulging eyes, and fangs, which further distanced the figure from a recognizable human form. These grotesque images differ from the modern caricature in that they do not identify a unique personality but, rather, try to reduce a human figure to a lowly type.

Leonardo da Vinci, Five caricature heads, after 1490, pen and ink on paper, 18 × 12 cm. (Gallerie dell'Accademia, Venice)

The English word caricature was originally a French word based on the Italian *caricare*, which meant "to exaggerate, load, or burden." Some of the first drawings to be called caricatures date back to the Italian Renaissance, and it is ironic that some of the most brilliant masters of humanist naturalism were also some of the first to experiment in caricature. Early caricatures by Leonardo da Vinci (1452–1519), Agostino Carracci (1557–1602), and Annibale Carracci (1560–1609) were used as amusements for the artists themselves, grotesquely parodying the pretensions and foibles of portrait sitters. Leonardo's tiny drawing of five heads from the 1490s has his characteristic delicacy of line contested by the crude, withered countenance of the monstrous characters. The absurd vanity of the old woman on the lower left is heightened by the way her hair is done in a girlish braid and by the small flower pressed against her withered bosom.

It is widely thought that the Carracci brothers were the first practitioners to gain public notoriety for their caricatures. Although none of the original drawings have survived, many of their students became notable caricaturists who initiated a thriving market for these distorted humorous drawings. Gian Lorenzo Bernini (1598–1680) made caricatures fashionable in Rome, but it was Pier Leone Ghezzi (1674–1755) who really excelled in the art and and built his career on more than 2,000 documented caricatures of people from daily life and notable social figures. These caricatures were not published or widely disseminated to the broader public, but they were a part of the trade in humorous portraits among elites.

In northern Europe, artists were experimenting in social critique through caricature, most notably in the work of Hieronymus Bosch (1450–1516) and later Pieter Bruegel the Elder (1525–1569), both of whom studied the homespun and quotidian manners of the day to make paintings that were both fantastic and startlingly real. Each painter was a master of the animated and distorted facial expressions that captured the vibrant passions of his subjects. Bosch's works were far more nightmarish than Bruegel's in their bold distortions of scale and the aggregation of disparate elements of humans, beasts, and everyday objects. The humor and social commentary of his work was, in many ways, a literal materialization of moral allegories found in church sermons and folk sayings. "The Ship of Fools" (1494), inspired by Brant's allegory, shows a number of commoners and clergy wildly singing as the boat is laden with precariously balanced objects. In this manner, Bosch represented the culmination of the classical and medieval grotesque traditions, which relied on the juxtaposition of human and animal characteristics; but Bosch went much further in blurring the distinctions between character and landscape, creating a whole world of allegorical madness. Although visually dazzling, Bosch's paintings tend to appear static when compared to the work of Bruegel, who more carefully rendered his figures to portray life as lived. Bruegel, too, had a penchant for copious detail, but his compositions have greater dramatic strength because of the spontaneous energy of a monoscenic narrative rather than the iconic power of a panoramic narrative. Hieronymous Cock (1510–1570) capitalized on the art of these master painters by creating etchings that captured the spirited chaos and social commentary of Bosch and Bruegel. Cock was the owner of the influential publishing house Aux Quatre

Vents in Antwerp and worked closely with Bruegel to render his drawings into print form. Evidence of their working process suggests Cock edited Bruegel's drawings in sometimes significant ways to make—what must have been to Cock's taste—a more marketable product. Cock's copy of Bruegel's "Rich Man's Feast" and "Poor Man's Feast" (both published in 1563) tended to gravitate toward more obvious contrasting sentiments and less subtle social commentary.

To his credit, Cock's publishing house had a significant influence on the development of print caricature. As the market for caricature flourished, many artists joined the burgeoning pool of talent to ply their wares. Jacques Callot (1592–1635) became justly famous for his caricatures of commedia dell'arte actors, which parodied and exaggerated the outlandish antics of the Italian improvised mask theatre. Although born in France, he lived in Italy for much

"What is this my son Tom" [*sic*], published by R. Sayer & J. Bennett, 1774. (British Cartoon Prints Collection, Library of Congress)

of his life and did hundreds of drawings of commedia characters. None of these drawings has ever been historically linked to an actual actor; thus, much of his work is regarded more as whimsical sketches based on commedia rather than caricatures of real players. Callot was also influential in his technical achievements in etching, developing techniques that allowed for more expressive lines and dynamic tonality, which were recorded and published by the Parisian Abraham Bosse in the first-ever manual for the craft (1654).

Despite a thriving underground market for caricature drawings in Italy throughout the 16th century, caricature as a visual style did not move into the popular press in Europe for over a century. There were a few notable exceptions, among them the work of George Townshend (1724–1807), who published loose and expressive caricatures of fellow members of society and government; but despite their momentary popularity and the shocking sensation they caused, they failed to generate a large number of imitators. The reason for this long delay in adopting the visual strategy of caricature was partly the dominant notion that caricature violated the "world of resemblances" by distorting the relationship between a real thing and how it was represented.[9] Prior to introduction of caricature in the "emblematic" way of describing the world, representations were not arbitrary or conditional but had an absolute value much like Plato's "theory of forms," wherein a representation transcended the actual object and the forms were archetypes of universal principles. The emblematic strategy for satirizing someone would be to make the person look foolish by putting the individual in the company of devils or having the individual vomit or defecate on him- or herself. Caricature directly challenged the unity and order of the world by foregrounding subjective and idiosyncratic ideas over social conventions and understood meanings.

As Amelia Rauser has pointed out, the emblematic notion of satirical prints finally fell aside with the satirical prints of the British macaroni fashions of the early 1770s. In these popular prints, the rakish youth of London were shown flaunting decorum by adopting an Italian fashion of exceedingly eccentric dress and powdered wigs that towered above all others like a huge plate of noodles. In the anonymous 1774 satirical print "What is this my son Tom," a middle-class father can scarcely recognize his macaroni-styled son. The print includes a humorous rhyme beneath it that concludes, "If thus the Taste continues Here, what will it be another Year?" The macaroni fashion was about celebrity and self-invention and pointed to a transformation in British society from one that focused on maintaining received social roles to one that was starting to accept a more fluid notion of social mobility and identity.

The new popularity for caricature in Britain captured what Oscar Wilde would say a century later about gossip in high society: "The only thing worse than being talked about is not being talked about." Although the caricatures were unflattering representations, they were memorable and indicated the level to which someone had entered society. To a certain degree, caricature and the macaroni fashion both emphasized the uniqueness of individuals over their capacity to conform to societal expectations. The broader change in society that would emerge from this realization—to which the macaroni fashions were mere symptoms—was that the true essences of things were not those qualities that were reducible to absolute types; they were instead the eccentric fleeting gestures and idiosyncratic qualities that embodied the notion of a person's distinct individuality in his or her caricature.

CHAPTER 3

Picture Stories

Graphic Narratives in Japan

China had developed the printing press before Europe did, but because of the way printing was employed by the government, there was a limited popular press. Such was not the case in Japan; for although Japan had adopted Chinese print technology along with many other aspects of writing and government in the Nara period (710–794), it developed a vibrant popular print culture. Combining this print culture with a rich tradition in storytelling and an indigenous brand of caricature (*toba-e*), Japan would lead the way to produce some of the most innovative graphic narratives that catered to a highly literate audience.

Picture recitation first appeared about the mid-eighth century in Japan with the arrival of Buddhist itinerant storytellers from Central Asia. Picture reciters carried scrolls (*emaki*) with drawings depicting both the rewards in the Buddhist cosmology for those who aspired to live a life of virtue and the punishments for those who rejected the Buddhist path of moderation. The *emaki* scrolls were brought to the emperor's court, where they were adapted to create a distinctly Japanese form of narrative art that emphasized expressive clothing, gestures, and nuanced awareness of social customs. The most famous of these early hand scrolls was the *Genji Monogatari Emaki* illustrating *The Tale of Genji* by Lady Murasaki Shikibu (ca. 973–ca. 1014). Despite the current decay of the original colors, the paintings reveal a compositional nuance that is truly astounding. The unknown team of artists who worked on the *Genji Monogatari Emaki* composed a series of monoscenic narrative images that summed up each chapter by focusing on the subtle, seemingly inconsequential moments that captured a fleeting sense of joy in ordinary things, tinged with a more somber recognition of the inevitable loss of such joy. The word for this feeling, *awaré*, is a highly refined and cultivated sentiment that permeates *The Tale of Genji* and its visual representation. Among the 20 surviving paintings, the one for chapter 50, "The Eastern Cottage" (*Azumaya*), expresses this feeling of *awaré* by capturing an idle moment in the story where the ladies of the court are airing out the royal spring residence. As Lady Nakanokimi is having her hair combed, there is a subtle suggestion of foreboding in the way a sliding screen in the background is left slightly ajar. It is from this small oversight in decorum that the rakish courtier Niou spies Lady Nakanokimi's half sister, Ukifume, whereupon he plots to take advantage of her. Because of Niou's actions, Ukifume eventually drowns herself in a river out of shame and sorrow. This still-distant tragic event is subtly prefigured in the flowing garments, hair, and ribbons that swirl around Ukifume in the scene.

Illustrations of *The Tale of Genji* establish the bedrock of what defined the women's-style painting (*onna-e*), where faces were rendered with extreme economy and the viewer peered into the scene from above. The contrasting men's-style painting (*otoko-e*) demonstrated a greater Chinese influence and tended to be monochromatic, or only lightly colored, with the focus more on natural figures that had a greater range of expression. The men's-style painting dominated the popular Buddhist narrative tradition of picture recitation, called *etoki*, which began in the Muromachi period (1338–1573), flourished during the Edo period (1615–1868), and is still occasionally performed today. Just as they did in India and China, earlier itinerant Buddhist monks and nuns carried on the picture-recitation tradition as a means to extol Buddhist virtues and collect alms for Buddhist charities. The story scroll of the Dojoji temple or *Dojoji Engi Emaki*, was one among hundreds of popular tales passed on in dozens of different renditions. It tells of a monk on a pilgrimage to the famed temple of Kumano who along the way meets a woman who tempts him from his ascetic path. The monk later avoids her on his return journey; and in her anger and frustration, she pursues the monk until she is transformed into a menacing serpent. In the final dramatic confrontation, the serpent woman finds the monk hidden under a temple bell. In a fit of passion, she wraps herself around the bell and the heat of her anger makes her burst into flames, consuming both the woman and the monk inside. Rather than condemning the woman for her actions, she and the monk both achieve salvation in the end. Virginia Skord Waters points out that the anarchic "anti-pilgrimage" the woman makes by pursuing the monk is not unlike the function of the picture recitation itself: where, through the theatrical performance of the picture recitation—with its passions and sexual overtones—the audience is given a religious experience.[1] Alongside the religious performers, there were also secular performers who told of great battles and heroic feats from *The Tales of the Heike*. Together, both secular and sacred stories established the vocabulary for popular literature and widely disseminated the stories that defined Japanese culture for centuries to come.

Unlike the earlier monoscenic narrative art of *The Tale of Genji*, in the *etoki* scrolls the emphasis was on representing the story with pictures that were more closely linked in a continuous fashion, emphasizing a sense of movement and transformation over time. One common stylistic trait that the *etoki* used was to begin the story formally and gradually adopt a looser, more vernacular style, which gave a sense of growing spontaneity and urgency. Despite the loose painterly style, there was a very sophisticated relationship between the words and pictures and the way the pictures were used to convey narrative events.

The narrative of the story was largely written at the beginning or end of the scroll with only small amounts of narrative and character speech written among the illustrations. The storyteller (*etoki hoshi*) would use the written text on the scroll as the framework for the story, which would be subtly amended to suit the audience at hand. Unlike in other parts of Asia, where picture recitation was predominantly a memorized oral performance with only a rudimentary text, Japan's picture recitation was a more a vocalized literature where the written source was given more development but nonetheless retained qualities that were designed to be read aloud.

Another important distinction in Japanese visual culture was the use of caricature to represent celebtities. Caricature had wide popular appeal in Japan, especially during the Edo period when woodblock prints depicted the notable figures of the teahouse district. These works became broadly known as *ukiyo-e*, or "images of the floating world," so called for the euphoric and unattached fantasies that the district inspired, but also because the teahouse district in Yoshiwara was literally a makeshift city built over a swamp outside of the city of Edo. The Yoshiwara district provided a powerful counterpoint to the otherwise regimented and orderly lives of the city's inhabitants. Early prints were sold to visitors to Yoshiwara as souvenirs of their favorite geishas, sumo wrestlers, and kabuki actors; as these personalities became well known in the district, their appearances were refined and abbreviated to a few expressive lines to reveal their striking beauty or humorous countenance. The captivating pleasure of an ukiyo-e print was not unlike seeing a candid paparazzi photo, where a celebrity was caught in a moment of partial undress—behind a folding screen—engaged in an idle pastime, as if he or she was a mere mortal. As purveyors of fashion, Yoshiwara personalities were described by their telltale eccentric clothing. Decorative patterns were rendered flat across the curving arcs of a figure's kimono, giving the body an animated beauty that conveyed both casual voyeurism and elegant formality. Ukiyo-e was closely watched and censored by officials of the Tokugawa shogunate, and yet the artists often pushed against those strictures that confined their talents and popularity to appeal to an audience that desired a novel way to break out from their social bonds and, as the poet Issa (1763–1827) wrote, "to walk on the roof of Hell and look at the flowers." To that end, there were a great many different kinds of caricature prints available: those that lampooned famous actors (*nigaoe giga*), but also ones that played on absurd customs and manners of the day. High-ranking government officials were strictly forbidden to be the subject of caricature, but portraits of Zen patriarchs tended to show the venerable Buddhist sages as goofy and childish. This was done not to insult their memory, but to instill Zen Buddhist humility and force the viewer to look for deeper meanings beyond surface appearances.

Comical prints were often called *toba-e* (Toba pictures) after the Buddhist monk Toba Sōjō (1053–1140), who was the supposed author of the satirical ink-drawn hand scrolls, the *Chōjū-jinbutsu-giga*,[2] which represented animals acting like Buddhist monks. In the early 18th century, when caricature was ascendant in Edo, collections of the *toba-e* print caricatures were sold as illustrated books (*ehon*). It was during this time that a number of such innovative caricaturists as Ōoka Shunboku (1680–1763) and Katsushika Hokusai (1760–1849) were working. Like many of the ukiyo-e artists, Shunboku was largely self-taught, though he was influenced by the Kano tradition that embraced the painterly Chinese work of the Song Dynasty. His vivid gestural brush strokes can be seen in "Men Trying to Catch a Flying Pestle" in the collection of his prints entitled *Ehon Te-Kagami* (1720). Each of the animated figures chasing the pestle has the same open-mouthed, excited, and foolish expression. By rendering the figures this way, the artist makes the object of the parody not a particular person but the whole of society that would desire the sexually suggestive pestle soaring overhead and out of reach.

Hokusai is best remembered for his dramatic landscapes of Mount Fuji, but he worked in many different styles and was a remarkable caricaturist who also has the distinction of having popularized the word "manga," which is now used to broadly denote all comic art in Japan. The Japanese word manga was based on the Chinese word *manhua*, which meant "impromptu sketches."[3] Although the word had been used infrequently before, Hokusai published a whole series of popular volumes of caricatures and studies from everyday life called *Hokusai Manga*. The first manga volume appeared in 1814, and 12 more volumes followed over the remainder of his lifetime, with 3 published posthumously by his students. The *Hokusai Manga* were published so that novice artists might use them as the basis of their own work. They contained every imaginable subject in varying poses, among them frolicking animals and people engaged in farming, hunting, sports, and games, as well as many eccentric and hard-to-imagine subjects such as gods, demons, ghosts, and blind people. Hokusai published these books as a means to promote his style of drawing among a wider audience, with the long-term hope that he would attract more students. The drawings have an energy and spontaneity that was prized in ukiyo-e art because it attempted to capture a fleeting moment or a passing fancy. What Hokusai's manga does not attempt to do is tell a story. Although storytelling with pictures has a long history in Japan, none of those traditions were associated with the word "manga" until the 20th century.

The earliest popular printed graphic narratives in Japan grew out of the caricature and erotic prints that were collected and sold as sets. The first print series that told an original story was the tale of *The Elegant and Horny Maneemon* (*Fūryū enshoku Maneemon*) by Suzuki Harunobu (1724–1770), appearing some time between 1768 and 1770. The main character for this story is a man who has been granted a wish by the goddesses of love that he be shrunk down to minuscule size so he can watch the sexual adventures of others. The humor was clearly intended for an adult audience and was part of a very popular tradition of erotic prints commonly called *shunga*, or "spring pictures." Each picture in the series is a monoscenic narrative with the kind of subtle attention to costume and social custom that was characteristic of the *onna-e*-style of *The Tale of Genji* but with much more vivid dramatic action and the expressive characterization of the *otaku-e*-style narrative scrolls. In the 12th and final print of the second series, Maneemon is in a tree spying on a famous actor of the kabuki theatre, Segawa Kikunojo II (1741–1773), fondling an apprentice to a geisha. The geisha has just caught them in the act and is now looking daggers at him. Perhaps the geisha's sour expression is also a reaction to a foul odor because up in the tree Maneemon has passed gas. Maneemon mentions his flatulence by making an allusion to a famous Heian-era poem about the Nara eightfold cherry blossom. The literary allusions and poetic parodies show that this work was not a base diversion for the uneducated but a complex satire on the lifestyle of the nouveau riche in the courtesan district.

Suzuki Harunobu, *The Elegant and Horny Maneemon* (*Fūryū enshoku Maneemon*), ca. 1768–1770. (By permission of the Smithsonian Freer Gallery)

It was for this educated audience that the next step in popular narrative art evolved with longer original stories published in multivolume series with more closely linked sequential actions. These works were called *kibyoshi*, or "yellow books," for the garish yellow covers they sported. Appearing first in 1775, *kibyoshi* were immensely popular, although for little more than a decade, until they were suppressed through government censorship. Brilliantly witty word-plays and suggestive illustrations were the hallmarks of this upstart genre, which skewered all things serious, lampooned all manner of fashion, and mocked all else deemed self-important. The author-illustrator Santō Kyōden (1761–1816) was one of the stars of *kibyoshi*. His work *Playboy Roasted a la Edo* (*Edo umare uwaki no kabayaki*, 1785), about the misadventures of a spoiled dandy who imitates the affectations of a playboy, beautifully captured the self-referential comedy of manners that defined the genre.

It is tantalizing to consider just how close the *kibyoshi* publications came to realizing the form of the modern comic book. They were mass-produced popular serial publications that contained original stories which included caricature, romantic adventure, and satire—predominantly told through pictures—accompanied by written narration, dialogue, and sound effects. About the only element that was not comparable to the modern comic was the sequential relationship between the pictures, which typically used one picture per page or sometimes had one picture spread across two pages for dramatic effect. Each picture in the book represented a complete scene, and from one picture to the next, there was a loose causal relationship between the actions represented. The amount of time between the scenes was portrayed in a nonspecific, epic style, where the action seems to occur over days or weeks. One distinctive quality of *kibyoshi* was the way the pictures were overrun with the text. The story and dialogue spilled across the pictures and filled up the page with a crazy abandon that suggested something improvised or haphazard, when in reality they were subtly crafted to create just that effect of an unreliable narrator.

The *kibyoshi* artists also followed the ukiyo-e tradition by employing the Chinese idea of a balloon- or cloud-shaped form emanating from a figure to represent dreams and fantasies. Although this form bore a remarkable formal similarity to the speech balloon used in Europe, it represented a vision—often emanating from the spiritually potent region of the neck—and never a sound or voice, though it sometimes included written dialogue or narrative to accompany the characters depicted inside the dream. Two dream scenes appear sequentially emanating from the neck of the author Masanobu in the *kibyoshi* entitled *Those Familiar Bestsellers* (*Gozonjji no shōbaimono*, 1782). The initial sequence inside the spreading balloon allows the story to set up a fanciful premise whereby all the subsequent scenes are understood to originate from within the dream of the author. By depicting dreams, the *kibyoshi* artists gave themselves license to explore a broader fictive world outside the heavily censored realms of real life. *Kibyoshi* were not entirely escapist material though; like the popular theater of kabuki, they often brought up sensitive political issues through innuendo, as, for example, in the story of *The Thousand Armed Goddess, Julienned* (*Daihi so senrokuhon*, 1785), where the goddess was swindled out of her wealth at a ratio of 8 to 1 by a man named Tamura, which was a not-so-veiled reference to the regent named Tamura, who devalued the currency by one-eighth. It was these and other political comments that eventually led to the crackdown on *kibiyoshi* and other popular entertainments in 1790.

Kibyoshi's success, as Adam Kern has pointed out, was also in part responsible for its ultimate failure.[4] The witty, intellectual audience that created *kibyoshi* and to whom it appealed was made up of an elite group that was vulnerable to government sanction because its members were dependent on the government for their own status and economic stability. Also, the appeal of this frivolous and decadent type of publication found itself out of keeping with the new somber mood in the city of Edo that followed the harsh economic Kansei

Reforms. Less sophisticated humor books and adventure stories soon filled the void left by the disappearance of *kibyoshi*. Despite the ready market for popular publications in Japan, it would be almost 100 years before Western-style comics would arrive and create the impetus for a new form of graphic narrative, manga, which would rival the complexity of *kibyoshi*.

Early Graphic Narratives in Britain

Ingredients for the creation of graphic narratives had been in place since the early Renaissance in Europe but had failed to coalesce into form because of economic and cultural pressure that kept writers, artists, and printers in separate guilds, which meant innovations in one area did not easily cross over into other areas. That graphic narratives should first appear in the early 18th century in Britain is remarkable considering how British publishers at the time were only negligibly profitable and could hardly compete with better-quality imports from Germany and the Netherlands. This situation dramatically changed with the work of William Hogarth (1697–1764), who transformed the fledgling craft into a professional industry and was able, furthermore, to straddle the worlds of fine art, writing, and printmaking in ways few artists at the time could.

The rise of engraving as a popular medium in Britain was facilitated by Hogarth in several ways: first, by demonstrating that there was a large demand for popular secular prints; second, by training hundreds of new engravers to handle the mass production required because of the demand for Hogarth's work; and third, by pressing the government to give copyright protection over printed images. The first copyright act for written works, the Statute of Anne enacted in 1710, protected an author's work for a period of 14 years after first publication. Thereafter, the publication was regarded as belonging to the "public domain" and could be reproduced by anyone without having to compensate the original author. In 1730, Hogarth produced a series of engravings called *A Harlot's Progress*, which proved phenomenally popular; but as he argued successfully before the British Parliament, much of the profit for his work had been lost to more cheaply produced pirated imitations. Once the Statute of Anne had been extended to printed pictures, Hogarth resumed his work with the publication of a series called *A Rake's Progress* (1733), which secured his fame and made him quite wealthy.

Hogarth was also an accomplished painter, and his engravings were based on monumental paintings that were hung together in a public hall for a paying audience to visit. Having paid to see the paintings, the audience was then invited to purchase a set of prints. The paintings were very effective in promoting the engravings, although on their own they were never prized by collectors. Hogarth made persistent efforts to be recognized as a fine artist without much success. In publishing his 1753 treatise *Analysis of Beauty*, he hoped to promote himself as a fine artist and he challenged his fellow engravers to eschew tawdry forms of caricature and phylacteries and instead look toward more baroque ideas of beauty. Hogarth was not an elitist in this respect; rather, he sought to invest a noble beauty into everyday events and in common people. Few engravers actually followed his lead, and Hogarth would eventually exhaust his popularity and become the butt of the satirical caricatures that he had railed against.

There were many appealing qualities to Hogarth's work—the superb craftsmanship, the energetic compositions, the lively figures, the meticulous detail—but most striking of all was his ability to capture a theatrical moment that allowed the viewer to draw out a moral from a climactic scene. Hogarth's works were exquisitely complex, and audiences enjoyed pouring over the monumental paintings and engravings looking for clues. In the first print of *A Harlot's Progress*, Mary (Moll) Hackabout is a young woman recently arrived from the countryside to work as a seamstress in the city. She is met at the Bell Inn by Mother Needham, who encourages her to forgo honest work and join her brothel. The dead goose lying limp in a basket in the lower right has a tag on it which reads, "For my lofing cousin in Tems Street in London," which indicates that Moll was expecting to meet a cousin who has failed to show up. The bad spelling on the note indicates Moll's general ignorance; and though the goose is symbolic of a silly person, that it hangs limp in the basket more like a phallus is a sexual reference to the man in the doorway who is fondling himself in anticipation of a young new girl at the brothel. Other girls can be seen in the coach awaiting perhaps a similar fate in the city, and the parson who could help them find their way is instead on the back of a horse reading his letter of introduction to an important member of the clergy. His equally oblivious horse is feeding on some hay, upsetting a stack of buckets, which we see in midfall. The bucket captures in a frozen moment a whole array of seemingly ordinary events, which frame the drama and portend the eventual downfall of this innocent girl.

Unlike their namesake, *The Pilgrim's Progress* by John Bunyan, Hogarth's *Harlot* and *Rake* have a less obvious moral. For even as Hogarth forcefully describes the failings of the principal characters, we cannot help but sympathize with them as they are preyed on by unscrupulous people and left to their downfall by negligent others. Hogarth's later series, among them *Industry and Idleness*, were more

William Hogarth, *A Harlot's Progress*, plate 1, April 1733. Etching with engraving on paper.

decidedly moral and for that reason not as compelling as dramatic characterizations. Hogarth's works sprung from the popular idiom of the stage, and in turn, his work was translated back into theatrical productions. In March 1733, some 11 months after the first appearance of *A Harlot's Progress* in print, a "grotesque pantomimic entertainment was performed at Drury Lane,"[5] which took the sequence of prints and dramatized them with popular songs and Harlequin pratfalls.

With his "Modern Moral Subjects," as he called them, Hogarth had invented a concept for a new kind of graphic narrative that linked together moments in a dramatic way that allowed an original story to be told in pictures. Each picture represented a separate scene; yet unlike in cyclic narratives, Hogarth's scenes were causally linked, for the reader followed a few characters whose actions predicated the next scene. As the character's fortunes changed, so did their appearances and manners, leading the reader to deduce the arc of their fate. The amount of time between the scenes in Hogarth's *A Harlot's Progress* is certainly longer than a week, and more likely several months to a year has elapsed, but exactly how much time is hard to say and unimportant in considering the larger themes of the work. Like the *kibyoshi* in Japan, Hogarth's works had established an important step toward modern sequential graphic narratives, but they did not achieve the structure of dramatically linked sequential narratives, where the actions flowed, one to another, in closely related moments. It would take yet another 100 years for that idea to come to fruition.

British Masters of Caricature

Where Hogarth demurred for the cause of decorum and demonstrated restraint in natural appearances, James Gillray (1757–1815) rushed head-long into caricatured excess. Even the most pernicious political cartoons today pale in comparison with the irreverent satirical prints of Gillray, who rode the crest of an extended wave of nasty character assassination in the popular press. Gillray was a partisan Tory supporter in his prints and savaged the rival Whig Party, but this was perhaps less a matter of personal conviction than economic expedience; by 1797, Gillray was clandestinely on the Tory payroll. Despite this lucre, Gillray gave his caricatures a haunted

James Gillray, *Presages of the Millennium*, 1795.

life all their own that transcended political sloganeering. In his print entitled *Presages of the Millennium* (1795), the Tory leader William Pitt personifies naked Death riding a wild mare and wielding a flaming sword as he crushes his enemies before him. For Gillray, the politics of the day were merely the two planks he used to prop up his passion, and it is for this reason that his work continues to enthrall. Toward the end of his storied career, with failing eyesight, Gillray went insane and had to be cared for by his longtime publisher, Hannah Humphrey.

Thomas Rowlandson (1756–1827) was a caricaturist who became well known for his series of plates entitled *The Schoolmaster's Tour* (1809). First seen in Rudolph Ackermann's *Poetical Magazine*, these were later republished in 1812 in their own book as *The Tour of Dr. Syntax in Search of the Picturesque*. The publication quickly spawned several new series featuring the same hapless schoolmaster pursuing other quixotic ambitions: *Dr Syntax in Search of Consolation* (1820) and, finally, *The Third Tour of Dr. Syntax in Search of a Wife* (1821). Each story was accompanied with illustrative verses by Dr. William Combe, who composed his rhyming couplets to describe the story conveyed in the pictures. Dr. Syntax was the first celebrity illustrated character to be used to promote various brands of hats, coats, and wigs.[6]

As a character, Dr. Syntax was of a well-known stock and variety. In his comical exploits, he joined the ranks of such other mock epic heroes as Don Quixote and Hudibras, but in a decidedly middle-class manner, in which high ambition and lofty aspirations are met with teatime appetites and the flagging stamina of middle age. There are wonderfully prosaic moments, as when Dr. Syntax is drawing the landscape from the back of his horse in much the same way a tourist today would try to take a photograph out the window of a car while driving down the highway.

George Cruikshank (1792–1878) was the preeminent illustrator who took up the mantle as England's greatest political satirist after Gillray, but by then political satire had become far more chaste than the earlier work of Gillray. In keeping with the new moral sentiments of the day, Cruikshank successfully revived Hogarth's moral stories in pictures with a very popular series on temperance called *Bottle* (1847), which was soon followed by *The Drunkard's Children* (1848). Unlike Hogarth, Cruikshank employed text below his prints to tell the story and did not attempt the same kind of dense symbolic actions that invited readers of Hogarth's work to indulge in a wider speculation about the meaning of the story. To his credit, Cruikshank had a great knack for melodramatic action, as realized in the final image of *The Drunkard's Children* where the "poor girl, homeless, friendless, deserted, destitute, and gin-mad, commits self-murder." The utter helplessness of her figure plunging off the bridge has an absolute finality, which powerfully speaks to her desperation, and our helplessness, as we look on.

Across these three masters of caricature, an important change in the form of graphic narratives in Europe occurs. Gillray and his generation of artists had developed a wide range of expressive forms to visually communicate speech, which included everything from the medieval, fancy, scroll-like phylacteries to the simpler, round-ended emanata. The visual forms of speech were allegorical in nature and created an additional layer of commentary on the action by appearing as either bubbles, animal tails, wispy smoke, explosions, vomit, or banners blowing in the wind. By the 1820s, virtually all text had been removed from within the picture and placed below in descriptive paragraphs where the dialogue was placed in quotation. Why a system for expressing voice should disappear and be replaced by more densely written and less evocative narrative text seems, on the surface, odd. The change needs to be seen in light of a new sensibility, where the naturalistic details of the picture would appear compromised by intrusive emanata. Also, because of the growing impact of literacy, a voice was no longer understood as a distinctly different mode of expression than text. A few artists continued to use emanata, but the practice of representing speech visually would, by and large, almost entirely disappear from popular prints in Europe and the United States until the very end of the 19th century.

Rodolphe Töpffer's Picture Stories

What began as a schoolmaster's pastime for his pupils eventually became the impetus for the modern comic strip. The Swiss schoolmaster, novelist, and amateur painter Rodolphe Töpffer (1799–1846) devised an original format to encourage his students to be more engaged by their reading. Rather than use the typical visual strategy of employing one picture per scene, he used several images per page set apart by smaller frames. By doing this, he created for the first time a montage, a way of describing a single idea over several closely linked pictures, as if one were seeing the action unfold in a play.

Töpffer also utilized for the first time different-sized panels on the page to suggest different kinds of narrative pacing; for example, giving the impression of an action building in intensity or dissipating through meaningless repetition. The novelty of this narrative construction is Töpffer's greatest and lasting achievement, for it introduced a sense of momentum through more specific causal relationships between the pictures. How Töpffer came up with this idea is difficult to say, since he does not discuss the novel structural form of his comics in his essays, only his use of caricature. It is interesting to note that Töpffer employed this new method of constructing a graphic narrative just at the time that musical notation in Europe took its modern form with vertical lines (bar lines) to mark off the metrical units or tempo. Dietrich Nikolaus Winkel invented the metronome in 1812, and tempo notation began to appear in the music of Ludwig van Beethoven by 1817—all this, 15 years before Töpffer began to draw his first graphic narratives, or what he called *histoires estampes*, "printed stories." The impact of musical notation is also seen in one of Töpffer's early stories where Mr. Jabot dreams of mazurka music and, in what must be one of the first times ever in a graphic narrative, musical notation is used to represent the sound of music.

To help achieve spontaneity in his pictures, Töpffer jettisoned tightly rendered figures and landscapes and used a looser, sketchy style that focused on the essential action of the characters and their expressions. Töpffer was a competent, but by no means accomplished, artist who had given up his earlier ambition to be a painter like his father when his failing eyesight compromised

---

Box 3.1   The Lithography of Alois Senefelder

The invention of lithography by Alois Senefelder (1771–1834) in 1789 was a dramatic departure from printing methods of the past because it did not rely on cutting or carving the surface to create the design but rather used the natural tendency of oil-based inks to repel water. As the name implies (from *lithos* meaning "stone"), lithography uses special polished sandstone blocks. Originally, the artist drew directly on the stone to create the design using a wax crayon. Wetting the stone allowed oil-based ink to adhere only to where the wax crayon drawings were laid down. Lithography was easier to modify, faster to produce, and did not wear out the way relief carvings and engravings did. Lithographic works could also be reprinted thousands of times, whereas engravings were limited to several hundred copies. Slowly and powerfully, the impact of lithography led to the rise of high-quality popular prints throughout the 19th and 20th centuries. The artistic advantages of lithography were that the artist could work in a number of media and that the original work would transfer directly without the need for the image to be carved or recut by another artist. Because lithography more directly reproduced the work of the artist, it also encouraged the idea that a print was a work of art with its own unique virtues.

his work. Töpffer credits the freedom he had in his picture stories to his use of "autography," an early form of lithography (see box 3.1), which allowed him to produce his drawings directly for reproduction without needing to have them be engraved or etched by another artist. The handwritten text below the frame was also used sparingly, not just to clarify the action but also to complicate the visual scenes by adding ironic commentary.

The unmistakable novelty of Töpffer's picture stories is derived not only from the unique style and form but also from the narrative itself, which is part romance, adventure, fantasy, satire, and farce. In many respects, he was inspired by the narrative hijinks of the novel *The Life and Opinions of Tristram Shandy* by Laurence Sterne (1713–1768). Both used deadpan understatement to sell farfetched ideas, and both demonstrated self-satire and narrator incompetence to create a carnivalesque sense of whimsy. Perhaps one of the most remarkable features of Töpffer's picture stories, and something that was not widely imitated later, is found in his use of repetition. Throughout all of Töpffer's picture stories, characters seem unable to check their habitual responses and repeat themselves: "Mr. Jabot resumes his attitude," "Mr. Vieux Bois changes his shirt," and "Mr. Jolibois (for passion blinds, alas) attempts to pursue the unfaithful one." The repetitions create a link between disparate story moments and suggest narrative continuity as a *leitwortstil* (a purposeful repetition of words to establish a motif), but the mechanical repetitions also arrest a sense of narrative development as characters habitually demonstrate their shallow motivations and limited grasp of the situation.

Töpffer credited only Hogarth as an inspiration for the picture stories; but where Hogarth attempted to freeze time and expand it until it became an impossibly complex moment that oversignified the moral, Töpffer's characters jerk and gambol, hurdy-gurdy-like, from one picture to the next. In one sequence of three pictures where Mr. Vieux Bois has perched on a rooftop, it appears only a moment has passed from one picture to the next; but the story written below says he has been waiting in vain, first for a whole week and then, in the final picture, for another three days.[7] The conflicting time references between the words and pictures confuse the orderly sequence of the dramatic montage and make Töpffer's graphic narrative seem more like a mock epic than a true dramatic story unfolding before the reader.

Without the fulsome praise of Johann Wolfgang von Goethe (1749–1832), Töpffer's picture stories would most likely have remained a local novelty rather than an international phenomenon. Goethe was an unlikely patron of caricature sketches, which he had railed against in his publication

Die Propyläen (1799) for their distortions of classical ideas of beauty and their association with revolutionary propaganda. The picture stories were presented to Goethe by his close friends Johann Peter Eckermann and Frédéric Soret, who also was a former classmate of Töpffer. Töpffer's politics did not coincide with the elder Goethe's, but the ironic voice and action in the picture stories was disarming for its ability to make fun of classes of people—the ill-prepared militia, the petty scientist, the socialite dandy rather than specific individuals or institutions. The aging Goethe had mellowed some of his earlier opinions; but more to the point, he saw in Töpffer a new kind of caricature, as Soret later described in a letter to Töpffer, "where everything freezes and unfreezes as if it were in the spirit of imitation."[8] As David Kunzle has also noted, Goethe may also have been attracted to the circular nature of the stories that spiral about rather than follow a linear path.[9] Late in life, Goethe made such curvilinear designs a common theme in his research.

After receiving encouragement from Goethe, Töpffer eventually relented and published one of his volumes, *Histoire de M. Jabot* (1833), and because of its popularity published two more in 1837, *Histoire de M. Vieux Bois* and *Monsieur Crépin*. Fearing that such frivolous work might undermine his promotion to tenured faculty at the University of Geneva, he published these volumes anonymously but nonetheless included his initials, "RT," conspicuously on each page. The works sold well for several decades, and despite widespread piracy, Töpffer achieved sizable compensation for his work and went on to create five more stories before his death in 1846. British copies of *The Loves of Mr. Vieux Bois* (1839) were pirated under the title *The Adventures of Mr. Obadiah Oldbuck*, with no authorship attributed, in a business venture by George Cruikshank and his brother Robert in 1841. A year later, a New York newspaper, *Brother Jonathan*, acquired the pirated British edition and changed the format from one register per page to two. At 12-and-one-half cents a copy, the "cheap book" was billed as the first ever to appear in America, and it too continued to appear for sale in print catalogs for several decades.

Such better artists as Cham (Amédée de Noé, 1819–1879), Nadar (Gaspard-Félix Tournachon, 1820–1910), and Gustave Doré (1832–1883) attempted to improve upon Töpffer's innovation, but with much less success. Doré began at a young age to draw picture stories based on the layout of Töpffer's picture stories. As an autodidact prodigy, by age 15 Doré had an exclusive contract with the most prestigious of caricature publishers in Paris, Gabriel Aubert and Charles Philipon (1800–1861). Some of Doré's early experiments formed the basis of his

Immolation sur l'autel de Péroun des citoyens accusés et convaincus d'avoir parlé franchement.

Les anciens Russes adoraient Péroun, dieu de la paix, des moissons, des armées, de l'amitié, du commerce, de la guerre, de l'honneur, de la gloire, de la ruse, du mensonge et de l'orthodoxie, etc., etc., etc.

Cette religion ordonnait expressément qu'on respectât les serpents et autres reptiles.

Les prêtres ne négligeaient aucune occasion d'ajouter à ce précepte la sanction du fouet. Aussi est-ce de cette époque reculée que date le knout, mot qui, dans le dialecte laconique et expressif des Slaves, signifie moyen de persuasion ferme, constant, incisif et seul capable de dépouiller le vieux Russe de sa rude enveloppe.

Les anciens Russes faisaient grand cas des femmes, par lesquelles ils étaient d'avis de se laisser conduire en tout et pour tout.

Gustave Doré, *Histoire pittoresque de la Sainte Russie,* 1854. (Library of Congress) first published works, beginning with *The Labors of Hercules* (*Les Travaux d'Hercule*) in 1847. Doré had a confident drawing style that demonstrated a flowing-line quality and delicate modeling of the figures; he proved himself far more adept than Töpffer at rendering believable figures and giving faces more expressive form. Doré also innovated with the picture-story format and began to cut figures off within the frame, giving the scene a greater sense of animation. *The Labors of Hercules* resuscitated the five-year-dormant picture-story genre—what Aubert and Philipon called the "Albums Jabot" line after an early volume they pirated from Töpffer—but this work did not prompt another in the publisher's series. Despite the seeming lack of public interest, Doré experimented with a few more extended graphic narrative projects, most notably *Dis-Pleasures of a Pleasure Trip* (*Dés-agréments d'un voyage d'agrément*, 1851) and his most ambitious work, *The Rare and Extraordinary History of Holy Russia with Over 500 Illustrations* (1853). Doré, in his *History of Holy Russia*, created some of his most cynical and cruel images of a long, brutal, and senseless history; but also, following the examples of Rabelais and Laurence Sterne, Doré continually undermined his history of Russia by calling attention to its crude invention made up of unreadable, ink-smudged pages, numerous repetitions, and rambling digressions. At one point, while describing the bloody history of Ivan the Terrible, Doré startles the reader with the only color image: a whole page splattered with red ink. Not until the advent of *MAD* magazine almost 100 years later would anyone attempt to create anything so ambitiously irreverent, so preposterously extravagant, so absurdly pointless.

It is evident that in preparing his satirical polemic against Russia, Doré misjudged public sentiment about the Crimean War; moreover, as in his earlier experiments, he had not been able to engage a sophisticated audience for his visually innovative work. *Holy Russia* was clearly a labor of love that embodied Doré's Rabelaisian joy in the absurd; but with its poor public reception, the financially strapped Doré turned to illustrating classic works of fiction and never returned to composing graphic narratives.

As Töpffer astutely observed, technical skill was not a prerequisite in creating an effective picture story and in many ways skill proved a hinderance for more capable later artists whose artistry complicated the necessary easy flow from one picture to another. The other issue that plagued the picture-story genre was similar to what had earlier undermined the Japanese *kibyoshi* books: the audience for these works was not well defined, requiring people who were both frivolous and intellectual, impulsive and sophisticated. Graphic narratives as single-frame humorous anecdotes continued to grow in popularity through the 19th century, but they would need to wait for the advent of children's literature before they could reach maturity.

CHAPTER 4

Modern Art Graphic Narratives

For most of the late 19th and early 20th centuries, modern art that emerged in Europe avoided narrative as a relic of the 18th-century art academies that had been the exclusive arbiters of taste. The general rejection of narrative in modern art happened just as popular narrative illustration in commercial publications was growing by leaps and bounds. The gulf between these two worlds is characteristic of the changing relationship between modern artists and the general public, but it is also indicative of the ambivalence modern artists had toward mainstream tastes and values. For these and other reasons, narrative art largely represents a path not taken in the modern era. However, there were a few isolated artists who worked in opposition to the prevailing nonnarrative modernist ideals of art; for those few, narrative art offered an opportunity to invent new storytelling modes that dramatically questioned the visual formation of meaning. Although much of the work by these artists lay outside the major trends in romanticism, symbolism, expressionism and surrealism, in hindsight the works represent significant breakthroughs in the development of graphic narratives.

Blake's Illuminated Printing

William Blake (1757–1857) lived through the American and the French revolutions and saw his role as artist not as the purveyor of fixed classical truths but as a prophetic visionary communicating his unique Christian-based mythology (suffused with the philosophy of the Enlightenment) and the artistic aims of romanticism. At the center of his mythology were creator "Eternals" who represented spiritual aspects of the body of Christ and symbolically mirrored aspects of his own unique print processes, which—according to Blake—was revealed to him by the spirit of his deceased brother. The exact process Blake used to create his prints is still something of a mystery; it evolved to a certain degree over his lifetime, but it was a distinctive combination of techniques that were augmented later with hand-painted ink and watercolor, making each print a reproduction of his original drawing yet a unique work of art. Blake called this process "illuminated printing," indicating that he saw this method as a mixture of the medieval traditions of hand-painted or "illuminated" books and modern print technology. What lay at the heart of this process was a manner of rendering a drawing directly on a metal plate so that his own brush and pen marks were reproduced in the print. Print technology at this time was primarily a two-part process whereby an original drawing would be transferred to metal or wood and then the engraver would cut away, or acid etch, the surface so that it recreated the image. By rendering directly on the metal plate, Blake sought more control of the print process so he would not be compromised through collaboration or possibly leave himself open to censure because of the revolutionary nature of his poetry and images. In William Blake's time, few could appreciate the full gamut of his artistic output, let alone the radical ideas he held about his spiritual beliefs.

To appreciate the radical departure Blake took from his contemporaries, it is important to note that prior to the 19th century, artists who worked as painters and sculptors enjoyed exclusive prestige as artists: people with a unique vision and singular creations. Engravers such as Blake, on the other hand, labored to fill a growing popular market for prints and held a secondary status as craftsmen. The idea that prints could be regarded as works of art with their own unique aesthetic virtues would not be a widely accepted idea until late in the 19th century. A significant difference between elite painting and popular prints was the way painting was a purely visual medium, whereas popular prints engaged in a multimodal approach, mixing words and pictures together. Since the Renaissance, when artists attempted to reestablish well-defined ideas of classical beauty,[1] there was a general disdain for incorporating words and text together into a composition. In the visual culture of the 18th century, which continued to extol such virtues, Blake's hybrid word-pictures were quite an anomaly.

The act of writing in Blake's creative process is connected to the idea of prophecy. Most engravers were trained, as was Blake, to write backward so they could include small amounts of text into their prints. Blake developed this skill to a high degree and was able to write out in reverse dozens of pages of text in delicate italic script. With this technique, he was free to mix words and pictures in imaginative ways, and so the character and style of the words composed an organic whole with the pictures. Despite the strong visual unity between words and pictures, Blake often added ironic commentary and complexity through the use of contrasting symbols and words to engage the reader's imagination. Take, for example, Blake's print of the famous poem "The Tyger" (1794), whose words describe a tiger of "fearful symmetry," but whose image of the tiger is placed asymmetrically on the page and given a rather meek appearance. By obviously contradicting himself, Blake conceived a revolutionary prophetic voice that not only questioned the status quo but also encouraged readers of his work to be revolutionaries themselves and to question the authority of his own prophesies.

In Blake's most ambitious project, *Jerusalem* (1804–1820), Blake shows himself as a miniature scribe writing backward on a scroll that unfolds across the lap of the sleeping giant Albion, who represents both England and all humankind. That the print shows the text backward meant that Blake actually wrote the text forward on the metal plate; thus, the appearance of backward writing represents the idea of the original prophetic voice just as Blake would have written the message. Blake contrasted the idea of scrolls as original prophecy with the idea that bound books represented received wisdom and established law. Blake maintained this iconographic code at the same time as he subverted it through playful inversions. This approach is especially evident in one of Blake's early illuminated books, *The Marriage of Heaven and Hell* (1789–1793), where Blake set out to describe a cosmology where heaven represents reason, or passive and consuming forms, and hell represents energy, or active and creative forms. In one image that parodies Michelangelo's Sistine Chapel ceiling, a devil is seen reciting from a scroll and two scribes on either side slightly above him are writing the words down in books. The devil and the scribe on the right have stopped to look over at the scribe on the left, who is still working to catch up. In this instance, if the scroll is the source of knowledge, it is not clear who wrote it. Furthermore, while caught in the act of transmission from scroll to book, the text is unequally being received and recorded, further calling into question the authority of the books.

Blake was the forerunner of a new kind of publication, the art book, which sought the form of the book as a medium for creative expression. Art books were not books about art, however, but were themselves works of art which could be distributed among a wider audience. Like a book, they contained a deliberate sequence of works that the artist selected to form a narrative. The structure and form of the art book introduced the idea of reading art by approaching the work in a reflective frame where thoughts and ideas of the artist could be shared. Artists who experimented with this form invariably limited the print run to no more than a few dozen so that the rarity of the book helped maintain the perception of it as an art object.

Goya's *Los Caprichos*

In 1797, Francisco de Goya (1746–1828) began work on a brooding series of etchings designed to be published as a book which contrasted starkly with his lighter-in-tone portrait paintings of Spain's royal family. The common conjecture for this change in artistic temperament has to do with a severe fever he suffered five years earlier that left him deaf and more darkly introspective, but also the times were changing and the ideals behind the American and French revolutions were spreading to Spain. The first series of etchings had the disarmingly fluffy title of *Los Caprichos* (*Caprices*); but they were, in fact, bleak meditations on human folly and ignorance and contained scenes of lust, cruel debasement, torture, rape, murder, and religious hypocrisy. Goya's *Los Caprichos* followed in the tradition of Sebastian Brant's *The Ship of Fools*, where allegory and fantasy were used by the artist as a license to ridicule human pretensions. In this series, Goya abandoned all superficial sentiment and aristocratic elegance and adopted grotesque caricatures of humans as animals and monstrous gargoyles, in some instances making parodic reference to actual members of the royal family and clergy. The exquisite tonality and dramatic compositions of Goya's etchings highlighted the barbaric and vulgar characters preoccupied with their vices. Each picture in the series has accompanying text on the bottom, which was written as if it were in Goya's own voice. In some compositions, he asks pointed rhetorical questions—for example, "How can the pupil know more?" about a picture of a jackass professor teaching jackass students—or he makes an ironic understatement, saying, "They spruce themselves up," in a composition that shows demons clipping their clawlike toenails as if they vainly believed that they could appear attractive. David Kunzle has argued that there is a progression in the series from social realism to private fantasy, suggesting that Goya intended readers to move from the symptoms to the cause of human folly, thereby providing a deeper exploration of human fears and desires that drive superstition and ignorance.[2]

Goya had hoped that a new era of more liberal discourse was in the making with the ascendancy of one of his patrons, Gaspar Melchor de Jovellanos (1744–1811), who was a strong advocate for the Enlightenment in Spain. But this hope was short lived, for his patron was soon deposed and sent into exile. The abrupt end of Goya's opportunity to champion more open social discourse forced him to pull all the remaining copies of *Los Caprichos* from sale after just two days. Goya did not altogether abandon this project; 11 years later, he began a new series that became known as *The Disasters of War* (1810–1820). The original working title, "Fatal consequences of the bloody war in Spain with Bonaparte. And other emphatic caprices," shows how these engravings were closely linked to Goya's experiences in the Peninsular War (1807–1814); yet it also shows how he saw them linked to his earlier work, *Los Caprichos*. As in his first set of prints, Goya depicts poignant moments that convey powerful themes of human suffering and degradation, but now the images are far more brutal and set in a landscape format, which forces us to survey the carnage. The accompanying text is also more clearly personal, "I saw it" (43), and more closely linked from one image to the next, as in the serial rape scenes: "They don't like it" (9), "Nor do these" (10), and "Neither do these" (11). The series ends with two engravings, first "Truth has died" (79), followed by one that pointedly asks, "Will she rise again?" (80). In each, we see the forces of chaos and dissolution victorious as the light emanating from Truth first fades and then in the second print appears to revive. The question is unequivocally directed to the reader, who must decide whether to take action on Truth's behalf.

Goya's use of words and images in his prints suggests an overall cyclic narrative that joins the disparate events into larger themes. Janis Tomlinson has noted that Goya had a keen narrative sense of "serial iconography," which he developed in his earlier royal commissions that linked large compositions together through the use of gestures and glances.[3] This narrative strength is also evident in Goya's engravings which masterfully show dramatic action as it unfolds, as evident in "The worst is to beg" (55), where a young healthy woman has turned her back to avoid looking at a group of starving people as she walks toward a French soldier in the background. The composition sets up the duality between the principle characters (the starving group on one side and the lady on the other); and then, only later, is the lighter, half-hidden impression of the soldier visible behind the woman, thereby linking her healthy condition with the French soldier, who has accepted her sexual favors to become her benefactor. The text assumes the audience understands this relationship and goes further to vindicate those who would rather go hungry than sell themselves to the enemy.

Printmaking Becomes an Art

In the early 19th century, metal-plate etching for commercial publications was increasingly being replaced by wood engraving and lithography, both of which allowed for faster and more efficient means of print reproduction. By midcentury, there began a revival of older forms of print technology now being employed by artists to create original works. The Société des Aquafortistes, formed in 1862, was one of the early organizations to champion the cause of etching and to a lesser degree lithography, as a younger sister to painting. This movement toward less modern forms of print production would continue through the 20th century as a means to create forms of fine art that were more clearly handcrafted and at the same time able to reach a broader audience outside the sanctioned venues for elite or commercial work.

Odilon Redon (1840–1916) trained with one of the leading artists in the new etching revival, Rodolphe Bresdin (1825–1885), and later took up lithography as a way to capture the sketchy dark voids that defined his dreamscapes. With lithography, Redon found a medium that responded to his emotional and visionary temperament, which sought to metamorphose past literary symbols and metaphors to represent a subjective interior world of dreams. The first of Redon's lithographic collections, called *In Dreams* (*Dans le réve*, 1879), cemented his reputation as the "Prince of Dreams" and catapulted him into the public eye. The black-and-white images had the quality of chalk and charcoal drawings that showed nearly empty landscapes with bodiless heads that had large luminous eyes looking upward as if in revelation. Redon wrote that he sought to give "life to creatures of dreams, improbable beings [fashioned] according to the laws of the probable."[4] Bound as a collection with deliberate sequence, the work had no specific narrative but, rather, suggested the irrational transformation of a dream. Through the application of a select few realistic details, the repeated use of spheres, and atmospheric textures, the collection created enough unity to suggest a narrative just outside the realm of comprehension.

Redon's 1882 volume *To Edgar Poe* was a bit of a ploy to capitalize on Edgar Allan Poe's popularity when, in fact, the images and the captions had no direct relationship to any of Poe's works. However, it was characteristic of Redon's way of working to imply known literary texts and symbols and yet ultimately to return the meaning of a particular drawing back to the subjectivity of the viewer. Redon's captions were much admired by the symbolist writer Stéphane Mallarmé, who said, "I adore your captions, which consist of a word or two, but are so much to the point that they show the extent to which you penetrate the arcane aspects of your subject."[5] In Redon's iconic image of the eye balloon from the *To Edgar Poe* collection, the enigmatic title "The eye, a strange balloon, moves towards the infinite one" ("*L'oeil, comme un ballon bizarre se dirige vers l'infini*") identifies specific objects in the composition but suggests that these objects must be placed outside their ordinary reference to the natural world, and it allows them to take on new meanings as from a dream language where personal meanings trump accepted values.

As modern art continued to grow evermore abstract, narrative works became evermore arcane and rare. Wassily Kandinsky (1866–1944) was on the cusp of this epochal transformation in modernism as it eliminated the last vestiges of representation and embraced purely formal representations of color, shape, and design. In 1909, Kandinsky began work on a book of poems and woodcuts called *Sound* (*Klänge*), along with a few other short plays, as a part of his ongoing project to establish a synthesis among all the arts. Kandinsky was inspired in this goal by the composer Richard Wagner's idea of a "total work of art" (*gesamtkunstwerk*), but he sought to further interpenetrate the arts and unify them through primary forms and colors. The woodcuts in the book are primarily in black and white and roughly describe figurative forms in outdoor landscapes that fold into and out of each other. The language also employs a simplicity and repetition that recalls folk ballads and tribal ritual. The text does not translate the images literally but, rather, points out the distance between what is seen and what is imagined. A group of hills is described as "a mass of hills of all the colors you can imagine or care to imagine. . . . Just plain, ordinary hills, like the kind you always imagine and never see."[6] Events described in the poems—a running man beating a drum or a bull being massacred, for example—focus on small moments of confusion, transformation, and stillness.

At the end of the 19th century, the woodcut came back in vogue with the arrival in Europe of stunning Japanese woodcuts (ukiyo-e). The revival was also a result of the fascination that Kandinsky, Paul Gauguin, and others demonstrated for folk and medieval art. Central to all these interests was the notion of the "primitive," which was understood as something more essential, more at the core of human existence than those things produced in the modern age. For this reason, artists who explored primitivism were responding more to the loss of innocence and authenticity in modern art than creating an actual reproduction of the art of nonindustrialized people. So-called primitive styles of art questioned the central ideals and values of the elite art world and became a nostalgic way to evoke all things lost or displaced by the modern world.

Expressionist "Wordless Books"

The idealism of Kandinsky and other early abstract artists was soon shattered with the advent of World War I (1914–1918). Each side's nationalist propaganda promoting the war began to ring hollow as the casualties mounted and the chemical and mechanical warfare became bogged down in deadly and pointless trench skirmishes. An art of rebellion and resistance to the architects of the war developed from within such movements as expressionism in Germany, which sought to convey the horror and despair of common people and the callous indifference of the insulated upper classes. Expressionism was a wide-ranging art movement that involved not only artists in more conventional media but also playwrights, filmmakers, architects, and graphic artists. Like Kandinsky, Vincent van Gogh (1853–1890), and Edvard Munch (1863–1944) before them, expressionists sought to create a "total work of art." They differed politically, but what they all shared in common was a stark graphic quality that accentuated histrionic emotions, so that it seemed the natural laws of the world were overruled by human passion and fear.

Expressionism was involved in its own brand of propaganda, and print publications were one way to widely disseminate works among its ideal spectators, expressionists described as the "masses," that is, oppressed workers. More commonly, however, expressionism found its audience with sympathetic socialists in Europe and the United States. A unique form of narrative art, wordless books emerged from such expressionist artists as Frans Masereel (1889–1972), Otto Nückel (1888–1955), Helena Bochořáková-Dittrichová (1894–1980), William Gropper (1897–1977), and Lynd Ward (1905–1985). These wordless graphic narratives typically told their stories with one black-and-white picture per page with no accompanying text. The idea of wordless books was not invented by the expressionists, however. Early examples of pantomimic sequential narratives first appeared in German pictorial broadsheets (*bilderbogen*) of the 1860s and had for a while appeared in popular illustrations made by Adolphe Willette and Théophile-Alexandre Steinlen for the *Chat Noir* (1882–1895), a weekly art magazine from the cabaret of the same name in Montmartre, Paris.[7]

Expressionist wordless books, as Lothar Lang has noted, owed much of their dramatic tableaus and twisted scenery to such expressionist films as *The Cabinet of Dr. Calligari* (1920) and *Metropolis* (1927).[8] However, the progenitor of wordless books, Frans Masereel, created the first two such graphic narratives, *25 images de la passion d'un homme* in 1918 and *Passionate Journey* (*Mon *livre d'heures*) in 1919, a few years before the first expressionist films were produced. Thomas Mann once said that he thought Masereel's book was the most stimulating "movie" he had so far seen, but Mann was also keen to point out the medieval influences that lie at the heart of these narrative experiments. Both titles of Masereel's early books refer to medieval forms of narrative (versions of Christ's Passion and Books of Hours); furthermore, Masereel thought that unlike movies, which when viewed are consumed all at once with actions unfolding in a fixed sequence, these stories should be meditated on—like a medieval text—and through repeated readings guide the reader toward a better approach to life.

The most telling influence of medieval art on expressionist wordless books is the use of allegory, and this holds true not only for Masereel's early work but throughout his career and even later among his many imitators. Wordless books relied on a narrative strategy found in such medieval allegorical dramas as *Everyman*, where characters represent ideas: "Kindred," "Beauty," "Discretion," and of course, "Everyman" himself, who is anyone and everyone at the same time. By using these generic stereotypes, wordless books communicated the boundaries of the story and immediately established the essential conflict in well-established ideas. Another source for allegorical characters found in wordless books was the socialist agit-prop (agitational propaganda) theater that portrayed such stock characters as the "Factory Boss," "Corrupt Police Officer," and "Strike Breaker," which were performed at strikes and union meetings to rally workers to their cause. "Everyman" in Masereel's *Passionate Journey* is an easygoing, hatless man who is unattached to any class or occupation as he moves through society indifferent to status and hostile to pretension. He is, in essence, a modern Everyman whose particular identity is unimportant as he acts as our guide to understanding a better way to live.

One of the unique features of Masereel's work that was not imitated by later wordless-book artists was the way his pictures were not always linked in a dramatic way by the continuation of an unfolding action; rather, the common transition between images is from subject to subject. In *Passionate Journey*, the images frequently leap from one situation and action (for example, the man cooking) to another (the man riding a bike) so that what we glean from the story is not a causal sequential action—first he cooked and then he rode a bike—but a commentary on the kinds of choices this man has made in his life. The book ends with a provocative sequence of symbolic images where the man first appears with a skull for a face and stomps on his own heart as lightning flashes. The final image is of him stepping out of this world, barefoot, with a jocular wave of the hand in a scene reminiscent of

Frans Masereel, *Passionate Journey* (*Mon livre d'heures*), 1919. (© 2010 Artists Rights Society [ARS], New York / VG Bild-Kunst, Bonn)

Nicolas Camille Flammarion's (1842–1925) famous wood-cut illustration from 1888 of a "medieval missionary" looking out from the point where heaven and earth meet.[9] Although socialism is the underlying philosophy in Masereel's work, as Thomas Mann remarked, "His heart, not Socialism, made a revolutionary of him. . . . For the true revolution is not 'in principle,' not in 'The Idea'—but in the human heart."[10]

The expressionist painter George Grosz (1893–1959) was also widely known for his vivid caricatures of the corruption and social decay during the Weimar Republic in Germany (1919–1933). His caricatures appeared in a number of left-wing political newspapers and magazines and were first compiled into a book, *The Face of the Ruling Class*, in 1921. His sharp linear drawings depict cruel police, wounded soldiers, greedy bankers, and dissolute prostitutes swirling about in a confusion of interconnected and overlapping lines that make the scene appear semitransparent. His caricatures had a journalistic style reminiscent of Goya, in which he used captions for his drawings to call attention to the disparity between the propaganda in the words and the harsh reality represented in pictures. One new technique for visual quotation that Grosz employed was the use of collage, where advertisements and commercially printed materials were cut and pasted into his drawings for ironic effect. The idea of making collage art, cutting and pasting existing images together to create a wholly new image, came into its own under the Dada art movement, where it had been employed to disorient and divest images of known meanings and introduce ironic commentary on the new juxtapositions. Grosz was active in the Communist Party, and many of his illustrations were funneled through an international network of sympathetic publications, allowing his work to become one of the signature styles of the radical left-wing political movement.

Surrealist Narratives

Following Masereel and the expressionists, few artists had much success or interest in making graphic narratives. One of the last to undertake ambitious narrative projects was Max Ernst (1891–1976). Between 1929 and 1934, he created two long series of collage works compiled and published into books, which employed Victorian romance and scientific illustrations to suggest stories with mythic and alchemical themes. Ernst used collage for a more deliberately dramatic effect: he and his fellow surrealists explored the psychological and dreamlike impact of the Dada collages, which rendered literal interpretations absurd and opened up the composition to disturbing and evocative images. Many of the collages are reminiscent of Redon's dreamlike compositions, but Ernst's collages were made of much more familiar elements, albeit in a new and conflicted whole. Unlike some collages where the different elements remain autonomous, Ernst was inspired by the 19th-century illustrator J. J. Grandville to create bizarre images that had an internal visual logic that displayed an uncanny truth. To achieve this affect, he worked hard to make the individual cut-out images in the collage appear as seamless as possible, first by carefully cutting and assembling the pieces so that at first glance the image appears plausibly realistic, but also through photographing and mechanically reproducing the collages so that none of the cut edges or layered surfaces appeared in the reproduction.

In the first series of collages, entitled *The Hundred-Headed Woman* (*La femme 100 têtes*, 1929), there were titles for the collages that suggested a deliberate sequence of action, as, for example, "The failed immaculate conception," "The same for the second . . . ," and ". . . and the third time failed." Regardless of their titles, nothing in any of these collages suggests an actual continuation of an earlier action. Ernst further defines and negates the narrative by mentioning a reoccurring character, a bird named Loplop, but then he does not give that character any consistent visual form.[11] Here, as earlier with Redon, the idea of a story is conveyed through engaging the viewer's expectation of narrative continuity without providing an actual plot. Charlotte Stokes[12] and, elsewhere, M. E. Warlick[13] have argued that Ernst had a particular story in mind with his collages, but their nuanced arguments concerning myth and alchemy underscore the complex levels of signification that Ernst employed in order to suggest a narrative without being limited to a specific story. Ernst's antiquated visual elements, along with the ancient mythic symbols, suggest that he was concerned, not with conveying a coherent new story, but with creating the impression of a story that was half-remembered, just out of reach of recollection.

Ernst intensified the dramatic action in his collages by inserting additional characters and objects. Their placement in the scene had a certain visual logic; the close proximity of the incongruous elements created a heightened dramatic tension. This is especially true of the last of Ernst's collage novels, *A Week of Kindness* (1934),[14] where the gestures of the characters in the composition make each scene seem emotionally charged with a melodramatic pathos. Unlike the earlier collage novels that extensively used captions, *A Week of Kindness* had no captions and was arranged into seven sections, one for each day of the week. Each day is assigned a number of thematic elements (i.e., Thursday: blackness, Rooster's Laughter, Easter Island), which are outlined at the beginning of each section. The preface was clearly intended to invoke alchemical and occult readings of the images, as if they were not intended to represent real actions and events but were instead, as in an alchemical manual, symbols of mysterious processes that defied realistic representation. There are many more repeated elements and figures, but still the collages present the reader with a hermetic world where the scenes reveal dramatic conflict and confusion without positing a logical progression. Ernst also employs to great effect collage elements placed inside the already existing picture frames hanging on the walls. It is as if the images hanging on the wall are telling us something of the psychological state of the people in the scene, but the images in the frames are just as ambiguous as

Max Ernst, "The Court of the Dragon" from *A Week of Kindness*. (© 2010 Artists Rights Society [ARS], New York / ADAGP, Paris)

the scenes in the rooms they are hung in, resulting in no new revelation but instead layering one ambiguity on top of another.

There was no immediate successor to Ernst's surreal collages, and graphic narrative experiments soon all but disappeared from the modern art movement. One of the few major artists to engage in narrative art during World War II was Pablo Picasso (1881–1973), who created a pair of etchings to support the anti-Fascist movement in Spain. In these prints, entitled *The Dream and Lie of Franco I & II* (1937),[15] Picasso lampoons the Fascist general Francisco Franco (1892–1975) in a grotesquely satirical manner akin to Alfred Jarry's character Père Ubu (see box 4.1). The curious thing about each of these etchings is that the nine panels that cover the page were not reversed so they could be read normally from left to right; instead, Picasso created the images so they appeared right to left on the print. This disturbing backward

---

Box 4.1   Alfred Jarry's Pére Ubu

Pére Ubu was the creation of the artist Alfred Jarry (1873–1907), who featured this obese, self-important fool in a parody of Shakespeare's *Macbeth*, *King Ubu* (*Ubu Roi*). The play was first envisioned as a puppet show, but it was eventually staged with live actors and life-sized puppets in 1896 at Lugné Poe's symbolist Théâtre de l'Oeuvre. The riotous opening night and later critical condemnation of the perverse antirealist farce did not put an end to the character; rather, the reactions spurred Jarry and his collaborators to invent several more plays that were printed in limited-run art publications with illustrations of the notorious Ubu in evermore outrageous adventures. Jarry developed a childish and primitive way of representing Ubu with signature stylized facial features, which were roughly based on a bombastic grade-school teacher in Jarry's past. Ubu's pear-shaped countenance also echoed the caricature that Charles Philipon made of the French King Louis-Philippe in the 1830s. Pierre Bonnard in 1901 and later Jean-Édouard Vuillard continued to keep the character alive after Jarry's early demise from malnutrition and drug overdose. The reoccurring caricature of Ubu was the epitome of bourgeois pretensions and in this respect mimicked such popular-press comic characters as Dr. Syntax (1812) and Ally Sloper (1867) and is the first repeated cartoon character to emerge from within modern art.

---

reading heightens the sense of confusion and the unnatural development that traces Franco's rise to power. The poem that accompanies the images describes scenes of the civil war in Spain: "cries of children cries of women cries of birds cries of flowers cries of timbers and cries of stones" (no punctuation in the original). The last three panels on the second page were added as Picasso was working on sketches for his mural *Guernica* (1937), which was titled after the name of a small town in Spain that suffered a brutal aerial bombing by the German forces supporting Franco. The close resemblance to disfigured characters in the mural is indicative of the broader shift in Picasso's work toward establishing a more emotional core in his abstract figures.

Charlotte Salomon's *Life? or Theatre?*

The other major narrative artwork born of the pain and suffering brought on by the rise of fascism was Charlotte Salomon's *Life? or Theatre? A Three-Color Operetta* (*Leben? oder Theater? Drifarben Singspiel*) of 1942. This

Charlotte Salomon, *Life? or Theatre?* (*Leben? oder Theater?*), ca. 1941–1943. (Collection of the Jewish Historical Museum, Amsterdam. Copyright Charlotte Salomon Foundation)

semifictionalized autobiographical story depicts Salomon's coming of age and follows the lives of her aunt (after whom she was named), mother, and grandmother as they each succumbed to depression and suicide. Salomon (1917–1943) learned of her aunt's and her mother's suicides only in 1939, when she was 22 years old, after she experienced her grandmother's suicide firsthand. At that point, she was living with her grandparents in the south of France hoping to escape persecution as a Jew in Germany. Pulling herself out of her own depression and thoughts of suicide, she set to work creating nearly 1,300 gouache paintings on paper; of these, about 800 were sequentially arranged to tell her story, although the precise order is unclear.

Salomon called her work a "three-color operetta" and quite literally used only three primary colors (yellow, red, and blue) and white (no black) to create a vivid palate reminiscent of Postimpressionist painters who were at the time reviled in the fascist-controlled art academies in Germany. She imagined her paintings as a visual operetta where music plays a critical role in defining the emotional tenor, meaning, and physical form of the paintings. Notes that accompany most of the paintings make frequent references to musical passages by Beethoven, Bach, Shubert, Weber, Bizet, and other composers. Just as music had framed the work of Kandinsky, the music in *Life? or Theatre?* acts as a force of nature whose laws serve as a point of departure from strict realism, permitting the scenes to float freely across the surface of the work so they can fully embody the sound. Salomon varies her modes of representation more than Kandinsky does. At times, Salomon paints portraits of her characters—wrapped up in their world—seen in a telling moment we are meant to linger over, as, for example, when we see a multitude of images of herself attending to her mother lying in bed struggling with depression. Synoptically, the moments pour themselves out across the page, allowing us to see the unfolding actions as patterns in a tapestry. But no one of these intimate moments is allowed to last for more than an instant before it is followed by another, and then another, flickering across the page like the notes of a song. At other times, and especially toward the end, the locations and characters are stripped bare of all decoration and become more awkward, as if they have become more urgent yet less purposeful, straining against narrative continuity and creeping toward closure.

Salomon scarcely ate or slept while she worked on this project, but it was recalled that she was often heard singing to herself. Salomon had grown up in a musical household; her stepmother, Paula Lindberg, was a classically trained singer who sang professionally. Her father was a well-connected professor and medical doctor, and their house was the center of a diverse community of Berlin intellectuals. We can see their secular and cosmopolitan influence on Salomon, who freely and ironically quotes from Goethe, Nietzsche, and Schiller as well as from folktales and popular ballads. In keeping with the theatrical premise of the work, the characters that represent Salomon's friends and family were given fictional musical names fitting for an operetta. Paulinka Bimbam, Dr. Singsang, and Professor Klingklang are some of the more playful character names, but she also included less harmonious names such as Mr. and Mrs. Knarr, or rattle, for her grandparents. For her own parents and herself, she creates the Kann family, which means "able," suggesting a kind of pragmatism, but also a will to act. For her love interest and spiritual inspiration, the real Alfred Wolfsohn she calls Amadeus Daberlohn, after the composer Mozart, whose music was especially beloved in the Salomon household. The name Daberlohn, literally "without money," refers to Wolfsohn's financial dependence on the Salomon household as a music instructor. This job gave him not only his only income but also a work permit that shielded him from Nazi persecution.

Wolfsohn had developed special theories of voice that were in many ways reminiscent of the spiritual-physical ideas of Rudolf Steiner (1861–1925).[16] Whereas Salomon's stepmother took only a passing interest in Wolfsohn's theories, Salomon was consumed by them, and they lie at the core of her belief in reinventing herself through her art. Wolfsohn had narrowly escaped death as a soldier in World War I, and his recovery and spiritual rebirth were at the center of his music theory. He said, "I discovered singing is more bound up with life than anything else . . . one can imbue sound with an expression that can reveal the innermost feelings churning up the soul."[17] Wolfsohn went on to say that suffering can be transformed through the creative work of an artist, and he argued further that this transformation is essential to great works of art. Salomon seemed to hang on his every word and lets us see his face painted dozens of times per page as he philosophized about life and art.

Salomon used several different narrative techniques, none of which resembled any kind of comic art of the day but were instead more aesthetically akin to a film, with suggestive cropping and framing of the figures in a cinematic fashion. This too may have been an inspiration from Wolfsohn, who told her that "the movie was the machine of modern man as a means of going out of oneself."[18] In the first half of the work, Salomon often used a synoptic narrative style, with many repetitions of characters, with or without frames. She arranged the scenes within each frame in a meandering way. To aid the reader in interpreting the narrative flow of each composition, she made diagrams on tracing paper that recorded the dialogue, narration, and descriptions of music. The words on these pages expand and contract and flow about the page, visually expressing the emotional tenor of the narrative. Only in the second half of the narrative, introducing the philosophical Amadeus Daberlohn, does Salomon begin using words directly on the page, giving them the same visual and expressive weight as the pictures. Toward the end, as her story encroaches on the present, the pictures become more hurried as if responding to the very real and growing threat of Nazi arrest and deportation. The pictures also represent more painful experiences, including her grandmother's leap from a second-story window to her death.

Despite her deepening gloom and desperation, Salomon ends the narrative with a powerful affirmation of the beauty of life. She writes: "And with dream-awakened eyes she saw the beauty around her, saw the sea, felt the sun, and she knew she had to vanish for a while from the human plane and make every sacrifice in order to create her world anew out of the depths. And from that came: *Life? or Theatre?*"[19]

A few days after passing her collected paintings and writings to a family friend to watch over, Salomon—now four months' pregnant—and her husband were rounded up by the Gestapo and sent to Auschwitz. It was September 1943, and Salomon would be killed on arrival at the camp; her husband survived until January. After the war, her parents, who had found refuge in Amsterdam, reclaimed her work. With its graphic depictions of suicides and love affairs, it must have come as quite a shock for them to see their lives described in such a revealing manner. They held onto the paintings for 10 years and finally, in 1959, brought them to the attention of the Stedelijk Museum, where a broad selection of the work from *Life? or Theatre?* was first presented in 1961. After several subsequent exhibitions, a film documentary, and the publication of selections of the work, it was first shown and published in its entirety in 1981 through the auspices of the Jewish Historical Museum in Amsterdam, where the work now resides.

Salomon's complex and inconsistent numbering schemes suggest she frequently edited and revised the order of the images, inserted new paintings, and removed others many times over the course of her making *Life? or Theatre?* It is remarkable that she was concerned with the perception of the work as a coherent sequential narrative, especially when it is not clear for whom she intended this work to be viewed as a whole. The sheer scope of the project defies easy exhibition or publication, and in many of these logistical ways, she seems unconcerned with how the work would fit into a gallery or be reproduced in a book. One of the last changes she made to the order of the work is indicated by a note inserted on page N 8 T, which states, "The numbering does not coincide with the correct order." The note goes on to say that the paintings should be viewed in the order in which they are currently arranged. Unfortunately, that order was lost in the 1960s as selections of the collection were put on exhibition, and today it is impossible to reconstruct exactly how she intended the work to be read. This small loss does not greatly hinder our appreciation of Salomon's artistic accomplishment; however, it does rein in our full understanding of *Life? or Theatre?* and is a reminder of the terrible loss that will forever keep us at a distance from this monumental work.

CHAPTER 5

Humor Magazines

In the 19th century, graphic narratives ultimately came into being in their current form: dramatic sequential action organized into brief moments shown in panels across the page. Across Europe and the United States, no single artist or seminal event stands out that clearly marks the first instance of modern comic art. One thing is for certain, however, comics were a by-product of the newly emerging mechanized world. Not only was mass production critical for its wide dissemination, but also mechanization played a key role in establishing new ideas about time, space, and movement.

Nowhere was the changing notion of time more evident than in the growing profession of journalism that fostered new habits and expectations of reading for leisure. Weekly newspapers from early in the 17th century had evolved into biweekly and in a few instances triweekly publications by the century's end. By the start of the 18th century, daily publications appeared with the arrival of *The Daily Courant* published in England (1702). The increasing rhythm of news cycles, argues Carlos Franciscato, involved "breaking events into time fragments according to the periodicity of a publication,"[1] which was instrumental in defining new and evermore urgent conceptions of simultaneity, periodicity, and novelty.

Rodolphe Töpffer had captured some of this faster movement in his moment-to-moment montages, but his narrative designs still held on to vestiges of the past and did not include speech bubbles or other emanata to further speed up the reading experience and close the lingering gap between words and pictures. The gradual emergence of what we now call "comics" in the 19th century required greater plasticity in caricature and fluidity in action to achieve even finer gradations in sequential action. In an indirect

Box 5.1   Early Animation and Eadweard Muybridge

The earliest protoanimation toys, the phenakistoscope (1831) and the Zoetrope (1860s), created the impression of seeing a figure in motion by spinning multiple depictions of the figure that when focused on by the viewer as a single point seemed to move all by itself. The illusion of sequential motion was a technique that inspired comic artists to experiment with more accurately parsing sequential actions to convey motion. The vocabulary for this early animation work was infinitely expanded by the photographic experiments of Eadweard Muybridge (1830–1904), who in 1877 set up an elaborate apparatus of cameras with shutters coordinated by electric triggers to capture in sequence the natural motions of a horse. Muybridge went on to employ this technique to capture all manner of animal and human motion on film. Muybridge's work was published (1887), allowing artists to see for the first time the accurate stages of natural action.

way, the invention of photography would eventually help further advance communicating these ideas of movement (see box 5.1); but as David Kunzle has pointed out, photographs enhanced, but did not create, the notion of a fragmented perception of actions which was already evident in the comics themselves.[2]

The first step in the advance of modern publishing in the 19th century was the development of cast-iron printing presses and cheaply manufactured paper. With these innovations, there began a gradual widening and deepening of literacy across Europe and the United States that was spread further by urban population growth and education reform. The proliferation of inexpensive magazines and newspapers created the first truly mass media. The visual appeal of each publication was an essential component in enticing this audience to read for leisure. Furthermore, the intense competition among publications became a powerful driving force for innovation in graphic narrative.

One of the key technical developments in printmaking at this time was wood engraving, which used sturdy end-grain blocks of wood that were incised with delicate lines that closely resembled pen-and-ink drawings. The chief advantage of wood engraving was that it allowed pictures to be printed at the same time as the metal-typeset words, making it possible to reproduce images thousands of times without wearing out. The heavier pressure applied to the block also allowed for larger and more dramatic use of solid black in the pictures, which can be seen in the increasing use of silhouette and dark shadows. Wood-engraving blocks were also better able to withstand the pressure of the new steam-powered typeset press that first appeared in the 1830s and could reliably churn out thousands of prints in a few hours.

French Caricature Magazines

Despite the advantages of wood engraving, the French satirical magazines stayed with lithographic printing for much of the 19th century. Part of the appeal of lithography was the quality of line and more expressive use of blacks and grays. The technical limitations were that lithography kept words and pictures more or less separate in the publications. Small amounts of text could easily be handwritten on the lithographic stone, but publishers of newspapers had to print the metal-type sections first and then apply the lithographic artwork second. Such French Illustrated publications as *Le Nain Jaune* (1814–1815), and *La Caricature* (1830–1835) typically included lithographic illustrations and caricatures outside the text as an appendix to the typeset words, printed on cheaper paper, that made up the main portion of the magazine. This arrangement suited the censors, who were far more concerned about visual caricature than written satire and insisted on approving each caricature before publication.[3] According to the government, both caricature and the theater were reasoned to be more dangerous forms of mass communication than written satire because they could appeal directly to the preliterate lower classes and might have a more deleterious impact on social order.[4] By keeping the written portion of the magazine separate from the caricatures, publishers were able to make last-minute changes to the illustrations if a censor failed to approve them.

Honoré Daumier (1808–1879) has become the acknowledged master of caricature and satirical lithography who produced more than 3,900 lithographs in the 40 years he worked for *La Caricatura, Charivari,* and other publications edited by Charles Philipon. His early work demonstrated a plasticity of expression that wildly caricatured the leading politicians of the day, making them appear petty, dimwitted, and deceitful. Over time, Daumier moved away from the iconic caricatures that reduced a person to a foolish type; gradually, he found a more nuanced dramatic language that examined relationships and social conditions beautifully distilled with evocative gestures and body language. This change in his work was partially a result of the censorship laws, which made it increasingly difficult for caricature artists to render well-known people and forced them instead to caricature society in general. The

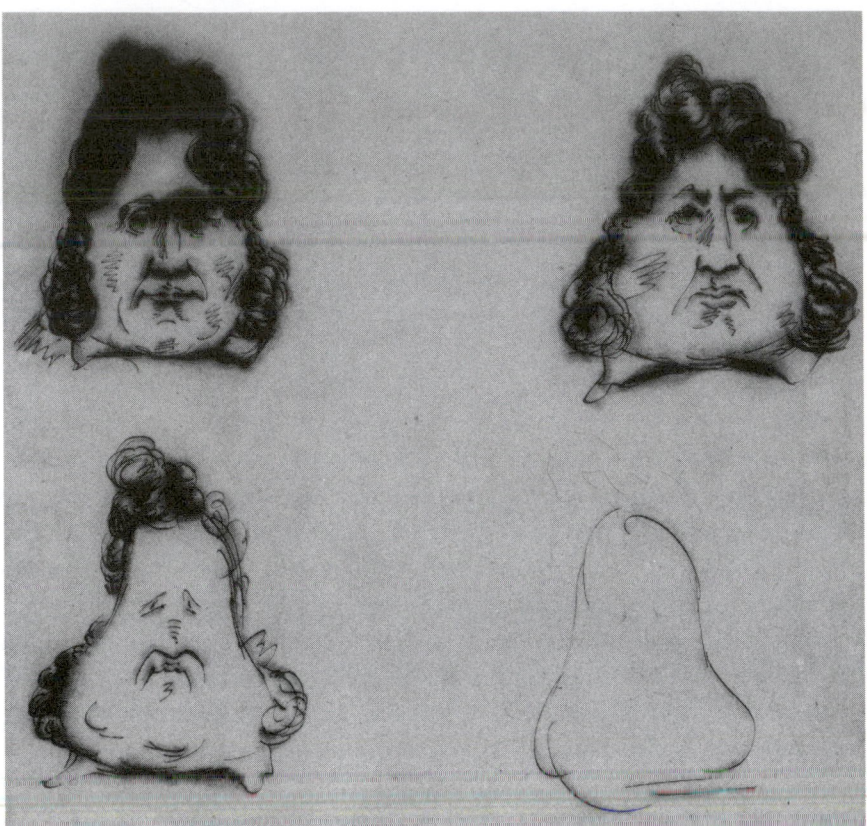

Charles Philipon, *The Metamorphosis of Louis-Philippe into a Pear (La Métamorphose du roi Louis-Philippe en poire)*, a drawing, 1831. (Courtesy of the Bibliothèque Nationale de France, Estampes et Photographie Department)

strength of Daumier's work and its lasting influence on caricature was his way of graphically rendering powerfully memorable scenes. Daumier's importance as a modern artist manifested very late in his life after he was celebrated by the art critic Charles Baudelaire in his 1857 essay, "Some French Caricaturists" (*Quelque caricaturistes français*). The ascendancy of Daumier into the ranks of fine art brought greater critical attention to the art of caricaturists, but as Alexander Roob has argued, it has distorted the actual history of the development of caricature and impeded an understanding of the more experimental aspects of the popular press and its influence on emerging avant-garde movements.[5]

In a courtroom in Paris in 1831, Charles Philipon was put on trial for publishing a cartoon by Daumier in which King Louis Phillip looked like a common workman. In his defense, Philipon argued before the jury that anything could be made to look like the king and that the court would have to ban all representations to uphold the censorship laws. To prove his point, he drew four squares on the page; in the first one, he drew a figure with a passing resemblance to the king, and then he continued to distort its appearance until in the last panel on the page it looked like a pear. In the common French slang of the day, a pear (*poire*) meant "fat head." His witty defense failed to convince the jury, and Philipon was sentenced to six months in prison and fined 2,000 francs. Philipon would return to court two more times to defend his publications from censure, and though he lost each case, his defiance and dramatic appearances served as publicity for his publications and made him a popular celebrity among the young Bohemian radicals of Paris.

The metamorphosis that Philipon employed to transform the appearance of the king was a common parlor trick, but one that took on new significance in the 19th century as caricatures began to expolre sequential action. One of the more inovative caracaturists who often used metamorphosis was the artist J. J. Grandville (Jean Ignace Isidore Gérard, 1803–1847), who also published with Philipon as well as illustrating books. Grandville initially created caricatures that broadly satirized society by putting animal and insect heads on human bodies (*Les Métamorphoses du Jour*, 1828–1829). This was an old idea that protocaricaturists had been doing for a long time, but Grandville's masterful technique in lithography gave the metamorphosed figures a quotidian naturalism that heightened the strangeness of their appearance. Energized by the success of this publication, Grandville experimented further with human-animal analogies with insects, mammals, machine parts, and humans all mixed up together in *Another World* (*Un autre monde*, 1844). In this work, he conceived of analogous shapes metamorphosing from one thing to the next, as seen in his "Apocalypse du ballet." Hearts and feathers fly up over the ballerina, metamorphose into wreaths, and shower down as money, which is finally transformed into confetti. The ballerina herself begins as a pair of stockings that change into a pair of dancing legs, which, after appearing for a moment as a ballerina, spin off as a top. All these transformations take place on a stage, giving the narrative a synoptic form and thereby allowing the viewer's eye to move around the complex composition over and over, as each image metamorphoses into the next. Grandville thus applied the distortions of caricature to describe a composite set of images that form a montage enlivened by motion. Unlike Töpffer, Grandville did not need

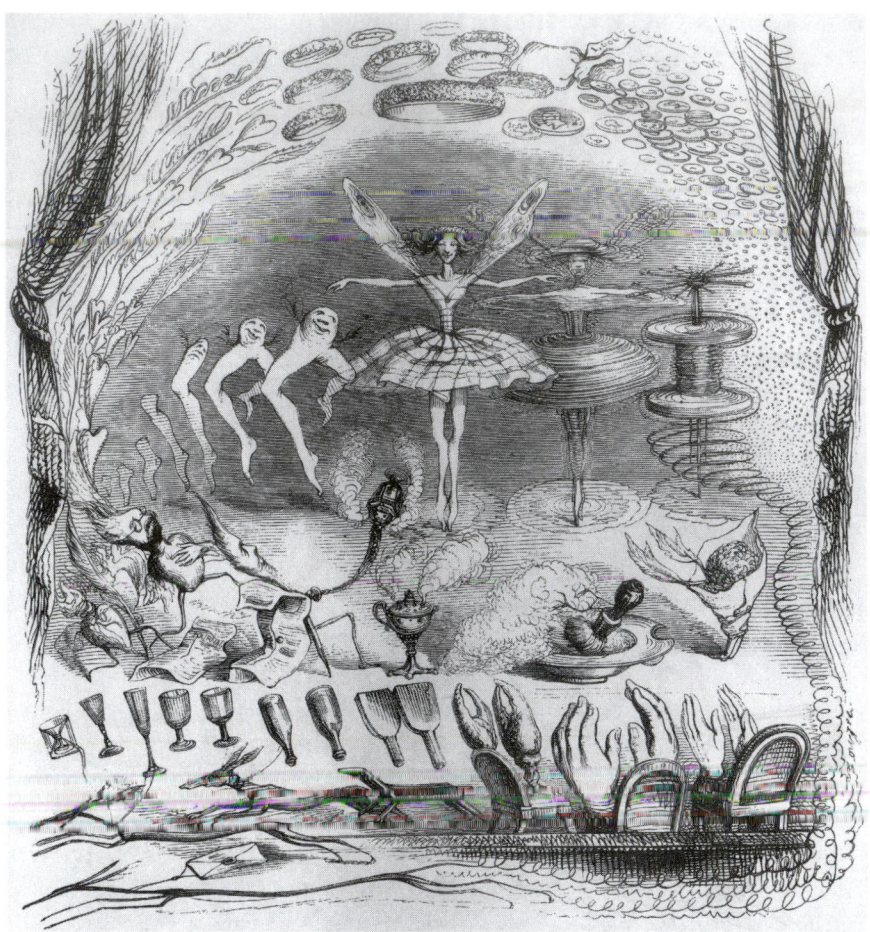

J. J. Grandville, "Apocalypse du ballet," from his collection *Another World* (*Un autre monde*), 1844.

separate panels or text to comment on the passage of time because the connections he makes are intrinsic to the forms.

One hundred years later, Grandville's dreamlike apparitions would be celebrated by the surrealist Max Ernst in his collage compositions and paintings. What Grandville accomplished that Ernst admired and imitated was not just the animal-human mix-ups but the primacy of an image that was not based on—or could be summed up by—a text. In the preface to *Another World*, Grandville has an artist's pencil say to a writer's pen, "You will let my wings move freely in space; in no way will you hinder my flight toward new spheres which I wish to explore. . . . You will record the impressions of a voyage you will have not taken."[6] What makes Grandville's metamorphoses seem truthful is this visual primacy and an internal graphic logic that makes the image seem undeniably true to itself.[7]

The notion of metamorphosis would eventually be grafted onto the modern idea of evolution put forth by Charles Darwin. The British caricaturist Charles H. Bennett (1829–1867) created a series of cartoons he called *The Origin of the Species* (1872), which closely imitated Grandville's type of social satire through metamorphosis. The continuity Bennett found between metamorphosis and evolution underscored the way science had also found meanings that were implausible to our minds yet undeniable to our eyes.

British Caricature Magazines

Following the caricature magazine format developed in Paris by Philipon, translations and adaptations of his *Charivari* publication appeared in Lyon as well as in Belgium, Germany, and Switzerland. In 1841, the Journalists Henry Mayhew, Mark Lemon, and Stirling Coyne joined in a new collaborative publishing venture with the engravier Ebenezer Landells, and the printer Joseph Last to found *Punch Magazine*, which was originally subtitled "The London *Charivari*" even though it had no connection to the French publication. The primary title, *Punch*, was based on the name of the offbeat lead character in the Punch and Judy puppet theater that entertained middle-class audiences along seaside resorts. The choice reflected the ideal audience for this new magazine: people who wanted a humor magazine with more playful jibes at society and a little less political rancor. *Punch* had at the outset a decidedly liberal bent that satirized royal excess and condemned oppressive employers. In the first decade of publication, *Punch* struggled to cover its costs. The liberal views eventually lost out to more conservative middle-class opinions, such as the famous attack on the Aesthetes in 1847, which gave the publication wider popularity and helped sustain it for the remainder of its 141 years of publication.

Punch used wood-engraved illustrations in its publication, economically allowing it to insert illustrations more liberally throughout. Just as in the French caricature publications, *Punch* also featured a large-format satirical print, called the "big cut," that took up a whole back page. For the big cut of June 24, 1843, Mr. Punch—the satiric icon of the magazine—mockingly submitted his own "cartoons" for a government-sponsored art competition taking place in London.[8] The word "cartoon" originally just meant a preparatory

John Leech, "Cartoon No. 1: Substance and Shadow," *Punch*, June 24, 1843.

sketch on inexpensive paper. What had before been called "Punch's pencillings" soon became known as "Punch's cartoons," and finally, simply "cartoons."[9] The word "cut," short for woodcut, was also used in the 19th century to mean a humorous illustration, even after the 1860s when woodcuts had been replaced by photomechanical reproduction. In the 1890s, the popular humor magazine *Comic Cuts* was one of the last to use the word "cut" before it was supplanted simply with the word "comic." In both instances, the terms "cartoon" and "comic" were not created through some deliberate effort to define a new medium; rather, they were by happenstance a simplification of common usage. Today, not all comics are funny nor are cartoons just preparatory sketches; indeed, because of their ambiguous meanings, it has proven very difficult to define these words according to their broad modern usage. (For more on political cartooning, see box 5.2.)

Blood and Thunder

Between 1820 and 1850, British publishers such as James Catnach produced the least expensive and most widely circulated publications, collectively called

> **Box 5.2** José Guadalupe Posada and the Retro-Folk Look
>
> José Guadalupe Posada (1852–1913) was a well-established illustrator and political cartoonist in Mexico when in 1889 he began work on the first of many prints depicting skeletons, known as *Calaveras*, acting as members of society. For the Mexican holiday Day of the Dead (*Día de los Muertos*), there was a long-standing tradition of displaying *calaveras* to honor the dead. The *calavera* is also a type of caricature, similar in effect to the common practice of making people look like animals to poke fun at their self-importance. Furthermore, *calaveras* underscore the notion that death is the great leveler of all ambition. Although Posada's *calavera* images represent only a small fraction of his total life's work, they beautifully capture the retro-folk look for which he is best remembered. Even though Posada used the latest photo-etching process on metal, his images were further engraved and manipulated so that they resembled the kind of rough-hewn woodblock prints that circulated in the countryside. This manner of working allowed him to maintain the advantages of metal print for mass production and at the same time appeal to sentiments and values rooted in the past as a critique of the emerging modern world.

catchpenny prints, penny bloods, or blood and thunders for their histrionic depiction of violent crime and natural disasters. These illustrated magazines were often only a few dozen pages long and could easily be folded into someone's pocket for casual perusal, giving rise to the market for "pocket literature." Each publication typically compiled a variety of short illustrated and sensational stories that could provide brief moments of diversion.

There were two impulses in 19th-century publications that drew them in seemingly contradictory directions: first, the need to capture a portion of the market and become popular; and second, the need to be recognized as a valuable asset to society by including explicitly educational material. Publications lived or died depending on their market share, yet there were strong public opinions about the need to demonstrate a didactic purpose for the good of society. The explicitly didactic direction could be seen in publications from the Society for the Diffusion of Useful Knowledge that in 1832 came out with a publication called *Penny Magazine*, which accrued a wide following with more than 214,000 copies in circulation. The *Weekly Chronicle*, on the other hand, favored a more sensational spin on the stories and saw its circulation soar in the 1830s with the publication of illustrations depicting serial murders. A publication that appeared extravagantly sensational would be attacked for pandering to the audience's baser impulses, whereas publications that took their educational aims too seriously were in danger of alienating a wide audience and failing economically. Successful publications were able to balance these goals, but not without compromises that would shape the direction and form of popular graphic narratives throughout the century.

Despite the huge popularity of these new publications and the large demand for illustrations, engravers earned very little for their skilled labor. The narrow profit margins the publishers worked under kept engravers' wages low, but their pay was low also because wood engravings were often reused from one publication to the next. Publishers borrowed illustrations from books and other publications, making only minor modifications to keep the public satiated with graphic news. As Thomas Gretton observed, the function of the illustrations "was not primarily the reporting of external facts but the triggering of associations and the arousal of emotions."[10] A picture's value in these publications was based on the illustration's ability to draw in a reader, and so its repetition did not seem to unduly diminish its entertainment value.

Variety in these publications was key to mass appeal. Thus, instead of one big cut, editors often resorted to using several smaller illustrations scattered across a page, commonly called a miscellany, or in French a *macédoine*. Miscellany pictures were sometimes thematically related, but they seldom told a single story; even when they did, the pictures were never arranged in any specific sequence. George Cruikshank was one of the early creators of the miscellany narrative style. The expansion of miscellany design schemes across all kinds of publications reflected the tastes of a public attuned to the variety acts found in music halls and vaudeville, where the panoramic narrative style gave the impression of abundance that assured buyers they were getting more value for their money.

Fueled by rumor and speculation, a number of remarkable recurring stories were circulated, such as the sightings of Spring Heeled Jack. The notorious character of Spring Heeled Jack was widely reported in 1837 and, with varying degrees of credulity, reappeared for the next 20 years as rapist, bandit, and vigilante. Spring Heeled Jack was described as leaping to great heights, having sharp, talonlike claws and flaming eyes or breath, being masked, wearing a tight leather suit, and having—inexplicably—a gold "W" emblazoned on his chest. If such a character as Spring Heeled Jack had not existed, then the often desperate and unscrupulous illustrated news magazine editors would have needed to invent such an ideal persona for their serial publications.

In 1888, embellishment was hardly needed in reporting the gruesome serial murders in London attributed to Jack the Ripper. The focus of the popular press shifted from more or less generically generated images to pictures that tried to visually recreate evidence that would appeal to the amateur sleuths looking for clues to catch the elusive murderer. *Illustrated Police News* was one of the more successful of these sensationalist magazines that mimicked the more respectable *Illustrated London News* but gratuitously indulged in the most graphic depictions of murder and mayhem. Over the course of the Jack the Ripper murders, the front page reproduced several vignettes of the murder scenes, suspects, evidence, and fallout from the events to create the impression of chaos and urgency. On the front page of the September 22, 1888, *Illustrated Police News*, for example, the graphic evidence swirls about a pair of "before" and "after" portraits of the eighth victim, Anne Chapman, highlighting the evident blood with forensic zeal. Even on this big-news day, the front page of illustrations does not confine itself to the Jack the Ripper murders but also moves lower down—in the spirit of miscellany—to pictures for stories about "An exciting scene at the Bestock and Wombwells Menageries" and "More Horrible Mysteries."

The fictional serialized stories that made Charles Dickens famous were broadly imitated in much cruder fashion in the penny bloods. The story of the murderous barber Sweeney Todd (1878) grotesquely characterized the angry desperation of the lower classes and the unscrupulous greed of the upper classes. There began an outcry against these publications for corrupting British youth, despite the fact they were never intended to be read by children. Edwin J. Brett (1828–1895), one of the most prolific publishers of the gruesome serial adventure stories, capitalized on the new anti–penny blood sentiment and made an about-face in 1865 when he published a scathing attack on fellow penny publishers and cleaned up his stories. In 1866, he launched *Boys of England*, which lasted in one guise or another until 1906. Brett's shift was only in part attributable to a more conservative morality, for it also indicated the growth in children's literature as a result of several landmark public education laws in Europe and the United States mandating compulsory primary education.

Illustrated Children's Literature

In 1796, Jean-Charles Pellerin (1756–1836) set up a printing shop in Epinal, France, and began producing broadsheets especially designed to appeal to young readers called *Imagerie d'Epinal*. Each large page told a complete

Cover, *Illustrated Police News*, September 22, 1888. (© The British Library Board)

story in a deeply abridged cyclic narrative style. The original format early in the 19th century included four equal-sized frames per page which gradually increased in complexity to include either a three-by-three or four-by-four

Jean-Charles Pellerin, "Don Quichotte," *Imagerie d'Épinal*, no. 36, ca. 1880. (Humoristic Publishing Co., Kansas City, Missouri)

grid of images by the late 1840s. Until the introduction of color lithography in the 1850s, these illustrations were originally hand stenciled with two or three colors. Each of the 16 pictures was captioned with a brief statement that explained the action. The simplicity and directness of the presentation invited early readers to become engaged in the story through the vivid graphic details. Beginning with religiously themed stories, Pellerin later expanded to include historic events, digested popular novels, folktales, moral fables, fantasy adventures, and cut-and-assemble toys. The ever-growing range of publications over the years mirrored the proliferation of children's entertainment across the 19th century that spread throughout Europe and the United States. A collection of 60 of these pages was translated into English and printed and distributed by the Humoristic Publishing Company in Kansas City, Montana, in the 1880s. The stories were hardly innovative or original, but they made accessible and acceptable the idea of stories in pictures for children.

By the middle of the 19th century, children's literature was still a rather meager genre that had not yet strayed too far from well-worn folktales and nursery rhymes. For Christmas in 1844, Heinrich Hoffmann (1809–1894) went to buy his three-year-old son a book, but he was dismayed by long-winded cautionary tales and the simplistic morals he found, so he came home with only a blank book to pen his own stories. His gift to his son that year was eventually published as *Struwwelpeter* (*Shockhaired Peter*) a collection of illustrated verses about children in trouble. As a physician in Frankfurt who dealt with psychiatric disorders, Hoffmann occasionally penned short stories and made humorous drawings to calm down young patients in order to get their trust so he could examine them. The stories he penned have an immediacy and intensity because of the way they focus on physical conditions and exaggerated actions, but the simplistic illustrations signal that these actions are playful and separate from any real threat of danger. Each verse ends with an obligatory moral, but the actions provide a fanciful turn from law-and-order to flirt with chaos: Cruel Frederick viciously teases animals only to have a dog bite him and steal his dinner; Pauline burns to death from playing with matches; Kaspar refuses to eat his soup, so he shrivels up and dies from hunger; and Flying Robert foolishly takes an umbrella outdoors in a storm and blows away, never to be seen again. The stories and drawings in *Struwwelpeter* established a new paradigm in children's literature, one that was based on the earthy folktales collected by the Brothers Grimm, but in a more condensed form with children as the focus—stories that were not intended as merely preludes to adulthood, but as cautionary fables to help survive childhood.

Through artless rhymes and simple drawings, Hoffmann established an important precedent in children's literature that emphasized character and

> **Box 5.3** The Whimsical Work of Edward Gorey
>
> Edward Gorey (1925–2000) captured the spindly line and histrionic character of Victorian and Edwardian illustration in his numerous small-format art books and anthologies which have been perennial bestsellers since the 1960s. His world of neglected topiary gardens and ballet revivals conveys peculiar anachronistic sentiments that cannot be easily dismissed as merely gothic-style camp. Gorey is especially effective at creating whimsical and absurd fables that create a discordant relationship between his deadpan prose and awkward, self-conscious artwork.

action over plot and verisimilitude. This shift allowed for greater freedom in graphic narratives because it let the illustration carry more of the weight. But even as the illustrations would become more critical to understanding the story, they also became simpler—even simplistic—refusing to make any more sense than was necessary to suggest the characters in action. Creating an unstable relationship between words and pictures was the first step toward embracing more carnivalesque fun in children's literature. Wilhelm Busch (1832–1908) was the first to fully capitalize on this new paradigm, and it is his work that laid the foundation of modern comics for children. (See also box 5.3.)

An academic painter who trained in Antwerp and Munich, Busch began to publish illustrated rhymes for local publications (*bilderbogen*) in 1858. His work became enormously popular after he published a series of short comical episodes about two naughty boys, *Max and Moritz* (1865). Using the same treacle-sweet rhyme schemes as Hoffmann, Busch employed a heavier dose of irony and irreverence, allowing his impish boys to wreak havoc on middle-class propriety with their pranks and teasing voices. The onomatopoeic sounds of the story animate the action of the pictures: roasted chickens pilfered up a chimney go "Schnupdiwup," bugs creeping across the bed go "Kritze kraze!" and in the end Max and Moritz are ground up in a flower mill that goes "Rickeracke rickeracke." The rubbery actions of the characters, coupled with these sounds, have the full abandon of the storyteller's art, giving vivid fun to the boys' antics.

Busch, like Töpffer before him, used a rounder, more flowing line in his caricatures, which simplified the anatomy and exaggerated expressions, gestures, and postures. Busch went further to flatten the figures with even less shading, letting the outline of the figure convey the movement. This technique gave his pictures an elastic quality that further emphasized the action. Perhaps the most important of Busch's visual innovations was his experiments in conveying physical pain through radiating lines and the way he sought to convey action through multiple depictions of limbs flailing about. It is in these examples that we see his most daring attempts at creating a visual code unique to graphic narrative.

Looking back over the past century, many commentators have noticed the similarity between Busch's comic creations and the agonistic antics of the cat-and-mouse team Tom and Jerry, as well as Sylvester and Tweety, Road Runner and the Coyote, and many others—where the physical world is injected with equal doses of justice and irony to game the laws of physics, make light of graphic pain, and ultimately celebrate the crushing defeat of the aggressor. This can be seen in Busch's later story of the frog who narrowly escapes two hungry ducks by slipping through a fence (*Die beiden Enten und der Frosch*, 1862). The ducks get stuck in a fence and are caught and carried off by a cook. In the last picture, the frog is seen bandaged, but smoking a pipe, happy to be alive. Children revel in this incipient anarchy because it appeals to a sideshow-like joy of watching a weak opponent achieve victory through wit and levity. By pitting a poor frog against a pair of hungry ducks, Busch has created a drama wherein there is no doubt about the veracity of the contest; in the very nature of the contestants, as Roland Barthes observed about professional wrestlers, there is "a seed that contains the whole fight."[11]

Busch was not content to endlessly recycle childish antics, however, so he applied his signature graphic style to a range of different genres, including a religiously themed parody, *St Anthony of Padua* (*Der Heilige Antonius von Padua*, May 1870), for which he was brought up on charges of blasphemy and pornography. (The publication was subsequently banned in several Catholic regions across northern Europe.) Examining the pictures today, one may consider them tame compared to the grotesque satires of the Catholic Church in the 16th and 17th centuries, but they do include many absurd situations that undermine the sanctity of the religious themes, for example, in the admission of Saint Anthony to heaven with his beloved pet pig. Some of the criticism of the work was based on the fact that Busch did not faithfully tell the story of the life of Saint Anthony but mixed and matched saints' lives for his own satiric ends. The pornography charge was largely related to an episode toward the end when the aged saint is tempted by a ballet dancer in a skimpy tutu. The legs of the ballerina are sensuously

Der Frosch kämpft tapfer wie ein Mann,
Ob das ihm wohl was helfen kann?

Die beiden Enten raufen,
Da hat der Frosch gut laufen.

Schon hat die eine ihn beim Kopf,
Die andre hält ihr zu den Kropf.

Die Enten haben sich besunnen
Und suchen den Frosch im Brunnen.

Wilhelm Busch, *The Two Ducks and a Frog* (*Die beiden Enten und der Frosch*), 1862. Münchener Bilderbogen Nr. 325.

curved to the point of absurdity; but also, as one perturbed critic pointed out, the beard of the old saint has the disturbing suggestion of male anatomy.[12] It is important to note here that Busch's animated lines were provocative not for their proximity to realistic human representation but for their power of suggestion.

In defense of his work, Busch, a pragmatic Lutheran, disavowed any malicious intention toward Catholicism and blamed the tense political climate for the charges against him. Busch was eventually acquitted and even though he subsequently avoided making any works that implicated specific people who could charge him with libel, he showed little contrition and seemed to thrive on the publicity, seeking out other projects with equally provocative social commentary, among them *The Napoleon Game* (1871), *Pious Helen* (1872), and *Father Filucious* (1872). Although these later works did not have the same lasting and widespread popularity as his children's *bilderbogen*, they do speak to the artistic range of Busch, who did not narrowly circumscribe the genre to what he created exclusively for children but saw the picture story as a new form of entertainment relevant for all ages.

British Comic Magazines

Following on the popularity of *Punch Magazine*, a number of humor magazines, including *Fun* (1865), *Judy* (1867), and *Funny Folks* (1874), tried to break into this intensely competitive market with even less expensive and more heavily illustrated publications. To accomplish this, they relied more on advertising, promotional gimmicks, and the creation of reoccurring comic characters. In the past, a few characters had been revisited in limited ways over a series of publications. For example, Dr. Syntax had been used to sell other goods; but beginning with the character Ally Sloper (1867), reoccurring characters became a widespread synergistic marketing strategy that would define a whole new role for comics into the next century.

To be a "sloper" in the British slang of the day was to be someone who ducked payment by sneaking out the back ally when the rent came due. A visceral embodiment of this expression could be found in the character of Ally Sloper, who was a cheapskate drunk—often seen clinging to a lamppost for balance with a bottle in his back pocket—with small piggy eyes and a bulbous rosacea nose that poked out from under a bent stovepipe hat. His waistcoat, hat, and umbrella suggested not so much a genteel man who was down on his luck, as they did a huckster who had unfeasible aspirations. Ally Sloper inspired so many later characters, from W. C. Fields to Andy Capp, it is hard to look back and recognize Sloper's one-time popular distinction. He was most likely drawn from Charles Dickens's petty schemer Wilkins Micawber, but clearly his newfound popularity came from the way he was pressed into the service of situations way beyond his qualifications. In the pages of *Judy*, Sloper was seen hobnobbing with the natives of Africa, getting lost in the casbah of Morocco, and being expelled from the Paris Exhibition for masquerading as a food critic. As he gained celebrity, Ally Sloper became the unlikely icon of the age, who represented the awkward visibility of the working poor in the new urban society that provoked so many collisions between different classes and cultures.

Charles H. Ross invented the Ally Sloper character for the magazine *Judy*, but it was his wife, the French-born Isabelle Emilie de Tessier (b. 1850–?) working under the pen name Marie Duval, who first built the character Ally Sloper into a popular phenomenon. Marie Duval was a rare talent to emerge in the male-dominated world of popular publications. She had had a brief career as a provincial actress before a stage accident made her end public performance and take up illustration. As a self-taught artist, she had in her work a daring and panache far beyond her basic artistic skill. Duval's

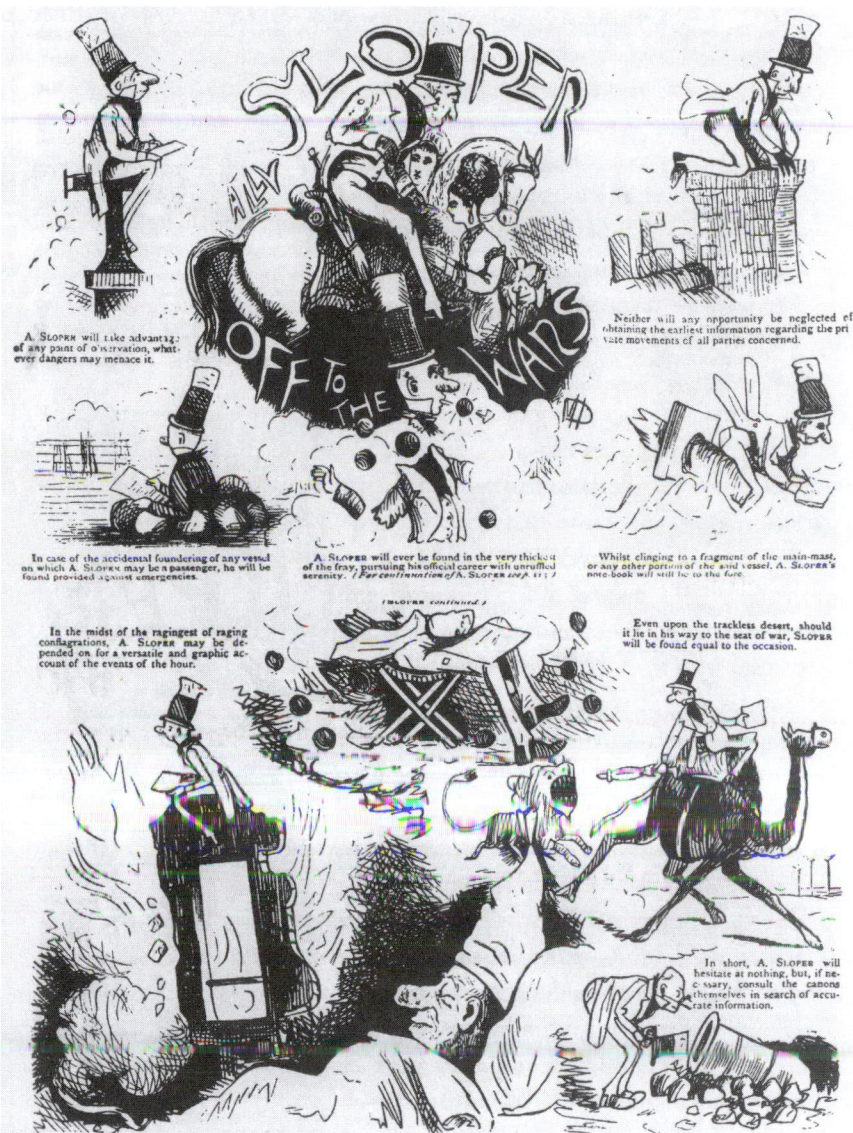

Marie Duval and Charles Ross, "En Route for Suez," *Judy*, December 1, 1869.

untutored style underscored Sloper's absurdity, making him appear like a poorly articulated puppet. It also gave him a naïve quality that allowed readers to sympathize with him during his comic misadventures. Seven short collected volumes of Ally Sloper were reprinted from the pages of *Judy*. This republication further enhanced his visibility and proved his viability as a character apart from the magazine that spawned him. Duval eventually lost the opportunity to keep her creation going when, in 1872, the magazine was sold to a new publisher, Gilbert Dalziel, who passed the character on to William G. Baxter and, later, to W. Fletcher Thomas. Under Baxter's pen, the figure of Ally Sloper filled out his rumpled attire and achieved a classic form that appeared on countless merchandise, including bicycles, doorstops, watches, medicine, cooking sauce, and cigars. With his growing popularity and his proven market power, Sloper was the first comic character to be given his own serialized magazine, *Ally Sloper's Half Holiday* (1884), named after the Saturday afternoon break that was legislated in Britain for all working-class people.

Ally Sloper's Half Holiday eventually succumbed to numerous imitators and less expensive competitors, ceasing publication in 1916, but not before radically changing the landscape of the popular press by introducing novel promotional strategies that included product placement inside the comic, competitions among readers, fan clubs, celebrity endorsements, and even one-time railroad insurance for traveling patrons.[13] One of the publishers whose magazines eventually eclipsed Sloper was the newspaper tycoon Alfred Harmsworth (later known as Viscount Northcliffe, 1865–1922), who jump-started his publishing empire by selling what he billed as more wholesome, family-oriented reading for half the price of the penny press. With linotype printing and even cheaper paper to cut costs, Harmsworth made his profit from greatly expanded circulation. By 1893, his five weekly half-penny publications had achieved 1.5 million copies in circulation.[14] *Comic Cuts* (1890) was followed quickly by *Illustrated Chips* (1890), each issue offering eight pages of comic illustrations in a format similar to Pellerin's *Imagerie d' Epinal*, where the descriptive text below the illustrations was in many instances deliberately redundant to help children learn to read. British publications maintained this pedagogical format long after it had disappeared from comics in the United States. Like most of his competitors, Harmsworth was able to cut costs further by pirating foreign comics that he translated and published without attribution. Wilhelm Busch was widely pirated in British humor magazines; but in the 1890s, it was American comic artists who began to appear as a valuable source for new material.

Comic Magazines in the United States

The success of *Punch Magazine* in London was not lost on publishers in other parts of the world, and soon imitators cropped up all across the former and current British Empire. The magazines *Judge* (1871), *Puck* (1876), and *LIFE* (1883) became the first to sustain some measure of profit and stability in the United States. In these magazines, words and pictures danced around each other in lively and innovative ways. For the most part, graphic narrative sequences were either without words or the narrative text was placed below the image. On rare occasion, comics used emanata to convey dialogue; but as the cartoonist Jimmy Swinnerton recalled, "It was not the fashion to have balloons showing what the characters were saying, as that was supposed to have been buried with . . . Cruikshank."[15]

Palmer Cox (1840–1924) immigrated to the United States from a Scottish settlement in Quebec and eventually arrived in New York in 1875 to look for work as an illustrator. In 1883, in the pages of one of the leading children's magazines, *St. Nicholas* (1873–1940s), Cox introduced the first comic story about Brownies—a Scottish variant of fairy lore—in a piece called "The Brownies' Ride," where he captured the mildly mischievous antics of a small tribe of Brownies taking a farmer's horsecart for a midnight joyride. Cox's Brownies had a boyish charm—there were no girls among them—with large luminous eyes and with spindly arms and legs attached to a compact and portly head and body. Despite some reoccurring characters in the group, the text never identified any particular Brownie by name but always referred to the Brownies collectively, creating the impression of a closely knit rabble of folk who more or less think and act as one. Brownies were in many ways the embodiment of the Victorian miscellany, offering a palate of various characters to enjoy; but they also constituted a unified collection with certain peripheral eccentricities that were clearly identifiable. Brownies were culturally heterogeneous and included a wide range of ethnic identifiers, making them the ideal representation of the United States' motto *E pluribus unum*. Indeed, many of the actions of the Brownies were also closely tied to American patriotic themes, including a cloyingly sweet story drawn from the U.S. war in the Philippines (*The Brownies in the Philippines*, 1904), where the impish chorus experiences various island flavors and terrors. All the later franchises that followed this enduring model—Rose O'Neill's *Kewpies* (1909), William Donahey's *Teenie Weenies* (1912), Peyo's *Smurfs* (*Les Schtroumpfs*, 1958), and Ken Sugimori's *Pokémon* (1995), for example—would capitalize on the collectable nature of a diminutive population.

The Brownie franchise quickly grew to include several books: *The Brownies: Their Book* (1887), *Another Brownie Book* (1890), and *The Brownies at Home* (1891), followed by eight more titles by 1906. In 1891, Cox took advantage of the revised U.S. copyright laws in an attempt to protect his work, but piracy still continued. Several companies paid Cox licensing fees for his work to appear on toys and games, but many did not, including the large Kodak Company, which used Cox's illustrations without permission from 1900 to 1906 to sell its immensely popular Brownie Camera.[16] This piracy continued despite invocation of the law, because the laws protecting the duplication of art work considered only the copy of original works and not the broader idea of a copyrighted character used in a new and different way. Cox never attempted any legal means to rein in the pirated works; perhaps he was all too aware of the difficult legal hurdles to prosecute and win such cases.

CHAPTER 6

Comics in the Era of "Yellow Journalism"

Fierce competition among United States newspapers provided the forum—if not the impetus—for the metamorphosis of comic art from illustrated anecdotes and puns to sequential framed action with emanata. Elsewhere in the world, comics were published almost exclusively in humor magazines; but in the United States, newspaper editors regularly used political and social comics in their pages. Even the statesman Ben Franklin was not above using allegorical political cartoons to make his point in his newspaper, and over the years comics became a part of the formula for providing entertainment and enhancing the visual appeal of the paper. Most notable from this era was the great graphic genius Thomas Nast (1840–1902), who was the first to render the Democratic Party as a donkey and Saint Nicholas as a jolly old elf. Nast was especially effective in his caricatures attacking the corrupt political machine organized by William Marcy Tweed (1823–1878) who ran the New York State legislature from a social organization known as Tammany Hall. The potent caricatures that Nast made of Boss Tweed and his cronies were able to rally and focus public outrage on some of the most visible manifestations of a deeply dysfunctional political system.

Political caricatures were effective at editorializing news while there were significant political events to describe, but with the growing competition, newspapers needed to distinguish themselves by providing unique content above and beyond the events of the day. Whimsical cartoons that parodied daily life had a distinct advantage over other kinds of illustrations of news, sports, or fashion shows because the papers themselves could create and control the content independent of any external news event. Cartoons did not have to appear in a timely way and could be inserted where needed and as space allowed. Therefore, cartoons were a chance for the paper to flaunt its visual appeal and create a sensation on demand. Such practices became known as "yellow journalism" and were not entirely reputable because they elevated the marketing of the paper over the dissemination of real news with some degree of objectivity. The *New York Times* and a few other newspapers stayed far away from cartoons to avoid this perception, but many more exploited their popular appeal, graphic excitement, and easy recognition to unleash what would become the marketing juggernaut of the 20th century.

Enormously influential to the development of U.S. publishing was the career of Benjamin Henry Day (1810–1889), who was the first to introduce the British publishing strategies of the penny press with the *New York Sun* in 1833. Day also was responsible for publishing in the United States the first (albeit pirated) copies of Rodolphe Töpffer's work in his *Brother Jonathan* magazine in 1842. Perhaps most influential to the visual character of newspapers was his 1879 patent for the halftone process named after him called benday dots. This technique allowed printers to mix colors through the careful application of varying amounts of primary colors applied as a field of small dots. On close examination, the colors remain distinct, but at a casual distance, the reader's eyes mix the colors. As the technique developed, benday dots allowed for an infinite pallet of colors to be reproduced with only four basic ink colors: black, magenta, yellow, and blue.

The Color Sunday Supplement

A leisure-oriented "Sunday supplement" began in the *New York Herald* as early as 1841. As competition increased, newspapers strove for evermore attractive means to lure readers. By 1890, 250 papers had Sunday supplements filled with as many extravagant and comical illustrations as the newspaper could afford. The competition increased another notch with the introduction of high-speed rotary color presses, first used at the *Chicago Inter-Ocean* in 1892. By 1894, the *Inter-Ocean Weekly* had a section especially for children that featured a variation on Cox's Brownies called *The Ting-Ling Kids* by Charles Saalburg (1865–1947). Saalburg held a patent on the four-color print process he used and in 1896 went to New York City to work for Pulitzer's *New York World* to print a colored Sunday supplement. It was there Saalberg printed cartoons by Richard Felton Outcault (1863–1928), who would go on to create the comics phenomenon known as the Yellow Kid.

Outcault was from Lancaster, Ohio, and after a brief stint as a marketing illustrator for Thomas Edison's workshop, he made his way to New York. The immigrant urban poor fascinated Outcault, and he spent time wandering the city drawing the occupants of tenement buildings. As far back as the 1870s, Michael Angelo Woolf (1837–1899) had established a popular genre of street urchin–themed cartoons in the pages of *Wild Oats* and *Harper's Weekly*. Outcault's initial contribution to this genre was his willingness to be less sentimental and more outrageous than Woolf, to push the antics of his cartoon characters to the brink of what was shocking. Outcault's cartoon for the *New York World*'s strip *Hogan's Alley* (first published February 17, 1895), was like Cox's Brownies in that it did not focus on any particular character but, rather, depicted the street that the kids ruled over. He effectively captured the tumult and chaos of the city in his illustrations, which featured a cacophony of signage and childish pratfalls which grew in complexity until he had achieved a wildly panoramic narrative style. Just as with Ally Sloper in Britain, the kids of Hogan's Alley crudely mimicked high society, reveling in their failure to achieve the grace of good breeding.

From the beginning of the cartoon, among the various children on the street, there was a mongoloid-looking, bald child in an ill-fitting, grubby nightshirt; his presence in the comic became increasingly pronounced, especially after his shirt was colored bright yellow in early January 1896. The Yellow Kid, who would later be called Mickey Dugan, anchored the page and typically stared blankly back at the reader with an idiotic smile. On his bold yellow shirt was written his voice in a broken street pidgin. Speech bubbles had appeared from time to time in Outcault's comic pages, often as a means for giving human voices to animals, but they made a dramatic return to comics in a *Hogan's Alley* comic strip making fun of Edison's phonograph (October 25, 1896). For this comic, Outcault dropped his typical single-frame format for a series of frameless pictures where the Yellow Kid talks with a phonograph. Just as before, the Yellow Kid's voice first appeared on his shirt, but this time the "voice" of the phonograph floated out from the horn in bubble-shaped emanata. At the end of the comic, the Yellow Kid falls over in shock as a parrot pops out from inside the phonograph. The Yellow Kid's final words no longer appear on his shirt but now emerge from his mouth as a speech bubble.

Outcault's comic captured visually a change in the culture that had been happening for nearly a decade. Large audiences now embraced Edison's phonograph, a new means for recording a voice that before this time could have appeared only as words on a page. Walter Ong has called this change the

Richard Felton Outcault, "The Yellow Kid and His New Phonograph," *Hogan's Alley, New York Journal*, October 25, 1896. (From the San Francisco Academy of Comic Art Collection, the Ohio State University Billy Ireland Cartoon Library & Museum)

second, or postliterate, orality, where recollected experience is no longer bound by the written word but is given a renewed immediacy through the direct recording of sound.[1] In an attempt to recapture the voice as a distinctive means of expression—different from words on a page—Outcault returned to the speech bubble. Emanata were originally conceived in medieval times as a means to visually represent the dynamic nature of voice in a culture still dominated by oral cultural values. Outcault most likely had no idea that emanata were first used in this context, yet he gave the vibrant and visual presence of the voice a new immediacy that better captures the raw urgency that is found in the phonograph. After his comic parody of the phonograph, Outcault continued to move back and forth between Victorian and modern comic styles, occasionally using speech bubbles and sequential action, as in his phonograph comic, and at other times reverting to his older panoramic narrative style. It was other comic artists working at the time, among them Rudolph Dirks (1877–1968), Frederick Burr Opper (1857–1937), and James Swinnerton (1875–1974), who picked up on the new sequentially dramatic narrative style and never looked back.

Dirks was a relative newcomer to William Randolph Hearst's paper the *New York Journal* in 1897, when he was asked to create a comic version of the Max and Moritz stories by Wilhelm Busch. Dirks created a pair of prankster boys and called them the Katzenjammer Kids, after the German word for cats yowling and also a vulgar term for a hangover. Dirks's *Katzenjammer Kids* proved to be a great hit and not only refined the formula of demon boys who terrorize their parents but also established the clean-line, action-driven forms around which American comics would flourish. The new, more sophisticated halftone printing with benday dots allowed for soft color washes that made the surfaces sparkle with life and vitality and reduced the need for grays from cross-hatched surfaces, a holdover from the days of wood engraving. By expanding on Busch's caricature style, Dirks further emphasized bold outlines, flying sweat drops, and radiating zip lines to accentuate the action. Originally, the strip was a silent one (see box 6.1), but by 1900 the characters were talking in a German-English pidgin. Their banter included such memorable lines as "Society iss nix" and "One iss just as bad as both der other ones."

As comics began to speak up, they had an indelible effect on the development of American English. Thomas "TAD" Dorgan (1877–1929) made the earliest use of such popular superlatives as "the cat's meow" and "the cat's pajamas" and coined such expressions as "for crying out loud," "Nobody home," "You tell him," and "Yes, we have no bananas." We can thank Dorgan for

---

Box 6.1   Silent Strips

So-called silent strips were comics that had no speaking characters but relied purely on visual gags to tell their stories. Some of Wilhelm Busch's early works include such picture stories without words as *The Flea* (*Der Floh*, 1865), featuring a widely used style of comic art that was popular through the end of the 19th century. In the 20th century, following the broad reintroduction of emanata, only a few comic artists had success with the challenging formula of the silent strip that is wholly dependent on pantomime. Some successes of this genre include Otto Slogow's *Little King* (1931) and Carl Anderson's *Henry* (1932); in Denmark, Henning Dahl Mikkelsen's *Ferd'nand* (1937, first U.S. publication 1947); and in China, Zhang Leping's *Sanmao* (1935). Aside from their silent main characters, what all these comics shared in common was how their silence conveyed a childlike innocence confronting the modern world.

naming the "hot dog" after the suspicious contents of the sausages sold on Coney Island and even further for turning the word "hot dog" into a common expletive. H. L. Mencken, in his pioneering study of American language in 1919, observed the way comic strips were instrumental in forming new words and phrases and noted the rapid invention of such new onomatopoeic terms as "zowie, bam, socko, yurp, plop, wow, wham, glug, oof, ulk, whap, bing, fooie, and grrr," concluding, "Their influence upon the general American vocabulary must be very potent."[2]

Because of the demands of deadlines, compromises with editors, and collaborations with printers, few of these early cartoonists regarded what they did as "art," for most considered themselves illustrators, journalists, or entertainers. Many in their careers worked the vaudeville circuit, performing what were popularly known as chalk talks. Clare Briggs, Rudolph Dirks, Winsor McCay, Sidney Smith, Rube Goldberg, and Milt Caniff were a few of the comic artists who joined the vaudeville circuit, where they would appear alongside a host of other variety acts. These performances would often include quick caricatures of people in the audience, a drawing that would evolve from one picture into another, or a finished drawing from a spray of dots on the page. Harlan Tarbell's book *How to Chalk Talk* (1924) sums up the goals of chalk talking much the same way Rodolphe Töpffer described his picture stories 100 years earlier. Both recommend that the artist-performer consider the theatrical impact of the drawing and increase the visual clarity by using a minimum of lines.[3]

Imitations, piracy, and the unlicensed use of comic characters for marketing was still largely unrestrained by copyright law. The problem of imitators was exacerbated by the battle between William Randolph Hearst (1863–1951) and Joseph Pulitzer (1847–1911), who repeatedly lured talented comic artists, journalists, and editors away from each other with the promise of higher pay. Hearst brought Outcault over to his paper in October 1896 to reprise his popular character in a newly titled comic, *McFadden's Row of Flats*; meanwhile, Pulitzer continued the Yellow Kid feature with George Luks (1867–1933). There were not only dueling Yellow Kids but also dueling Katzenjammer Kids, which also got caught up in the row between the newspaper giants.

Though Pulitzer and Hearst filed suit against each other and their cartoonists for breach of contract, there is no evidence that any legal means were used to rein in the proliferation of comic-character imitations and spin-offs before the turn of the century. The title of a comic could be protected under copyright law, but any newly published comic, even when it was done with the same characters and style as before, was considered a new work of art. In 1895, Outcault had even made fun of Cox's copyright of his Brownies in an early cartoon from the *Hogan's Alley* series, but in time, he would surpass all others at aggressively marketing and protecting his creations. Beginning with *Buster Brown* (1902), Outcault successfully marketed the character to the Brown Shoe Company to become one of the longest-lived comic brands in history. Whereas most comic artists coordinated their own business dealings, Outcault had in his personal employ a lawyer and two secretaries to manage his creative assets, and they successfully brought 30 cases to trial to protect his popular brand.[4] From this point forward, hugely successful comics could generate more income from licensing than from publishing the comics themselves.

Outcault solidified the idea of the formula strip in Buster Brown, whereby the basic plot ingredients were well established and the strip would always feature the same concluding panel—in this case, a warped homily under a placard entitled "Resolved," where Buster gave with mock seriousness the "moral" he garnered from his misadventure. This formula created greater continuity in the comic strips. It also liberated comic artists from having to reinvent their strips each week; and if the formula proved popular, it was because the little twist rewarded audiences who came back for more.

Winsor McCay (1867–1934) was a largely self-taught comic artist who drew from the visual vocabulary of circus sideshow posters to create some of the most dazzling comic pages ever rendered for a newspaper. McCay's *Little Nemo in Slumberland*, his most famous strip, featured daring and spectacular visual qualities that readers of the *New York Herald* poured over on Sundays from 1905 until 1911 and later in Hearst's *New York American* from 1911 to 1914. McCay did not follow the common trend of the day by filling out his comic with colorful characters who returned from week to week. The emphasis was always on the richly detailed dream world of King Morpheus, rendered from the vivid memory of Winsor McCay, who claimed he could recall how to draw anything, at any time, having only seen it once before.[5] Nemo, whose name means "nothing" in Latin, was merely a cypher—an *everyboy*—who was largely acted on by McCay's dream world of Slumberland, which spun, stretched, and gamboled like a fairground funhouse. In the last panel of each comic, we often find Nemo startled awake, confronting the reality of the day, tossed from his bed by the vividness of his dream experience in Slumberland. By making this rather ordinary child appear as the real "author" of these incredible visions, McCay reminds us through little Nemo of the latent power of imagination that lies within us all.

McCay was himself something of a "Nemo," a modest and conservative man; for unlike many of his peers in newspaper publishing and vaudeville who had more gregarious lifestyles, he seldom spoke much of himself and lived a quiet family life. Apart from a few minor early strips and later editorial cartoons, McCay was fascinated by the dream world, where he could display his virtuoso technique for illustrating graduated metamorphosis. Like the U.S. comic artist A. B. Frost (1851–1928) before him, McCay was far more interested in the way something happened and frequently relied on formulaic concluding panels, which merely signaled that the dream was over. McCay also clearly did not expend a great deal of thought about the words on his page. The dialogue seldom added much to the visual action and was often stuffed into ill-fitting emanata, seemingly as an afterthought.

McCay's lesser-known comic *Dream of the Rarebit Fiend* (1904–1919) was a more adult-oriented comic with darker, anxiety-ridden nightmares born from people suffering from poor digestion after having feasted on cheese fondue (welsh rarebit) the night before. In these strips, McCay's formula was to begin with an absurd condition—for example, elephants dropping from a hole in the ceiling or two ladies' mink stoles getting into a fight—and have it grow exponentially until it overwhelmed the dreamer. Many of the pages of *Rarebit Fiend* are whimsical, as is the fashion illustration that is obscured by progressively worse ink smudges; but a few explore more disturbing fears—fears of

Winsor McCay, *Dream of the Rarebit Fiend*, no. 286, May 1907.

being buried alive, or of a child whose mother is planted in the ground and turns into a tree. McCay's constant moral message was that the alcohol-laced cheese fondue represented the decadent, soft, and alluring culture of the urban world that encouraged indulgence and excess. On the last panel, like a member of a temperance meeting, the dreamer regrets eating the rarebit and promises a more wholesome lifestyle based on moderation.

Few artists were able to achieve, and none could surpass, Winsor McCay's elegant and sophisticated rendering. Even those artists with far more training, such as Lyonel Feininger (1871–1956), had a rough time creating a popular comic page. Feininger struggled for a year in 1906 to create some art nouveau–inspired fantasy comic pages for the *Chicago Tribune*; yet even though the drawings were fanciful and imaginative, they failed to tell a compelling story. Other artists, such as Gustave Verbeek (1867–1937) and Henry Grant Dart (1869–1938) also created visually imaginative worlds, but their efforts were short lived. Few besides McCay could work quickly enough and sustain the energy necessary to create such highly crafted and imaginative panels week after week. McCay eventually also found it taxing to sustain and ended *Little Nemo* and spent the bulk of his later career as an editorial illustrator for Hearst. As the insatiable demand for comics continued, the prevailing trend was for artists to adopt simpler and more efficient ways to render their figures and the world they inhabited, giving greater emphasis to the actions of the characters and less to the unfolding landscape through which they traveled. Such changes were almost inevitable as popular comic strips began to appear not just on Sundays but in the daily papers as well.

By 1902, Sunday comic supplements were between 32 and 86 pages in length, and on special holiday editions they could be up to 130 pages. Comic artist Roy McCardell noted that the three largest of the New York papers, the *World*, the *Journal*, and the *Herald*, "realized that their patrons were spectators rather than readers."[6] The humorous essays and stories in the Sunday supplements were no match for the comic art and so were eliminated to create more space for comics. The huge demand for new material created a large corps of illustrators and comic artists, and although several great talents emerged to create comic characters that would last for decades, hundreds of other nameless artists flourished for a while and disappeared. In this dynamic and competitive field, comic artists were inspired, not by a handful of talented leaders, but by a huge population of feverishly active artists struggling to make deadlines.

Many of the newspapers and humor magazines that held out against the new comic onslaught from the Sunday supplements were swept aside and folded, while others scrambled to accrue staff cartoonists to help them compete. National syndication of the comics began in 1906 to help defray the costs of publishing, and soon popular features in New York could be found in papers all across the country. Syndication gave stability to the business of being a comic artist and allowed American comics to become a national, and eventually an international, phenomenon. Syndication also allowed comic artists to make one popular title their speciality and refine their craft to develop a fairly narrow signature style.

Over the years, newspaper comic syndicates grew increasingly cautious and conservative, relying on an ever-shrinking handful of titles to appeal to as broad an audience as possible.[7] The full trajectory of newspaper comics, from spectacular and whimsical full-page entertainment that could be read for hours to superficially differentiated, shrunken, momentary diversions, was a by-product of the expansion and eventual consolidation of newspaper syndication. For just as fierce competition drove newspaper publishers to develop spectacular Sunday comic sections, the lack of competition among papers and shrinking advertising revenue from the advent of such competing media as radio and television all but doomed the comics page to future obscurity. (See also box 6.2.)

Daily Comics and the Origins of Continuity Strips

At the time of the upsurge in comics' popularity, most papers used artists to illustrate sports events because camera film and lenses were still too slow to capture the action. As these artists were enlisted to fill out the comics pages, they brought with them much of the male-dominated humor of sports journalism and created characters who were, like themselves, quite at home at the racetrack and in the pool hall. Clare Briggs (1875–1930) had a long and influential career as a comic artist after he got a break developing a sports page comic at the bequest of editor Moses Koenigsberg. Called *A. Piker Clerk* (1903), it sporadically appeared in a Hearst paper, the *Chicago American*, for about six months. The strip followed the misadventures of a lanky gambler who fictionally placed bets on actual horse races; the strip played off the actual results of the races. Koenigsberg later explained the sudden departure of the strip by saying the gambling theme was a little too vulgar for Hearst. Whatever his original motives were for ending Briggs's comic, Hearst did not balk at hiring Harry Conway "Bud" Fisher (1885–1954) three years later to capitalize on his new popular strip, *A Mutt* (short for "Mutton Head"). Mutt, like Piker before him, was an impulsive horse gambler who wore pants that hung around his ankles, and for the first time in comics, his absurd schemes continued on in

Box 6.2   Comics of the Machine Age

Comics were born of the machine age, and their novel way of parceling out units of time across the page made them ideally suited to describe the action and energy of machines both real and fantastic. In Britain, William Heath Robinson (1872–1944) had a long career as an illustrator whose work often included large makeshift contraptions that precariously accomplished small and inconsequential tasks. At various places along his machines, there are signs of wear that have been addressed with a patchwork of half-hearted repairs. The actual mechanics of Robinson's machines remained relatively simple—a giant spike for making holes in a golf course, a motorized pulley for "self-rising" suspenders— but very often it is the self-satisfied air of the people who attend the machine that best conveys the sheer absurdity of the whole enterprise. In the United States, Rube Goldberg (1883–1970) created many comic pages, as well as political cartoons, but nothing is quite so well remembered as his farcical inventions. Goldberg, inspired by the memory of one of his college engineering professors, created absurd machines powered not just by gravity or pulleys but by all the forces of nature and conditions of human sentiment. His machines represented not just the absurdity of our mechanical dreams and aspirations but also the frail human weakness at the heart of these devices.

the sports pages from one day to the next. Fisher originally created *A Mutt* for the *San Francisco Chronicle* sports page, but had been savvy enough to copyright his work for himself, so he was able to defend and keep his creation to himself even as the *Chronicle*'s publishers tried in vain to hire another artist to keep the popular strip going in their own pages. Fisher maintained this autonomy with his copyright after leaving Hearst's syndicate in 1913 for the Wheeler Syndicate, successfully suing Hearst to stop imitating his comic in a case that went all the way to the Supreme Court. With copyright and trademark controls in place, Fisher would become the first staggeringly wealthy comic artist. In the long term, however, Fisher's victory was an anomaly against a growing trend denying cartoonists rights over their work. Cartoon syndicates continued to consolidate their power over the industry in the 1920s and 1930s and were able to insist on work-for-hire contracts with new comic artists that gave the syndicate copyright control over the characters the artists produced. This work arrangement limited the artists' artistic autonomy, since the comic strips they drew could now be passed on to another artist at the discretion of the syndicate.[8]

Bud Fisher is also credited with establishing the strip format that would run across the width of the page rather than down one column. This arrangement gave his feature a visual prominence and clarity that broke up the long vertical columns of text in the newspaper. In 1908, the distinctive, long-lived features of the strip finally came into place when Mutt was paired up with a squat foil to Mutt's designs, Jeff. Fisher gave the pair the brisk slapstick repartee of earnest rivals and co-conspirators, and would go on to introduce many of the narrative devices that have became the stock-in-trade of the comic strip. Longer stories began to appear, and each new episode in the series would end on pivotal moments in a court case, a marriage, or a divorce. Mutt was also the first comic character to attempt to run for president, a stunt imitated by scads of characters ever since. Despite the ongoing drama that circulated through their fictional lives, the characters never aged, granting them that essential protection from mortality that comedic characters require. Fisher was a restless man who seemed to bore of the strip and, soon after winning his suit with Hearst, passed the job on to his assistant, Ed Mack, who passed it on after he died in 1932 to Al Smith, whose name did not supplant Fisher's on the strip until Fisher died in 1954. This continuing of the strip long after the artist retired has become the accepted practice for nearly all popular comic strips to the present day. The upshot of this practice has been that heritage strips have crowded out space for new material, making it harder and harder to break into the business.

By the 1920s, newspaper comic strips were regarded more as family entertainment than merely sports page diversions. One of the early family-oriented strips was Sidney Smith's *The Gumps*, which dominated the Chicago Tribune Syndicate from 1917 to 1959. *The Gumps*—with blowhard father Andy, pragmatic defending mother Min, precocious child Chester, and an assortment of eccentric pets—defined the prototype comic family characters for several generations. *The Gumps* featured longer, more complex narratives and a much larger cast of supporting characters than seen in earlier strips. The characters did not age with time, but Sidney Smith was willing to introduce more human drama and—despite the huge protests of his loyal readers—dared to kill off one of his major characters, Mary Gold, in 1929. In a reflective panel, Andy considers the fate of the youthful Mary: "Queer freaks—this old world—there is nothing you can nail down. Just when you think you have something—something happens—the flower you admired by the wayside yesterday—withers overnight. Foot prints in the snow—foot prints in the sand—nothing lasts—life; a puff of smoke." Such a frank and resolute statement was rare and bracing. In the face of an uncertain future foreshadowed by the economic crash that would produce the Great Depression, comics rose to the challenge and gave narrative continuity over and above the daily shocks and dislocations of the day.

That need for continuity inspired thousands to follow the bachelor Walt Wallet as he struggled to raise a foundling child he discovered on his doorstep in 1921,[9] count off each day of Dagwood's 1933 hunger strike to force his parents to consent to let him marry Blondie,[10] and pour over every detail of Jiggs and Maggie's 1937 transcontinental trip through every state in the union.[11] It also prompted New York Mayor Fiorello LaGuardia to read *Little Orphan Annie* on WNYC Radio during a week-long newspaper delivery strike in 1945. Comics became a type of glue that allowed strangers in a city to bond through their common adventures. As the stories expanded and aged, they also provided the fodder for nostalgia against the oftentimes brutal and unsentimental changes of urban life.

The continuity and ubiquity of popular comic strips, appearing in every major newspaper and adorning every imaginable form of merchandise, gave these creations a sheer force that often took over the lives of their creators. George McManus (1884–1954) found tremendous success with his family strip *Bringing Up Father*, which by 1952 had 80 million readers in 46 countries, amounting to more than 500 newspapers in 16 languages. In a *Collier's* article, McManus clearly and unequivocally stated, "I am not Jiggs. Maggie is not my wife. I have no daughter," saying these were answers to questions he was asked almost every day. People assumed wrongly that McManus's marriage, like his comic strip, was a wreck or that he had been divorced many times, none of which was true. McManus's model for his strip was, in fact, a 1895 hit comedy called *The Rising Generation* starring Billy Barry—a comedy he had seen many times in the theater where his father was the manager. Still, the editors at *Collier's* could not resist dressing McManus up to look like Jiggs for his photograph, as if his fictional character demanded a more corporeal presence than imagination could provide.

The humble beginnings of George Herriman's (1880–1944) *Krazy Kat* began along the lower margin of his comic strip the *Dingbat Family* (1910). There, in the seemingly inconsequential, narrow portion of the strip, Herriman began to explore the odd humorous banter between a twee cat and an unsentimental mouse as a counterpoint to the antics of the family above.[12] In the June 24 strip of 1910, the mouse became exasperated by the foolish talk of the cat and hurled a brick at its head. The effeminate male cat took these missiles as signs of love and thus was born the kernel of nonsense that would be spun out for decades to come. Herriman once admitted he had considered making the cat a girl and even drew up some strips with her pregnant. In the end, he decided this was too much like a soap opera and thought of Krazy as a "Sprite or Pixie" of no consequential gender and therefore free to do as he or she pleased.[13]

As the actions of the cat and mouse began to prove popular, the strip was briefly renamed *The Family Upstairs*. Finally, on October 28, 1913, the cat and mouse were featured in their own strip, *Krazy Kat*. At first, the early strip was almost devoid of any background and there were wide margins between the panels as if this were a way for the strip to retain its original status and character as an ancillary comic strip. Even as *Krazy Kat* rose in reputation, Herriman continued to create more typical gag-oriented humor strips; the most lasting of these was *Stumble Inn*, which ran from 1922 until 1926. These other comics featured the same fine technical brilliance he brought to *Krazy Kat*, but they were more conventional in character: light-hearted situation comedies that relied more on jokes and pratfalls for their comic punch. These other strips had charm, but they did not have the ironic self-reflexive humor that Herriman explored in *Krazy Kat*. It was as if by creating other more conventional comic strips, Herriman allowed *Krazy Kat* to continue to abide in the margins, so to speak, having no greater consequence, no higher significance than the ink and paper required for its existence.

Although never hugely popular compared to such other imaginative strips as *Polly and Her Pals* by Cliff Sterrett and *Thimble Theatre* by E. C. Segar, *Krazy Kat* appealed to many cultural critics, artists, and poets who lauded the strip for its uniquely modern and American sensibilities. The most famous of these accolades came from the writer Gilbert Seldes (1893–1970) in his 1924 essay on *Krazy Kat*, where he proclaimed it "the most amusing and fantastic and satisfactory work of art produced in America today. . . . It is wise without pitying irony; it has delicacy, sensitiveness, and an unearthly beauty."[14] Aware of the strip's unique appeal, Hearst put the comic in the entertainment section of the paper, where it was printed in black and white for most of its history. Week after week, until the day he passed away in 1944, Herriman flauted the conventions of realism with the daring of a cubist painter, twisted his words with Joycean flair, and paraded a cast of eccentric characters as vibrant as any Charlie Chaplin film.

To attempt to explain the *Krazy Kat* comic strip is to go down the rabbit hole of reverse logic and babble in George Herriman's unique krazyspeak of Dickensesque Cockney, Yiddish, Spanish, French, and Navaho. The irrepressible Krazy Kat is the first point of the triangular relationship between the pragmatic mouse, Ignaz, and the stoic dog, Officer Pupp. The cat fawned over the mouse as "a lil ainjil," who actually wanted nothing more than to hurl bricks to "crease that kat's kranium"; in turn, the cat said, "In [my] hour of mellon kolly [Ignaz] soothes me with a brick—missil of love and iffection." Officer Pupp secretly loved the cat and was ever vigilant to defend Krazy by jailing Ignaz for his brick tossing. Ignatz never learns his bricks are seen as tokens of love, Krazy never recognizes Officer Pupp's affections, and Officer Pupp never acknowledges that Krazy wants to be hit by the brick. Because the characters each have their own singular motivations, they remained oblivious to changes that might make them evolve. Thus, the farce is endlessly repeated, each iteration a new variant on the absurd theme.

The great poetic genius of Herriman's *Krazy Kat* was that it was all about itself as a comic, true to what only comics are true about, inspiring the kind of awe at virtuosity that comes from gazing at an elaborate painting on a grain of rice. From one panel to the next, Herriman shifted backdrops, skipped across the time of day, the seasons, and moved the frame of reference from an outdoor wilderness to a stage set to a deck of cards. The characters' ongoing patter largely ignored these changes, unless it suited their immediate needs—such as when the mouse, Ignatz, explained to Krazy the reason why he had a black brick was that in the third panel, the sky was black. Just as predicted, the panel is black except for the cat being flung back by what we can only assume is Ignatz's brick invisibly finding its mark. In the last panel, Ignatz takes a deep theatrical bow and thanks his "boss" for the extra ink.[15] The imagined collusion between character and creator was just one of the many ways Herriman had of winking at the reader, reminding us that Krazy Kat was nothing more, or less, than a drawing on a page. Whereas other popular comics aspired to step out of their frames and enter into the real world as explorers, newlyweds, and presidential candidates, *Krazy Kat* had no other ambition than to be a comic.

What saved this small drama from complete inconsequence was the way it was keenly aware of its artifice; it stretched all bounds of continuity to create ever new and fantastic means for these characters to explore their singular ambitions. What often is described as the Ur-myth of Krazy's brick fetish is in a comic page published in 1919; in a "reverse news reel" from 1919 BC, Kleopatra Kat receives love notes from Marcantonni Maus by means of messages chiseled into a brick that he tosses lovingly at her head. The conflation of the dates is not the only clue that this is not an insight into the present from the past but, rather, just a repeat of what has gone on since the dawn of time. In 1922, another origin myth was told of a "million million years ago" when the first brick was formed in a primordial sea and Ignatz flitter mouse, now flying on batlike wings, finds the brick while looking for something to fracture the foolish face of Krazy Katfish. Thus, Krazy Kat's history is not a past from which the present is a result; it is just another reiteration of the present.

The original setting for *Krazy Kat* was a nondescript and seemingly arbitrary and whimsical collection of faraway buildings, mountains, and trees. As early as 1911, Herriman began to make reference to Coconinio County out in the Monument Valley region of Arizona, and its unique landscape of flat-top mountains jutting dramatically out of the wide, flat plains began to appear in 1926. Herriman most likely learned about this part of the United States from his friend and colleague Jimmy Swinnerton, who had traveled out to the region in 1903, but he also knew it from first-hand experience. Starting sometime in the mid-1920s, Herriman and his wife and daughter were regular visitors to the area, where they took in the sights and culture. The preposterous and grand landscape in Monument Valley, which could look either like haphazardly strewn toy blocks or a chaotic city skyline, proved to be a perfect fit with *Krazy Kat*, giving it its signature character: a world without scale.[16]

As the narratives of daily comics continued to incrementally evolve over the years, artists invented hundreds of characters that peopled large imaginary worlds. Whether it was the cavemen in V. T. Hamlin's Kingdom of Moo (*Alley Oop*, 1932), or the hillbillies from Al Capp's Dogpatch, Kentucky (*Li'l Abner*, 1934–1977), or the eccentric animals found in Walt Kelly's Okefenokee Swamp (*Pogo*, 1948–1975) the immersive quality and complexity of these worlds was not achieved through any initial grand design by the artist. They were more often born from the happy accident of numerous stopgap inventions used to meet ongoing newspaper syndicate deadlines.

The Impact of Animation on Comics

Like comics, early animation found inspiration in vaudeville-style short humorous sketches. J. Stuart Blackton (1875–1941) was one of the pioneers of animation who experimented with moving drawings with his short films *Enchanted Drawing* (1900) and *Humorous Phases of Funny Faces* (1906), which mixed drawing with live action in the spirit of a vaudeville chalk talk. Animation and comics also both used visually striking simplified graphic shapes in strong outlines, which allowed for easy-to-read fluid action and easily repeatable renderings. Émile Cohl (1857–1938) was the first to take animation beyond the level of trick photography to develop a mercurial style of humor, where the pictures acted in a fluid, rollicking manner, which would dominate animation for the next 30 years.

Despite their obvious affinity in narrative content and visual style, there were relatively few comics that became animated cartoons and, similarly, few animated cartoons that became newspaper comics. Comics were frequently made into live-action plays, musicals, and movies, but animation was developing its own optical gimmickry that did not translate easily into or out of the nonanimated comic pages. Winsor McCay was the first to use his own characters in an animated short, *Little Nemo* (1911), but he did not try to recreate one of his comic pages; rather, he used them for visual hijinks that showed off the spectacle of the animation. One of his *Dream of the Rarebit Fiend* comics, "How a Mosquito Operates," was made into an animated cartoon the following year, but this was not one of his reoccurring comic characters, and it largely emphasized the sort of visual play that animation excelled at. McCay was most famous for his film *Gertie the Dinosaur* (1914), where he engaged the animated cartoon within the context of a live vaudeville performance. The novelty of Gertie was that it was an animated character who had personality. It was Cohl who made the first animated feature based on a comic strip when he produced—all by himself—13 short films based on George McManus's comic strip *The Newlyweds and Their Baby* (1913–1914). These popular features were the first of this new genre to be called by the term "animated cartoons."[17] Until the 1920s, crossovers between comics and animated cartoons were still relatively rare. It was not until August 1923 that the animated character *Felix the Cat*, after nearly 30 animated movies, appeared in the Sunday comic supplement. The first few years of the daily newspaper comic strip of *Felix the Cat* that began in 1927 were taken directly from the animation cells used in the movies, until 1931 when original material was developed for the comic strip.

It was only later, as animation began to move beyond the stunts and gags of its own design, that it began to develop longer and more complex narrative action. Walt Disney (1901–1966) was a significant innovator in this regard. Disney closely plotted the dramatic action and timing of his films, especially as he began integrating recorded sound with the action, as seen in the early Mickey Mouse animated cartoon *Steamboat Willie* (1928). To control the tempo of the action further, Disney trained his animators to begin just with the key poses, or key frames, in an animated sequence and then fill in the transition pictures later. The standard practice in New York animation studios until then had been to start at the beginning and animate the whole sequence straight through to the end. The Disney method allowed for greater flexibility, and it meant that talented animators were given the key poses to draw while beginning animators would work on the in-betweening, or "tweening" as it is now often called. By lining up the key poses and posting them on a bulletin board for all to see, the Disney animator Webb Smith in 1933 invented the idea of storyboards to plot out the entire action of an animated feature. Today, the storyboard has become such an indispensable tool to the film industry that it is difficult to imagine that conceiving a film as a series of key pictures in a sequence—like a comic strip—was not always self-evident.

Disney's impact on comics would continue to grow as the animation style he developed became ingrained in the popular culture. This was in part a result of an aggressive marketing campaign for his animated characters that went far beyond anything that had been attempted before. Part of that plan was to push the characters into comic strips and comic books. The initial Mickey Mouse comic strip appeared early in 1930 scripted by Disney himself and visualized by the art of Win Smith. By April of that year, Disney had passed the duty on to a relatively new employee, Floyd Gottfredson (1905–1986), who continued to write and draw the Mickey Mouse comic strip until 1975. Compared to the animators at Disney, Gottfredson had great autonomy in developing the plots for his comics and even went on to introduce new characters. A similar situation arose with Carl Barks (1901–2000) who, starting in 1943 with a story called *The Victory Garden*, went on to create more than 500 Donald Duck comic books. Although their work was attributed to Disney, the two men gained international fame for their great comics and helped establish the Disney style worldwide.

CHAPTER 7

Graphic Narratives in Asia

In the late 19th and the early 20th centuries, the advance of European and American colonialism brought about broad social and cultural upheavals in India, China, and Japan. This contentious period also introduced into Asia modern graphic narratives, including Western-style caricatures, cartoons, and comics. On the one hand, comics came to represent the advances of Western-style democracy and a free press, but on the other hand, they represented the oppressive wrongs of colonialism that threatened traditional values and social autonomy. The dual identity of modern comics in Asia provided new forms and venues for modern stories that provided humor and insight into a changing world.

The Hindu Heroes of Indian Comics

Early in the 17th century, commercial trade from the British Empire expanded into the Indian subcontinent and slowly began to replace the crumbling authority of the Muslim Mughal Dynasty. To manage their affairs, the British needed a corps of clerks and officers in India, and it proved more efficient to train high-caste[1] Hindus rather than import people from Britain. These Western-educated Hindus formed one of the first middle classes in Asia and were collectively called *babu,* after the honorific they adopted to mark their unique status. Those of the babu class were some of the first to read newspapers and seek out more secular forms of entertainment. The lifestyles of the babu were among the more visible signs that India was changing, and they became the subject of many early satirical prints and drawings (*kalighat*) that made fun of their colorful eccentricities.

After the failed Indian Rebellion of 1857, the government in Britain began to exert deliberate force to shape Indian society by banning child marriage and widow burning (*sati*) as well as other religious practices that contravened British morality. The ensuing clashes between traditional and secular lifestyles spilled over into the early popular press and framed the debate about the future of India.

Following the well-known formula established by *Punch Magazine*, British expatriates introduced Western-style humor magazines with the *Indian Charivari* in Calcutta (1873). One year later, political cartoons demonstrated their growing influence when the Bengali newspaper *Sulav Samachar* created a scandal by depicting a dead Indian servant attended by his weeping wife while a Western doctor concludes a brief postmortem and the guilty party merely smokes a cigar. The comic alluded to the collusion between wealthy European landlords and corrupt government officials who did not defend the native workers from their cruel bosses. Such cartoons as these eventually provoked the British to impose vernacular press censorship in 1878. The colonial censorship laws were broadly defined and were more draconian than the laws in Britain with harsh penalties that essentially forbade the depiction of British subjects in India and abroad. The result of these restrictions forced Hindu cartoonists to turn their gaze exclusively toward self-mockery; common themes included the dangers of women's emancipation and the excesses and indulgences of the Hindu priestly caste, the Brahmins.

An interesting feature of early Hindu political cartoons was the willingness to represent Hindu gods in secular ways. In 1874, the comic magazine *Busuntak* had the powerful British police commissioner Sir Stewart Hogg depicted as the boar-headed avatar of Vishnu, Varaha. The cartoon not only made fun of Hogg's name but also parodied Hogg's godlike powers to bestow gifts to the wealthy while crushing underfoot the common Hindu. There was also the humorous depiction of Durga, the goddess of death, who is usually seen bare chested, sporting Victorian dress and walking on a smiling prone babu who seems to be enjoying his degradation at the hands of a woman. This cartoon was intended to make fun of the new propriety laws that dictated proper dress codes. The willingness to use Hindu religious iconography in topical political commentary served two purposes: first, it supplied a vast arena of shared symbolic meanings that were well known to Hindus; but second, the meanings were more cryptic to the British and less likely to provoke censorship.

One of the early political cartoonists in India was Gaganendranath Tagore (1867–1938), the nephew of Nobel Prize winner Rabindranath Tagore, who in the late 1910s and 1920s published biting social satires and

Vidyasagar, "Society for the Prevention of Obscenity," published in *Basantak*. (Courtesy of Bangiya Sahitya Prasad, Kolkata, West Bengal)

caricatures. One of his political cartoons, entitled "Caste Machine," shows an obese Brahman sitting on a millstone that is crushing the skinny lower-caste people. A skeleton representing death assists the Brahman, who appears oblivious to the suffering at his feet. Gaganendranath's published work in cartoons was limited compared to that of a far more influential cartoonist, Shankar Pillai (1902–1989), who had a much wider audience and a much longer-lasting impact on the development of cartoons in India. Shankar was active through the turbulent years of World War II and the ensuing struggle for independence and was even something of a celebrity among the people he pilloried in the popular press. Shankar started one of the first satirical magazines in India, called *Shankar's Weekly* (1948–1975), which became a training ground for some of India's next generation of cartoonists.

Following Indian independence in 1947, comics slowly began to appear more regularly as the country regained its stability. Lee Falk's *The Phantom* was one of the popular imports to be repackaged in India by Indrajal Comics, published by the *Times of India* under the editorial direction of Anant Pai (b. 1929). For readers in India, the Phantom, who was at home in both the jungle and the modern world, had an unmistakable appeal, especially as many of the adventures took place in India. Lee Falk, who had never visited India, introduced several characters and situations into the strip that had to be amended by the editors in India to keep from offending their audiences. The fanciful "Bengali tribe of pygmies" had to be changed to the "Denkali tribe" so that it did not reflect negatively on the large population of Bengalis in western India (none of whom are pygmies); and the comic's evil 20th Phantom, "Rama," was actually the name of a prominent deity in Hinduism and needed to be changed to the more ubiquitous Indian name of Ramalu.

Anant Pai, who had seen the popularity of *The Phantom*, worried that Hindu culture was quickly disappearing against the steady tide of Western comics and came up with an idea for a Hindu version of *Classics Illustrated* as a way to present the familiar stories from Hindu epics in the new medium of the comic book. Eventually, the publication was picked up by India Book House and published in 1967 under the title *Amar Chitra Katha*, which means in Hindi either "immortal picture stories" or "our picture stories." Anant Pai was a shrewd businessman who marketed his comics in urban areas to parents who wanted to bestow Hindu culture on their children in a simple and accessible way. Adopting a paternal view to what he saw as vanishing Hindu culture against Western secularism, Pai promoted his *Amar Chitra Katha* so that the comics appeared both educational and religious; through these efforts, he now has a legion of children who know him only as "Uncle Pai." One valuable strategy Pai used in the 1970s was to have prominent religious leaders and politicians promote the unveiling of new stories, thereby lending them an air of sanction and respectability. Prime Minister Rajiv Gandhi released the issue called *March to Freedom* about the fight for independence; and Cardinal Simon Pimenta, the archbishop of Bombay, released the story *Jesus Christ*, which has proven to be one of the most popular *Amar Chitra Katha* stories ever published.[2]

The *Amar Chitra Katha* series, which includes 384 stories of largely Hindu and Buddhist legends, myths, and historical figures, has been a long-lived success with some titles being translated into as many as 38 languages.[3] The success of the series, as well as the nature of the content, brought increased scrutiny from all quarters of Indian society. Conservative critics thought the dress and manners too barbaric and believed the stories did not go far enough to erase the vulgar elements; liberal critics, on the other hand, thought the editing too severe and claimed that all the cultural nuance had been taken out of

Box 7.1 Wayang Comics

In the country with the largest Muslim population in the world, Indonesia, the ancient Hindu epics of the *Mahabharata* and the *Ramayana* remain popular in a form of traditional shadow puppetry known as *wayang*. The wayang puppet theater had a resurgence of popularity in the 1970s following the publication of a series of comic books based on the wayang stories by the artist R. A. Kosasih. Kosasih, like Anant Pai before him, was inspired by the *Classics Illustrated* comics and decided to make his works both educational and entertaining by diverting from the story and comparing the differences between Indian and the Indonesian renditions of the stories. Kosasih often eliminated regional variations of the wayang stories and emphasized the Indian origins rather than the Indonesian derivations that had developed over the centuries in the wayang. The characters in the wayang comics appear costumed like the puppets, but they are given more natural facial features, so the style of the drawings approaches that of early American superhero comics such as *The Phantom*. The wayang comics became so popular with young audiences that puppeteers (*dalang*) began to change their performances to incorporate some of the comic book innovations. By the late 1980s, the fad for wayang-based comics had largely died out as the Indonesian market had been crippled by censorship and competition in comics from Hong Kong, South Korea, and Japan.

the stories and replaced with crude ethnic and gender stereotypes such as the devoted and sacrificing wife, the selfless Hindu warrior, and the greedy and disreputable Muslim. To counter these and other criticisms, the *Amar Chitra Katha* developed an editorial process that removed any idiomatic expressions or slang. Despite the rather generic realism that has been promoted at *Amar Chitra Katha*, a few of the artists have gained recognition for their exceptional work, among them Yusuf Lien's sensual *Mirabai* and P. B. Kavadi's *Tales of Narada*. (See also box 7.1.)

Badahur (Hindi for "the courageous one") by Abid Surti first appeared in 1976 and was an early attempt at creating an indigenous superhero. The character Badahur had a distinctive modern Indian look of blue jeans and a saffron homespun shirt (*kurta*), which gave him the symbolic force of Western proletarian pragmatism coupled with Hindu nationalism. Badahur battled bandits (*dacoit*) based on those who were actually terrorizing villages in northern India for much of the 1970s and 1980s, and at his side was a remarkably liberated girlfriend named Bella, who was both a student of history and biology as well as a black belt in karate. Bella frequently appeared on the cover and was featured inside the comic as an active force in moving the story forward. Indrajal Comics, which published *The Phantom* along with *Badahur* and a few other superhero titles, eventually closed shop in the early 1990s. The primary reason stated by the management was lack of profits because of competition from TV.

Populist Graphic Narratives of Modern China

The push toward modernization was alternately opposed and supported by several different classes in 19th-century China, leading to painful and destabilizing transitions with reoccurring civil wars. As China struggled to throw off feudalism, these disruptions were also felt in changes to traditional print culture. When lithography first appeared in Shanghai in the late 1860s, it provided a means for cheaper and faster printing, which, in turn, made individual prints and small books accessible to a much wider audience than ever before. The impact of lithography on China was more dramatic than its appearance in Europe some 60 years earlier because the technology that arrived was fully developed and far in advance of any existing print technology in China. Typically, one woodblock printer could produce as many as 600 prints in one day, whereas the output from a manual lithographic press could produce as many as 1,500 prints in two shifts, and an electric press could produce as many as 16,000 prints in the same amount of time. The mechanization had a deleterious effect on the cottage industry of woodblock print production; where once there were thousands of artists producing hundreds of designs, there would now, under the new mechanization, be only hundreds of artists producing dozens of designs. Although lithography did not entirely replace woodblock printing, the dominance and cultural significance of the older technology was quickly on the wane.

With fewer publishers producing the majority of the prints, government officials instituted greater censorship over the print designs, creating even greater movement toward standardization among publishers. Early government control, however, was not unified or well coordinated, resulting in uneven enforcement and contradictory rules. There were also some fledgling efforts to co-opt traditional print production for political messages. Peng Yizhong belonged to a movement of scholars who were pressuring for changes in the academic world, and he seems to have been one of the first to use traditional woodblock prints to promote modernization. In an effort to promote the idea of women's education, a collection of prints entitled *Girls Ask for Education* (ca. 1906) represented a common theme of a group of women undergoing military training. On horseback or sporting rifles in military formation, these young women are dressed in a traditional *cheongsam* but have their small bound feet in American-style cowboy boots. Taken altogether, the images create a curious mixed message of modernity, Western culture, and erotic fantasy.[4]

Lithographic illustrated stories began to appear in print as early as the late 1890s in China. The typical format consisted of relatively small, pocket-sized publications bound on one side so they were easy to carry. These illustrated "little books" (*xiaoshu*) proved widely popular among the urban lower classes, but they were shunned by established booksellers. Instead, *xioshu* established itself as popular entertainment, commonly sold or rented in market stalls or on the street outside theaters just as chapbooks had been in England a century before. By the mid-1920s, the growing sales of illustrated stories attracted more established publishers and the length and quality of the publications began to improve dramatically. The World Book Company published a rendition of the popular classic novel *Romance of the Three Kingdoms*, calling the book a "*lianhuan tuhua*," or linked-picture book. The emphasis was now on the drawings with a minimum of text to convey the story. The book's format was widely imitated, and the term "*lianhuanhua*" (without the *tu*) became commonly used to describe the new genre.

The early 20th century was also the heyday of Chinese traditional theater, Beijing opera (*jingju*), which had already proved for many years to be a popular subject for single-sheet New Year's pictures (*nianhua*) and later as lianhuanhua. The first illustrated Beijing opera story was based on a Shanghai production of *Exchange the Prince with a Leopard Cat* (*Limao huan taizi*) in 1918. For publishers, Beijing opera provided readily accessible material: the figures and backgrounds were copied from the costumes and stage sets, and the well-known story made it easier to convey the action in a few pictures. Although the images were clearly derived from Beijing opera, there was no effort to capture a specific performer or a particular performance, as was commonly done earlier in Japan with ukiyo-e images of kabuki. Often given very short notice about the pending playbill, Beijing opera stories were drawn, printed, and sold before the opening night of a performance at a cost that was less than the price of a ticket to see the show. The speed of production compromised quality and accuracy, but the popularity of the theater productions virtually guaranteed an audience for the cheap publications.

Western-style satirical cartoons and caricatures first appeared in *The China Punch* (1867) by British expatriates based in Hong Kong. *The China Punch*, much like the British magazine it imitated, provided conservative nationalist views in a humorous and satirical manner. Though written in English, the magazine served as a prototype for other humor magazines with different political agendas and audiences. The autonomy that Hong Kong enjoyed at this time as a British territory provided greater license for political dissent than found in other Asian markets and was home to many revolutionary publications. When an anti–Qing Dynasty magazine called *The Journal of Current Pictorial* was banned on the mainland of China in 1905, it promptly moved to Hong Kong and published nearly a dozen more issues before international pressure forced its closure.

In 1925 in the magazine *Literature Weekly*, Feng Zikai (1898–1975) introduced a beautiful fusion of Song Dynasty–style painting and contemporary elements in a series of cartoons entitled *Zikai Manhua*. By titling his work as *manhua*, or "impromptu sketches,"[5] Feng used an 18th-century Chinese literati term that had become popular a century earlier in Japan as manga. Feng was in part inspired by the quick character sketches of the Chinese literati artist Chen Shizeng (1876–1923) and, after spending time in Tokyo in the early 1920s, by the Japanese artist Takehisa Yumeji (1884–1934). Over the years, Feng's name became closely identified with the emergence of this new looser style of cartoon art, where the drawings were more suggestive and allegorical, but with just enough detail to ground them in the modern world of urban Shanghai.

The first successful manhua magazine, *Shanghai Sketch*, appeared in 1928 as a slim eight-page tabloid with four pages dedicated to two-color-lithographed manhua drawings. With 3,000 copies a week in circulation, *Shanghai Sketch* developed a few serial characters, including Ye Qianyu's *Mr. Wang*, who first appeared in 1928. The character Mr. Wang was derived from the Western comic idiom with all the familiar tropes of family life in the city. The surge in interest in manhua that buoyed *Shanghai Sketch* created an opening for a few women to emerge as cartoonists, including the notable example of Liang Baibo (ca. 1911–1970), who took the pen name "Bomb"; she later changed her name to just the sound of a bomb, "Bon." Her best-known comic was about a thoroughly modern woman, *Miss Bee*, which first appeared in 1935.

Another character that appeared for the first time that same year was an orphaned street urchin, *Sanmao* or "three hairs," drawn by Zhang Leping (1910–1992) and published by Xiaochenbao. Sanmao was always drawn without speech balloons, and in his silent world he was a sympathetic character similar to Charlie Chaplin's little tramp character, reflecting the growing class-consciousness in China and providing a running commentary on the disparity between the rich and the poor. *Sanmao* was shockingly frank in its portrayal of poverty, hunger, police brutality, and corruption. The character Sanmao was constantly battling for survival as a shoeshine boy or a house-servant; but despite the constant humiliations, this plucky three-haired kid persevered. Generous to those less fortunate, eager for education, warm when comforted, and defiant against injustice, Sanmao had a strong moral core, which is not surprising considering his name was a pun on the Chinese Buddhist term for the teachings of Buddha, *sanbao* or "three jewels."

Through the 1930s, 17 different manhua magazines competed for readers in Shanghai, the most prominent being *Modern Sketch*, edited by Lu Shaofei, with a very clean art deco style and full-color lithographic prints. The inaugural issue of *Modern Sketch* sported an ink bottle knight on a horse made of pencils preparing to joust with his pen. Manhua was now decidedly political, and this cover by Zhang Guanyu signaled that with its illustrations, the magazine was willing to take on the evils of society. Feng Zikai's work represented the brutal realities of the time with a subtle grace that revealed his strong humanist concerns for social justice and deep sympathy for the plight of children. Even in his most graphically violent work, as in the lianhuanhua based on Lu Xun's *The True Story of Ah Q* (1937), Feng does not demonize the culprits or exaggerate the suffering but lets the simple brutal facts of the Japanese invasion of China speak for themselves. With the capture of Shanghai, manhua artists fled to Hong Kong to continue their anti-Japanese manhua until, in 1941, Hong Kong, too, was occupied by the Japanese and soon all manhua publications were stopped.

In retrospect, the 1930s proved to be a brief period of respite between the wars, riots, rebellions, upheavals, and crackdowns that had shaken China and would continue to affect the country for many years to come. In that time, a great outpouring of creativity in the comic arts occurred because they were able to infuse the Old World traditions and icons with New World issues, sentiments, and styles. At the end of the war with Japan in 1945, hostilities resumed between the Nationalists and the Communists and would continue for the next four years. In the cities controlled by the Nationalist Party, publishers were forbidden to publish works critical of the government. To circumvent the restrictions, cartoonists took their work directly to the public in exhibitions done in impromptu galleries. To protect themselves further from government persecution, the artists adopted fanciful and mythic localities for their political commentary. Liao Bingxiong

(b. 1915) presented his scathing commentary on the Nationalist Party masqueraded in a story called the *Cat Kingdom* (*Maoguo Chunqiu*), which toured public exhibition halls to large audiences in 1946.

The Chinese Communist Party and the Expansion of Print Propaganda

The Communist intellectual Lu Xun (1881–1936) championed popular literature and was one of the first to propose the idea that lianhuanhua could be used as propaganda to educate the populace about Communist ideology. Rather than embrace the now common lithographic process, Lu Xun was enamored of the older woodblock print technology that had deep roots in rural life and aesthetics. As early as 1929, Lu Xun promoted contemporary Japanese and Western woodblock prints in his journal, *Morning Flowers of the Garden of Art* (*Yiyuan chaohua*), and in 1931 he organized a workshop on modern woodblock printing, which prompted several intellectual artists to take up the challenge to create woodblock prints similar to the work of expressionist artist Frans Masereel. The project became a focal point for left-wing artists in China, and over the next five years, 15 different woodblock print societies formed, eventually becoming the Committee of Shanghai Woodcut Artists in 1936. This group would include some of the more influential artists of the Chinese Communist Party, who continued their work while in exile in Yenan during the civil war. Early on, these artists established a style that emulated the decorative celebratory qualities of the older nianhua but also, as a result of their art school training, infused their work with greater realism.

The urban European expressionist-style socialist art eventually fell out of favor as Mao Tse-tung (1893–1976) put forward his own agenda in his closing remarks at the Yenan Forum on Art and Literature (1942). Mao favored Lu Xun's approach to positive proletarian imagery that celebrated labor and valor while it erased feudal history and interpersonal relationships. Reforming traditional print iconography often proved challenging, especially as it was often invested with sentiments that were contrary to Communist doctrine. The nianhua print entitled *Brother and Sister Open Wasteland* shows young male and female figures briskly dancing in a manner common in the popular *yangge* drama. Although the print had a positive and proletarian message based on local customs, it was sharply criticized because it was mistakenly read as "Husband and Wife Plow the Fields," a reading that had sexual connotations which the Communist Party was eager to avoid. Another, more disturbing trend was the effort to transpose Communist leaders into the place of folk gods. The 1949 calendar from the Masses Art Society closely mimics a traditional stove god calendar design, with the portraits of Mao Tse-tung and Zhu De replacing the traditional figures of gods as the twin icons of the Revolution.

An early example of this new Chinese Communist–style graphic narrative was Mi Gu's lianhuanhua entitled *Young Blacky Gets Married* (*Xiao erhei jiehun*). Mi Gu, an enthusiastic supporter of Communist ideology, graduated from one of China's two most prestigious art schools. Prior to his work with the Chinese Communist Party, Mi Gu published manhua for some anti-Nationalist publications in Shanghai during the Sino-Japanese War. Mi Gu later moved to the Communist base in Yenan, where he took up producing lianhuanhua. The lianhuanhua of *Young Blacky Gets Married* promoted the fairly common theme of love marriages over arranged marriages, but what made the work unique for the time was the use of realistic figures and backgrounds rendered in bold lines. Shadows done with crosshatching were eliminated and there was an emphasis on contour and a minimum of decoration. In this manner, the figures were realistically rendered but often had a flat quality with open space reminiscent of classical Chinese painting. This approach was an attempt to appear folksy without the typical cultural trappings and reliance on obvious character types. Widely distributed and reprinted, *Young Blacky Gets Married* stood as a model for future Communist Chinese works simply called "new" lianhuanhua.

At the end of the civil war, the Nationalists retreated to Taiwan and the Communist Party took control of the mainland, instituting radical reforms and abolishing many established traditions the Communists regarded as feudal. Mao's comments on art in Yenan were pivotal in defining the future direction of Communist art in China for more than 30 years, not only by giving artists direction but also by serving as a weapon to use against artists who did not conform to the party ideology. The Communist Party was able to establish Mao's views soon after assuming control of the government by consolidating all the remaining Shanghai publishers into two large publishing houses under direct government supervision. Because of these and other changes in the economy, the only work available for most artists in Shanghai was to go into publishing, where one of the early projects was an effort to develop new lianhuanhua that were ideologically and culturally in tune with the Chinese Communist Party. Needless to say, with vast resources at their disposal, the general quality of the lianhuanhua improved significantly as leading artists took up making picture stories for the masses. Indicative of the new optimism for the Communist agenda, the popular character

Sanmao returned in a new adventure called *Sanmao Yesterday and Today* (*Sanmao Jinxi*) in which the street urchin had suddenly been delivered to a socialist paradise where all his material and emotional needs were met.

Lianhuanhua, with its older epic narrative style (similar to kibyoshi), was deemed more appropriate to convey Chinese Communist ideology than the more modern multipanel manhua because lianhuanhua was associated with the working classes and was essentially Chinese in origin, whereas manhua was derived from Japanese and American comics more commonly found in urban areas. A new lianhuanhua was still expensive for most Chinese; depending on the length and quality of the print, one might expect to pay anywhere between between 12 and 35 fen (five to fifteen cents). Gino Nebiolo describes traveling by train in China in the 1950s and being given a lianhuanhua along with her evening tea. She noted that the passengers eagerly read the comics, which were shared among the passengers until the end of the ride, when they were collected by the conductor.[6]

Circulation numbers of the new lianhuanhua are hard to estimate because there were many editions, some of which were only produced and distributed locally. Among popular titles, it was possible to have as many as several million copies sold with dozens of reprints. One of the early ambitious works of lianhuanhua was the serialized story of resistance fighters called *Railroad Guerillas* (*tiedao youjidui*) by Ding Bingzeng and Han Heping, which was based on a novel by Liu Zhijia. Compiled between 1954 and 1962, the completed series was published in 10 volumes with more than 1,000 drawings. It remains one of the most successful lianhuanhua publications, having been reprinted at least 36 times and selling almost 4 million copies.

Desiring to keep the Revolution alive in the memory of younger Chinese, the Communist Party was especially interested in producing stories that covered the Sino-Japanese War and the overthrow of the Nationalist Party. The story of the *White Haired Girl* was an early favorite and reputedly the real story of a girl who had been rescued by Communist Chinese forces during the civil war whose hair had turned white as a result of all the atrocities she had experienced at the hands of the Nationalists. As early as 1945, the story was made into a Beijing opera and later, in 1950, a movie. Hua Sanchuan (b. 1930) created a new lianhuanhua for the story in 1963 based on the popular film version. The new lianhuanhua were primarily used as way to disseminate the message of the movie to rural areas where films were unavailable.

A critical turning point in all Communist Chinese art was the Cultural Revolution (1965–1976), which viciously attacked all art not explicitly endorsed by Communist Party propaganda officials, led most visibly by Lin Biao and

Mao's fourth wife, the former Shanghai actress Jiang Qing (1914–1991). The Cultural Revolution was significant for elevating the cult of Mao. All pretense to historical accuracy or traditional conformity was laid aside, and every artistic production had to sing the praise of Mao at a fever pitch. Older works were banned or radically altered so that they would conform to the new exaggerated style that allowed for no nuance regarding the Communist cause. Older artists suffered the indignities of having to publicly retract and apologize for earlier works, many of which were destroyed under the new dictum that the people should destroy the "four olds: old ideas, old customs, old culture, and old habits of mind." As a result of the Cultural Revolution, many publishers closed and the number of new lianhuanhua dropped significantly. As a devout Buddhist and a scholar of classical literature, Feng Zikai was increasingly out of place in Communist China and, near the end of his life, quietly endured the pains of the Cultural Revolution when hundreds of his original drawings and paintings were destroyed and he was branded a "counterrevolutionary."

At the death of Mao in 1976, the Cultural Revolution came to an end. Four leaders close to Mao known as the "Gang of Four" were pilloried as responsible for the abuses and atrocities, and the country slowly began to regain stability. Many banned works returned, but artists were fearful of reprisals and it was still frowned on for an artist to seek individual recognition for his or her work; hence, many new lianhuanhua were published anonymously or as a collaborative effort. Liao Bingxiong demonstrated extraordinary daring in 1979 when he organized a group exhibition called Self-Deprecation, that directly criticized the Cultural Revolution. More than 10,000 people each day attended the six-day show. Liao's own iconic contribution was a self-portrait showing himself wrapped tight in a fetal position, deep misery on his face, and though the ceramic jug had broken and fallen away, he still held the shape that he had been forced into. The text above states, "The downfall of the Gang of Four was followed by the criticism of their deeds. My own self-criticism was necessary too."[7]

Between 1978 and 1987, lianhuanhua returned in popularity. At its peak, Lu Fusheng (b. 1949) created *The Phoenix Hairpin* (Chatou Feng), 1983, which explored in 72 painterly scenes on silk a story about Lu You (1125–1210), the great Southern Song Dynasty poet. The work has no connection to the earlier dictated socialist realist style and instead returns to the more painterly qualities of the early manhua illustration by Feng Zikai. *The Phoenix Hairpin* is in many ways a sentimental reminiscence from the past, based not on a movie or even a Beijing opera but on an older style of theater called *kunqu*, which had all but died out in the 20th century. Lu Fusheng, a connoisseur of *kunqu*, included many of the actual lyrics from the original play in his work. The oval shape of the frame is reminiscent of Southern Song Dynasty fans, on which similar abbreviated lyrical images were often painted.

Communist propaganda comics have reappeared from time to time in China, although their effectiveness seems to be waning. As recently as 1999, a comic entitled *Li Hongzhi: The Man and His Evil Deeds* was published by the China Art Museum Press to attack the leader of the outlawed Falun Gong movement. The comic used stereotypical exaggerations to vilify the leader and his followers, painting them as extremist hypocrites whose backward ideology was reflected in their clothing that was drawn to look 30 years out-of-date. The intense propaganda campaign was shocking to some who could scarcely believe the comic book's claim that the Falun Gong spiritual group could spread "an apocalyptic view that created social terror." As one businessman responded to the comic to a *New York Times* reporter, "It's as though we are reliving a bad dream."[8]

Japanese Modernization and the Invention of Manga

During the Edo period (1603–1867), Japan had long maintained its isolation from the rest of the world, and the authority of the ruling shogun rested in part on his ability to maintain social order by keeping foreigners out. Commodore Matthew Perry's arrival in Japan in 1856 forced the country to open up to the rest of the world and created a rupture with the traditional past that effectively eroded the feudal system. After the subsequent collapse of the shogunate and the restoration of Emperor Meiji in 1867, Japan pursued an ambitious plan for modernization that would transform it from an agrarian society into a world power in less than 50 years. Through that era of turmoil and transformation, the new comics industry, inspired by Western-style caricature and satirical prints, was a mix of Old World aesthetics and new modern forms. All the arts were emerging from under the heavy-handed censorship of the shogunate, and there was enthusiasm for trying new ideas. There was also some self-repudiation by artists seeking to distance themselves from the feudal past.

An eccentric correspondent for the *London Illustrated News*, Charles Wirgman (1835–1891), was the first to bring comics ashore. One year after his arrival in Japan in 1863, Wirgman abandoned his original employer from Britain, and self-published *Japan Punch*, which was released more or less monthly until 1887. Each 10-page issue was produced in the same manner as traditional woodblock prints, which had been available in Japan since the early 16th century. Wirgman tailored his humor magazine to the growing expatriate audience in Yokohama by showing cartoons in a manner typical of the British satire of the time. The ethnocentric humor focused on the many weird and ironic ways Japan was adapting to modern Western culture, including, for example, Japanese who politely removed their shoes when entering a train only to learn they were left on the platform when leaving the station. Wirgman so effectively established the cartoon genre in Japan that even long after *Japan Punch* ceased publication, cartoons were called *ponchi-e* or "punch pictures." Wirgman settled permanently in Japan, became quite proficient in Japanese, and over time played an important role in defining the character and purpose of comic magazines in Japan. For his efforts, Wirgman is still fondly remembered in Japan as the progenitor of Japanese comics, and every year a memorial ceremony is held at his grave.

In 1874, the artist Kawanabe Kyōsai and the novelist Kanagaki Robun published the first Japanese comic magazine, *Eshimbun Nipponchi*, which is a pun that could be translated as either the illustrated "land of Japan" or the "Japanese Ponchi." The magazine lasted a mere two issues, but it demonstrated interest among Japanese artists and intellectuals in the new cartoon medium. In 1877, Nomura Fumio returned from four years' study in London and brought back several volumes of caricatures and several issues of the magazine *Punch*. Together with the artist Honda Kinkichiro, they created a political comic magazine called *Marumaru Chimbun*. *Marumaru* in the title referred to the little circles that Japanese censors used to delete offensive material, and *chimbun* was both a pun on the word for newspaper (*shimbun*), and a word that suggested "strange tidings." Technically, the magazine was far in advance of earlier publications; by using the newly available zinc-etching process, the magazine had higher-quality prints appearing every Saturday with a circulation of 15,000. The captions for *Marumaru Chimbun* were published in both English and Japanese in an effort to appeal to intellectual Japanese as well as an expatriate audience. The magazine employed some of the leading illustrators of the day and was a significant innovator in comic art. This new venue for political discourse was not without its problems. In 1880, a political cartoon critical of the government by Honda landed the editor in jail for a whole year.

George Bigot (1860–1927) was another influential foreigner in the early Japanese comic industry. He introduced the French *Imagerie d'Épinal* comic style in his publication *Tôbaé*, which appeared biweekly from Yokohama starting in 1887. Bigot came to Japan to study art and worked for a while as a cartoonist at *Marumaru Chimbun* before beginning his own French-Japanese magazine. The title, *Tôbaé*, was the traditional Japanese word for comic caricature (*toba-e*), which in the magazine was represented as a character appearing much like the French commedia character Pierrot, who would from time to time appear inside the editorial cartoons to give his own ironic opinion of matters. Bigot dealt with the intervention of censorship officials by caricaturing them in the magazine. In the 1887 cartoon entitled "Tôbaé at Police Headquarters," the editorial staff of all Western-style newspapers appear kneeling, bound, and gagged at the foot of a scrawny officer who is lecturing them on what it is permissible to print. *Tôbaé* ran for about 70 issues, and though it was considerably more expensive than other magazines of the time, it was essential to the popularization of multi-panel comics in Japan.

It was only in the 1920s when comics in Japan took the now commonly used term "manga" derived from the Chinese term "*manhua*." Rakuten Kitazawa (1876–1955) created some of the earliest serialized comic strips that were called manga and went on to become one of the premiere comic artists in Japan and one of the few who can boast having a museum dedicated to his work. Kitazawa began his career in 1896 as an assistant to the Australian artist Frank Nankivell (1869–1959) at the American magazine *Box of Curios*, where he was exposed to the latest techniques in cartooning. A few years later, in 1902, Kitazawa was the editor of *Jijishimpo* newspaper's Sunday color comic supplement, which was the first in Japan to capitalize on the idea popularized by Pulitzer in the *New York World* six years earlier. In his first comic strip for that supplement, entitled *Tagosaku and Mokubē Sightseeing in Tokyo*, Kitazawa used colloquial speech and gesture to communicate sight gags featuring two country bumpkins lost in the big city. Kitazawa's great popularity came about through his work on the color comic magazine *Tokyo Puck*, which he founded and edited from 1905 to 1912. Based on the American humor magazine that began in the 1870s, *Tokyo Puck* was opinionated and provocative, with such shocking political cartoons of world leaders as an unflattering depiction of Teddy Roosevelt writhing to reach the "anti-Japanese wasp" on his back (1906). With a circulation of more than 100,000, *Tokyo Puck* was an astonishing success; but Kitazawa's more significant contribution to Japanese comics came later when he left off imitating the tight, illustrative European-style comics and began working with a brush in a looser, more traditionally Japanese manner.

The painterly quality that marks the aesthetic of the Taisho era (1912–1926) was first introduced by graphic designer Takehisa Yumeji, who inspired Kitazawa, as well as the Chinese artist Feng Zikai. In 1928, Kitazawa effectively used this calligraphic-like brushwork technique in his serialized comic strip, *Tonda Haneko*, about a precocious little girl who has a fascination for all things Western. Wearing a short skirt, she joyfully demonstrates her ability to dance the Charleston, much to the dismay of her more traditional elders. The

Rakuten Kitazawa, *Tonda Haneko* (*Miss Haneko Tonda*), 1928.

Japanese text is written in Katagana, one of the four Japanese syllabary that are specifically used to write foreign words and to add dramatic emphasis. Here, it is employed to express the sound of Haneko's vigorous dancing. The extraordinary length and complexity of the sounds that describe the energetic Charleston rhythm is a reflection of the Japanese language, which is rich in onomatopoeic sound expressions.

Japanese comics followed American trends and increasingly became oriented toward children's themes. Translation of American comics reprinted in Japanese magazines began in 1923 with George McManus's *Bringing Up Father* and then quickly expanded to include such American strips as Cliff Sterrett's *Polly and Her Pals*, Bud Fisher's *Mutt and Jeff*, and Pat Sullivan's *Felix the Cat*. Yutaka Asō's *Easy-going Daddy* (*Nonki na Tōsan*) was an obvious imitation of McManus's *Bringing Up Father*, where the father figure, Uncle Nontō, takes on a variety of odd jobs that of the modern middle-class world. The strip first appeared a few months after the devastating Tokyo earthquake of 1923 and was created at the request of the editor of the *Hōchi* newspaper to help people forget their worries.

The trend toward children's comics was also related to the increasing censorship of political discourse and the violent intimidation of left-wing political activists. Under the Peace Preservation Law passed in 1925, many artists and editors were jailed, tortured, and even killed for expressing ideas critical of the government. Masamu Yanase (1900–1945) was one of the leading ideological cartoonists who, following the lead of the German artist George Grosz, depicted the extreme class differences in modern Japan. Yanase's own 1929 parody of *Bringing Up Father* was entitled *Bringing Up a Rich Man* (*Kanemochi Kyoiku*), which underscored the willful ignorance and folly of the rich in contrast to the dedicated resolve of the working classes. Yanase's political cartoons were a particularly vivid portrayal of the times with their scratchy lines and biting caricatures of rampant militarism, indifferent industrialists, and excessive censors. Under the increasingly ultranationalist government, Yanase frequently suffered arrest and persecution for his comics and political activities with the leftist modern art movement Mavo.

Leading the way in children's manga were the hefty children's magazines, which included serialized comic stories beginning early in the 1930s. Each monthly episode ran for about 20 pages and consisted of a complete story in the ongoing saga of the characters' lives. In a manner similar to the way comics were developing in Europe at this time, these manga were compiled into hardcover editions that were printed in color on good-quality paper at about 150 pages in length. One of the early popular favorites of this era was Suihō Tagawa's *Black Stray* (*Norakuro*), which ran serialized in *Shōnen Club* from 1931 to 1941. The hapless black stray dog had numerous misadventures until he eventually stood upright and joined the army. In fanciful military battles against farm animals, Norakuro unwittingly became a war hero. *Norakuro*, which bore some resemblance to Pat Sullivan's *Felix the Cat*, was an enormously popular image that was widely exploited for numerous merchandising opportunities. Despite the pro-military message in the comic, the Japanese military was actually not too pleased to have Norakuro's support, and so the comic faded from view as the Pacific War of World War II began to heat up. The other children's comic with a pro-military message was Keizou Shimada's *Dankichi* (1935–1938), which had the more disturbing racist plot of a young boy becoming king of a Pacific island and teaching the dark-skinned natives to make war on the invading white foreigners with coconut bombs and cannons that could shoot live tigers. *Fuku-chan* (1936–1971), by Ryuichi Yokoyama (1909–2001), appeared for the first time in the 1930s and, contrary to the pro-military comics of the day, actually had a rather innocent and tenaciously upbeat character that has made it the longest-lived comic in Japan's history.

The rise of military power in Japan and the subsequent Pacific War had a devastating effect on popular print publications. Between 1937 and 1944, the overall number of publications fell from 16,788 to 942. By 1943, all paper was rationed by the government; then a year later, all comics were banned from newspapers, which were ordered to report only "essential" news. Emerging from this period was a growing popular trend in picture recitation (*kamishibai*) and rental kiosks (*kashihonya*), both of which allowed alternate means to circulate cheaply produced graphic stories to a wide audience.

The live *kamishibai* performances were conducted by a solo performer who rode about on a bicycle and set up a little stage attached to a small case over the rear wheel. The *kamishibai* performers used a series of individual cards printed with sensational stories set in a frame and revealed the pictures, one after another, as they told the stories. Performers also used clapper sticks or drums to announce the show and add a dramatic flourish to their sensational and humorous stories. The performance was free, but the people who stayed to hear the story bought a candy from the performer after the show. Just as in ancient times, when poor Buddhist monks and nuns told stories from painted scrolls (*etoki*), the *kamishibai* performers would travel far and wide disseminating current events along with myths and legends to rural areas cut off from other forms of mass media. Before the mid-1950s, it is estimated that as many as 10,000 performers of *kamishibai* roamed the cities and countryside playing to an estimated 5 million people a day. Most of the performers were people from the low *burakumin* caste, who had few other economic opportunities.

Kamishibai during World War II owed a great deal to earlier silent films from the 1920s that employed performers (*benshi*) to recite all the dialogue live before the audience, in a manner that was similar to the famed *bunraku* puppet theater of Osaka. The bold, hand-painted color illustrations used in a *kamishibai* performance employed a cinematic vocabulary of close-ups, worm's eye views, and long shots, but also zip lines that show force and highlight the direction of the action. Performers rented a set of six to eight pictures from publishers who contracted writers and artists to compose the stories in a wide range of styles including children's folktales, movie adaptations, adventure serials, and current events. During the war, the *kamishibai,* like all other means of mass communication in Japan, was closely regulated by the government, and special war propaganda stories were printed and widely disseminated.

One of the most popular of *kamishibai* characters was the serialized adventure story of the *Golden Bat* (*Ōgon Batto,* 1931), created by the writer Ichiro

Suzuki and illustrator Takeo Nagamatsu. Golden Bat is the first costumed superhero, appearing several years before Lee Falk's Phantom and before even the earliest attempts by Seigle and Schuster at creating Superman. The peculiar cross-eyed and skull-headed hero wore a high-collared coat and a long red cape similar to the costume worn in Lon Chaney's film appearance as the Masque of the Red Death in *The Phantom of the Opera* (1925). Golden Bat announced his arrival with a spooky laugh and swooped down to dispatch the villains with lightning from his staff.

Following the Pacific War and the growing availability of television in the 1950s, *kamishibai* quickly waned in popularity, and many of the artists and publishers moved into the growing comic book industry. Shirato Sanpei (b. 1932) was an artist whose career followed the changing landscape of popular entertainment from *kamishibai* to serialized manga in rental kiosk magazines, and eventually to being an artist employed in the new growing market for manga magazines. Several popular *kamishibai* characters also made the leap to manga. The *Golden Bat* soon appeared as manga and eventually became a live-action movie in 1966 and an animated TV series a year later, which helped spread its fame outside of Japan where it also proved popular across Latin America, Italy, and Australia. Despite Japan's weak political influence after World War II, it would soon regain its economic stature, and with the growing popularity of its manga become an international cultural force that would eventually surpass America's dominant role in comic production.

CHAPTER 8

The Superhero and the Comic Book

The 20th-century phenomenon of the U.S. comic book was born from the convergence of two different media markets: first, a thriving popular fiction market of adventure, science fiction, and romance; and second, a less reliable market for newspaper comic strip reprints compiled into book form. Once firmly conjoined, the modern comic book with original adventure material was soon graced with a new breed of adventures starring superheroes. No longer constrained by the width of a newspaper page, the dynamic action of the superhero helped sustain the expanded narratives that could run "faster than a locomotive" to become the ideal masters of the modern world, with a power great enough to contend with the terrifying forces of industrialization. The identity of the comic book with superheroes has become so inextricably enmeshed in American culture that—even today—it is very difficult for some people to imagine that there was, or ever could be, a comic book that did not star a superhero.

Twentieth-century pulp fiction was a holdover from the 19th-century blood-and-thunder pocket publications that had cultivated a reliable formula for escape. Just as before, lurid covers enticed readers into reading shocking accounts of murder, mayhem, sublime love, cruel justice, and pathetic debasement. A relatively new genre to this market was science fiction, which was chiefly a product of the imaginative work of Jules Verne (1828–1905), H. G. Wells (1866–1946), and Edgar Rice Burroughs (1875–1950). In 1926, Hugo Gernsback (1884–1967) began the first magazine devoted to science fiction,[1] *Amazing Stories*, which bolstered the American market for science fiction and led to other magazines such as *Astounding Stories* in 1929. It was from the pulp magazines that such heroic characters as *The Scarlet Pimpernel* (1905), *John Carter of Mars* (1912), *Tarzan* (1912), *El Zorro* (1919), *Buck Rogers* (1928), *The Shadow* (1930), and *Doc Savage* (1933) would emerge and serve as the prototype of the new superheroes. The powers of these heroes were said to be so great they had to disguise themselves in order to avoid the corrupting influence of society and work undercover to dispense vigilante justice. These pulp fiction characters were all well enmeshed in popular culture through magazines, radio, and film, yet by the 1920s there was still no venue for them in the comics medium. Newspaper comics—now exclusively dominated by syndicates—had relegated comics to the confines of middle-class family-oriented humor. When pulp fiction characters slowly began to appear in newspaper strips, the format, conventions, and expectations of newspaper comics were already too constrained to allow their full fruition.

Adventure Comics in Newspapers

Charles Kahles (1878–1931) was the early pioneer of above-average heroes in comic strips. Even before his signature work *Hairbreadth Harry* (1906), he had created the first police comic, *Clarence the Cop* (1900), and the first aviation strip, *Sandy Highflyer, the Airship Man* (1902). Kahles relied a great deal on humor and melodrama to propel his brief plots, but he did introduce the first comic renditions of the damsel in distress and the cliffhanger at the strip's end. By 1924, kid strips began introducing more extended adventures, starting with Roy Crane's (1902–1977) *Wash Tubbs II*, followed a short while later by Harold Gray's (1894–1968) *Little Orphan Annie*. Wash Tubbs eventually became a sidekick to the more typical adventure character of Captain Easy. The plucky Orphan Annie always remained the focus of her strip; at the onset of the Great Depression, in her Dickensesque adventures she conveyed the no-nonsense determination of a little girl in hard times.

Adventure characters from pulp fiction began to appear in U.S. newspaper comics January 7, 1929, with the simultaneous arrival of comics based on Philip Francis Nowlan's (1988–1940) *Buck Rogers* and Edgar Rice Burroughs's *Tarzan*. *Buck Rogers* and especially the *Tarzan* franchise had already demonstrated a strong popular following in print and in movies, but they were only slowly introduced into the comics pages of a few dozen papers. The syndicates' reticence to try out this more serious dramatic material was based largely on the assumption that comics were supposed to be funny but also the large number of well-established comic strips made it harder for new material to appear.[2]

Tarzan and *Buck Rogers* were both based on a well-known formula that had wide currency at the time. In Washington Irving's *Rip Van Winkle* (1819), H. G. Wells's *The Sleeper Awakes* (1910), and Edgar Rice Burroughs's *John Carter of Mars* (1912), the hero is brought to another time or another world where he must contend with profoundly different realities. In recent retellings, the hero actually gains some new power from being caught between the past and the present. A dual identity was at the heart of Tarzan, who, through some twisted Darwinian logic, was superior because he was genetically an heir to a British lordship, yet raised in the wilds of Africa. This dual heritage gave him benefit of both good breeding and jungle bestiality. *Buck Rogers* was an even more flimsy story, which added nothing but hyperbole to the current stock of science fiction stories. Instead of 100 years into the future, as in *The Sleeper Awakes*, Buck Rogers was sent 500 years into the future; but the greater stretch of time did not result in a more radical reimagining of human society. The chief nemesis in these future worlds was typically a contemporary villain who had grown in power over the intervening centuries. In the case of *Buck Rogers*, Buck had to thwart the evil machinations of the Dr. Fu Manchu look-alike, Ming the Merciless. Buck's love interest, Wilma, was more modern in the way she appeared as a flapperesque picture of women's independence, though much of the drama in the strip concerned rescuing her from Ming's harem.

The quirky graphic style of *Buck Rogers*, developed under the artwork of Richard "Dick" Calkins (1895–1962), is often equated with the art deco style (1925–1939) with its bold geometry and streamlined shapes of flying spacecraft and futuristic cities. Art deco was an obvious fit for this futuristic tale, for it eliminated the last vestiges of Victorian cross-hatching from comics and introduced clean, flowing lines that made the figures appear to move and act with greater vitality. The chief visual appeal of the strip from the beginning was the way figures could float and jump with the help of their "jumping belts" filled with the special ingredient Inertron, which "fell upward." The jumping belts produced a near weightlessness that allowed the characters to jump great distances. A similar idea was at work in Burroughs's *John Carter of Mars* stories; but there, the hero had a natural advantage through the difference between the gravity of Earth and that of Mars. With the help of the jumping belts in *Buck Rogers*, the comic characters were no longer like actors on a stage but were instead now unbound by Earth's gravity, allowing the visual drama of the strip to became superanimated, spiraling out of the frame.

The initial *Tarzan* comic was a black-and-white comic drawn by the extraordinarily talented and influential Harold R. Foster (1892–1982). The Canadian-born Foster was working for an advertising agency in Detroit when he created some sample *Tarzan* pages at the request of a friend and colleague, Joe H. Neebe, who pitched the idea to some of the leading comic syndicates. Foster's *Tarzan* used equal-sized boxes to lay out the story in a scene-to-scene manner akin to the 19th-century French children's publications *Imagerie d'Epinal* by Pellerin. Both *Imagerie d'Epinal* and Foster's original *Tarzan* relied on heavily abridged versions of known stories, and both used brief passages of narrative and dialogue to sum up the action without the use of speech balloons or any other obvious comic-derived visual codes (aside from zip lines). Foster's artwork followed on the book illustration tradition of Howard Pyle (1853–1911) and N. C. Wyeth (1882–1945) and had far more naturalistic rendering of the human anatomy and studied cultural details in costume and locale. All this lent his work a kind of exotic gravitas rarely seen in comics at this time but something that had long been the mainstay of adventure illustration in story books.

As the abridged material for the *Tarzan* comic was coming to an end and new material needed to be developed, Foster expressed no interest in continuing to work on the strip, so the Metropolitan Syndicate (now known as United Features) passed it on to Rex Maxton, who proved unequal to the task. Maxton's contract was not renewed, and Foster was at last enticed to continue the new adventure with original material on September 27, 1931. When Alex Raymond's *Flash Gordon* appeared in 1934, it was thematically related to *Buck Rogers* as a science fiction–fantasy comic, but it was clearly molded after Foster's more naturalistic rendering and more significantly the *Imagerie d'Epinal* style that Foster had developed. Although this framed and largely narrated action lacked some spontaneity, it allowed for longer narrative sequences on the newspaper page that were inevitably interrupted by a cliffhanger . . . "to be continued."

As the economic depression deepened, humor strips took a darker turn and many began to flirt with adventure. Popeye became the standout character in E. C. Segar's *Thimble Theatre* shortly after his first appearance in 1929. *Thimble Theatre* had been only a knock-about family comedy strip before Popeye introduced a sea adventure and further enhanced the crazy energy of the slapstick with his high-power pugilism. Popeye represented one of Segar's best-distilled characters, easily recognizable yet wonderfully malleable, who could whip up a tempest of energy in the teapot-scaled comic strips. Segar's *Thimble Theatre* enjoyed a special kind of adventure-fantasy-humor that gave him license to introduce bizarre elements, like the fourth-dimensional creature the Jeep, the evil Sea Hag, and the Goon, but it was the no-nonsense Popeye who gave the strip its ballast.

Dick Tracy (1931) by Chester Gould was born out of the Depression era's obsession with flamboyant mobsters, which gave the strip a level of stark cruelty that had not been attempted before in the comic pages. Gould's distorted and surreal criminal faces—seething with malice and evil intent—were often awkwardly attached to tight, angular bodies dressed in a solid black that let them melt into the shadows. Both Segar and Gould continued to render their characters in a starkly graphic shorthand that resisted the growing trend toward greater naturalism in adventure comics, such as *Tailspin Tommy* (1928), *Secret Agent X-9* (1934), and *Prince Valiant* (1937). Milt Caniff (1907–1988) was the masterful artist behind *Terry and the Pirates* (1934) and later *Steve Canyon* (1947). Caniff framed his Oriental melodramas in a more cinematic fashion, and his characters moved with a fluid naturalism in richly rendered exotic locales. Caniff's work became the gold standard for adventure comics and was widely influential in inspiring a whole generation of comic artists on how to effectively communicate action and build suspense.

The new action strips began the work of teasing out longer and more complex narrative action, but they also began the process of creating a more complex visual language of dramatic action, one that tried out more challenging perspectives, more detailed environments, more compelling human anatomy, and more striking use of solid blacks. These were all incremental steps that moved comics away from the early dominant style based on vaudeville theater and began the gradual introduction of the dramatic style of pulp fiction, radio, and movies.

The next ingredient to transform adventure comics was the use of a costume to set the heroic character apart from the rest of society and visually define his role as a vigilante. Lee Falk's *Mandrake the Magician*, first appearing June 11, 1934, had many curious and improbable features which never seemed to undermine its wide and long-lived popularity. Based on the stage appearance of the Canadian-born magician Leon Mandrake (1911–1993), the comic character was dressed in a dapper suit-coat with tails, top hat, and cape. Mandrake always appeared impeccably dressed and groomed with his slicked-back hair and pencil-thin mustache, even when adventuring in the tropics, which had the curious effect of giving him an aura of transcendence and invulnerability. Mandrake's cape was an especially powerful visual form that flowed as if it had a life of its own, propelling him through the scenes and animating all his actions to make them seem larger than life. Mandrake was an illusionist who, with just the wave of his hand, had the power to hypnotically convince people that he had transformed objects and people into something strange. Although this does not seem like a real superpower, the impact on people and things was never circumscribed by reality and very often had real consequences in a way a mere illusion would not have had. For instance, a speeding car attempting to run over a woman was hypnotically made to appear to flip over backward, which somehow made the car no longer a real threat to her life.

Lee Falk soon passed the artwork for Mandrake on to Phil Davis and before long began work on another comic strip, *The Phantom* (1936), which would garner him worldwide fame beyond all other adventure strips. The Phantom was dressed in a skin-tight purple suit that covered his whole body with an opening for a narrow black mask like that of Zorro, which showed only the whites of his eyes. Falk later said the pupil-less eyes peering out from the mask gave the hero a more classical look, like Greek statuary. The purpose of the costume disguise was said to protect the character's individuality as he fought crime, but it was also meant to signal his allegiance to the role of the Phantom through the "Oath of the Skull," which had passed down from father to son for more than 400 years. Falk used the vigilante theme as a defining feature of the hero, who is no longer motivated by some specific altruistic cause but has now sworn an oath to fight all crime. Falk later explained in an interview that his use of a skin-tight costume was inspired by the leggings worn by Robin Hood as portrayed by Douglas Fairbanks Sr. in the 1922 silent film.[3] Though many today talk about the skin-tight suits as "spandex," there was no actual material that could be fabricated in the 1930s to maintain the kind of elastic, skin-tight clothing seen on the Phantom and later superhero characters. The absurdity of their clothing can be seen in the way they were talked about by comic artists as "long-john heroes." Nonetheless, it was this revealing and transformative costume that was the signature form that gave the heroes their unique presence and powerfully signaled their commitment to their extra-societal role. Unique, colorful costumes had other advantages for marketing, copyright, and brand identification that have kept long-john heroes returning long after the novelty has worn off.

The Golden Age of Comic Books

Comic reprints published in book form were a well-known strategy in Britain dating back to the mid-19th century, which allowed publishers a second venue to squeeze every pence they could out of their popular features. Late in 1902 in the United States, William Randolph Hearst began repackaging his popular comics and reprinting them as books when the color presses were idle early in the week. The original format of these cardboard-backed books varied in size from 24 to 60 pages and could be large (11 by 16 inches) or small (6.5 by 7 inches) and ranged in price from 20 cents to 50 cents. The Manhattan publishers Cupples and Leon were the early leaders in the comic strip reprint market between 1906 and 1934. They published some of the most popular titles of the day, including Outcault's *Buster Brown*, McCay's *Little Nemo in Slumberland*, and McManus's *Bringing Up Father*, to mention only a few. Adding nothing original aside from the cover on the book, the comic strip book publishers were essentially middlemen who bought the art proofs of the comics for $5 per page. Most of the original publications were compilations of a single title, but soon collections began to appear offering a wider sample of popular comic strips. Unfortunately for them, Cupples and Leon moved out of the comic reprint business to focus on their own popular fiction titles just as the comic book industry was about to take off.

The main problem facing the fledgling comic book industry was that the profit margins were too small and unpredictable, since the books appeared at irregular times and their content varied too much in quality to secure regular public interest. The Eastman Color Printing Company was engaged in publishing the Sunday color supplements for a number of East Coast papers when the marketing executive Harry Wildenberg proposed making promotional comics for such large corporations as Gulf Oil. Securing the money ahead of publication insured a profit for the publisher and the promotions were successful for the companies, but there were only so many companies in the Depression era of the early 1930s that had the wherewithal and inclination to use comics in a promotion. Wildenberg then teamed up with Max C. Gaines, and in 1934 they were able to come up with a formula that for the first time demonstrated that money could be made in comic books sold directly to the public through newsstands at the inexpensive price of 10 cents. By the mid-1930s, there was enough quality comic strip material being generated in the newspapers for a monthly half-tabloid-sized publication of 64 pages entitled *Famous Funnies* (July 1934), which contained several different newspaper comics series from different syndicates, all published in black and white with a flashy color cover.

By 1938, a handful of publishers vied for a market share, which prompted the introduction of more original content. After retiring from the army, Maj. Malcolm Wheeler-Nicholson (1890–1968) wrote a number of military-themed pulp fiction stories before embarking on a publishing venture in the new comic book industry. With all the popular newspaper strips already taken by other comic book publishers, Nicholson created *New Fun* in February 1935, the first comic book that had entirely original material. *New Fun* offered 35 pages of black-and-white comics in a variety of genres in a large tabloid size to imitate the scale and size of Sunday strips. Wheeler-Nicholson hoped some of the more popular comics he published would be picked up by the newspaper syndicates, but this scheme did not materialize. Sales were brisk enough, however, to keep the publication afloat and eventually spin off another title, *New Comics*, in 1936. Despite the modest success, Wheeler-Nicholson was an inconsistent businessman who was bankrupt by 1938. His editors, John Mahon and William Cook, left with half the art inventory to start their own comic book publications, and the remains of the business were sold to the pulp fiction publishers Harry Donenfeld and Jack Liebowitz, who latched on to one of Wheeler-Nicholson's comic book titles, *Detective Comics*, as the new name for their company. It was an important change because it signaled a decisive shift away from their former soft-porn titles as *Spicy Detective* and signaled a whole-hearted embrace of adventure comic books.

A Chicago entrepreneur, Harry Chester, opened the first comic art studio in an old tenement building in New York and served up new comic material for Nicholson and a few of the other fledgling comic book publishers. These studios, known as "packagers," operated like sweatshops, where it did not matter what kind of talent or skill you started with, artists could keep their jobs so long as they could keep up with the the huge volume of work. In Depression-era New York, it was not hard for Chester to assemble a team of artists to churn out material at roughly the same cost as it took to pay the newspaper syndicates for reprints. It was in these studios where the comic book industry took its germinal form, and many of the contemporary aspects of comics industry were established from this time forward.

The relatively small pay per page that comic artists received for their work and the lack of copyright ownership of the works they created meant the system was a highly derivative business that rewarded volume and novelty over artistry and originality. No one had time to use live models or do research to develop material, so these comics were notoriously imitative, relying on well-heeled formulas. The common trade in graphic material among the beginning studio artists involved "swipe sheets," which were drawings that were copied from previous pages, other artists' work, and inserted where necessary to render the anatomy of a pose or the fold of clothing, or to capture an expression. Jules Feiffer (b. 1929), like many comic artists who learned comic art in just such an environment, said, "Swipes, if noticed, were accepted as a part of comic book folklore. I have never heard a reader complain. Rather, I have heard swipe artists vigorously defended, one compared to the other: Who did the best Caniff, the closest Raymond?"[4]

In the packager system of comic production, few artists had art school training, and most picked up only the minimum skills they needed to survive. Since comics were displayed in newsstands with the covers facing out, the most skilled artists would often be set to work on the cover's design, often resulting in flashy cover illustrations that had very little to do with what was inside. Today, many collectors look at the covers as the greatest achievement of these comics and have often reproduced the covers while leaving much of the actual contents of the comic books to remain obscure.

The early years of comic books are often now generally referred to by comic book collectors as the Golden Age, and although there is no consensus as to when this age actually began or ended, most point to the publication of *Superman* as its origin. Joe Shuster (1914–1992) and Jerry Siegel (1914–1996) were a pair of recent high school graduates from Cleveland who tried unsuccessfully for five years to sell their idea for an all-powerful superhero called Superman. It was clearly not obvious to newspaper comic strip publishers at that time that the preposterously costumed and invincible hero from another planet would become one of the most popular comic characters of all time. It took a long time for Shuster and Siegel to get a break because their art and writing did not meet comic strip standards and their idea of a superhuman man was an even more outlandish and preposterous an idea than was acceptable for pulp fiction. These deficits proved ultimately to its advantage in the comic book medium, where the audience was drawn from a more narrow population of 10- to 12-year-old boys and where the less accomplished drawing made it seem more rebellious and more distant to the adult world. Also, the story of a superhero disguising himself by feigning incompetence, thereby allowing himself to be the object of both female worship and loathing, had a verisimilitude that powerfully appealed to this particular group.

Although the Superman story had many features similar to the stories of other heroes of the day—for example, the cape, costume, outsider origin, invincibility, and vigilante justice—it went further in embracing the notion of the hero having superpowers simply because he was an outsider, thus raising the bar on invincibility so that the hero was now a "superhero." At first, Superman's powers were far more circumscribed than they are today: he did not fly so as much as leap up to one-eighth of a mile, run faster than an express train, and deflect bullets off of his tough skin. Gradually, Superman was leaping longer and higher, but it was only when Max Fleischer (1883–1972) began animating the Superman story in 1941 that he asked to abandon the jumping for flying. The rationale for Superman's superiority was always couched in his alien origins, but ultimately it had to do with his role in usurping the power of modern technology: tall buildings, trains, bullets, and so on. It is significant that in the first show of Superman's strength on the cover of *Action Comics* #1 (June 1938), we see him holding a car above his head preparing to dash it to pieces. So long as technology grew in power, Superman would match its strength and reassert his superiority. By the 1960s, the powers of Superman had bourgeoned as Umberto Eco archly described them:

> He can fly through space at the speed of light, and when he surpasses that speed, he breaks through the time barrier and can transfer himself to other epochs. With no more than the pressure from his hands, he can subject coal to the pressure required to change it into a diamond; in a matter of seconds, at super sonic speed, he can fell an entire forest, make lumber from trees; and make a ship or a town; he can bore through mountains, lift ocean liners, destroy or construct dams; his x-ray vision allows him to see through any object to almost unlimited distances and to melt metal objects at a glance; his super hearing puts him at extremely advantageous situations permitting him to tune in on conversations however far away. He is kind, modest, and helpful; his life is dedicated to the battle against the forces of evil; and the police find him an untiring collaborator.[5]

This trajectory of powers is especially evident with the advent of Superman's most notable weakness, kryptonite, which was first used in the *Superman* radio drama in 1943 and introduced into comics in 1949, just as Americans were getting familiar with the notion of atomic radiation. It seems Superman's greatest nemesis was not an archcriminal but the indifferent science and technology of the 20th century.

The arrival of Superman in *Action Comics* signaled the moment when the comic book industry came into its own and embraced the advantages of a longer format with stories that directly appealed to a younger, male audience. Over the course of the next few months, as sales figures began to trickle in, it became increasingly obvious that large numbers of youths were buying Superman comics and that the popularity of this strangely costumed character was spilling over into other comic book titles.

Detective Comics (DC) editors rushed to field new superheroes of their own, and in 1939 they decided to publish *The Bat-Man* (*Batman*), developed by Bob Kane (1915–1998) and his friend Bill Finger (1914–1974). Unlike Superman who was created out of a plot idea, the character Batman was a costume first: a guy with ornithopter wings, perhaps inspired by the Hawkmen of

Flash Gordon. Bill Finger was a writer deeply steeped in pulp fiction, and he apparently suggested some of the bat themes from those sources and also some of the iconic costume details: the scalloped cape, the pointed-ear cowl, and the Phantomesque white-only eyes. Kane was a clumsy artist who could only roughly indicate the musculature of his characters; but despite the awkwardly grimacing faces, wooden gestures, and flat backgrounds, *Batman* was a huge hit from the start. Although it was Kane who took most of the credit for the work, Bill Finger went on to write many of the early *Batman* comics and conceived of many of the principle villains that would fight Batman and terrorize Gotham City with their eccentric plots.

Whereas Superman embodied the mythic spirit of the Luddite, with human supremacy achieved through the overthrow of technology, Batman embodied the spirit of Leonardo da Vinci, with the expansion of human abilities through individual perfection and innovation. Without intrinsic superpowers, Batman relied on the new cutting-edge technologies hidden in his utility belt, along with the bat mobile, the bat gyro (later the bat plane), and finally the bat computer (first introduced in 1964), to solve inscrutable crimes. To fund this appetite for the latest gadgetry, Batman became the alter-ego of the super-rich Bruce Wayne, who fights crime as a vigilante to revenge the brutal deaths of his parents. No other superhero has been more thoroughly subjected to pop psychoanalysis as the character of Batman. People have tried to explain in faux-Freudian terms how a childhood trauma might lead someone to stalk around at night dressed up in a bat suit. One must never forget that Batman, like many superheroes that would come after him, began just as a costume and that all other aspects of the person inside were merely a way to explain the outward form of that costume. What is truly remarkable about the Batman character is how an empty, glowering, and pointy-eared cowl has inspired so much imaginative content.

In the early adventures of Batman, the character had very little personality aside from a cruel streak, at one point shooting down his foe with a gun. Both Batman and Superman used tough-guy tactics to intimidate crooks into confessing. As the characters grew in popularity, editors at DC began to tone down the darker vigilante aspects of their superheroes and heighten the altruism. A year after his first appearance, Batman was given a little more color and a sidekick, Robin, to make him a more sympathetic character.[6] The idea of sidekicks soon grew in popularity and became a regular feature of many new superheroes (see box 8.1).

The third major superhero in Detective Comics' stable was Wonder Woman, conceived and written by William Moulton Marston (1893–1947) in collaboration with his wife, Elizabeth Holloway Marston (1893–1993) and

Box 8.1 Fletcher Hanks

Fletcher Hanks (1887–1976) was an enigmatic comic artist who produced some of the more outlandish superhero characters and stories, among them *Stardust, the Super Wizard* and *Fantomah, Mystery Woman of the Jungle*, in a style full of lurid designs and a histrionic narratives that are strangely affecting. The omniscient narrator of "Stardust the Super Wizard" intones, "In his tubular spacial, traveling at terrific speed on accelerated supersolar light-waves, Stardust starts his race to save the earth from destructive conquest." The oddly proportioned faces and bodies often seem unnaturally stretched or twisted; but instead of just looking clumsy, they seem to embody the narrative excess in a deep, fierce play that transcends anatomical and grammatical form. Though widely admired by comic aficionados today, Fletcher's style was an eccentric anomaly, a path not taken in the longer trajectory toward greater naturalism in adventure comics. Fletcher's influence was also cut short by his relatively brief career as a comic artist. A heavy drinker and an abusive father, Fletcher disappeared from the comic industry in the 1940s only to finally reappear in the winter of 1976, frozen to death on a bench in Central Park.

DC editor Max Gaines. Both Marston and his wife were researchers in psychology and were instrumental in the development of a lie detector based on systolic blood pressure. Marston was introduced to the comic industry when he had been asked by DC to join an executive board to evaluate the educational value of their publications. Marston saw an opportunity to provide a new role model for girls by creating a vigorous and bold female archetype in comic books. Wonder Woman was not the first female adventure hero, costumed crime fighter, or superhero. Although she was superseded by *Sheena, Queen of the Jungle* (1937) by Will Eisner and S. M. Iger, *The Woman in Red* (1940) by Richard E. Hughes and George Mandel, *Fantomah* (1940) by Fletcher Hanks, and *Miss Fury* (1941) by Tarpé Mills, Wonder Woman was the first conceptual superhero specifically designed to send a feminist message.

Many later female superheroes, among them Super Girl, Bat Girl, and She-Hulk, were derived from direct male predecessors, as if they were Eve made from Adam's rib; but Marston created Wonder Woman using the classical prototype of the Amazon warrior and overlaid that with further inspiration from his wife, Elizabeth, and their mutual lover Olive Byrne. With her bright red, white, and blue costume emblazoned with a golden eagle across her chest drawn by Harry G. Peter (1880–1958), Wonder Woman was a patriotic icon similar to the enormously popular Captain America, who just appeared the previous year in Timely Comics (later known as Marvel). Wonder Woman, as an Amazon, was rooted in a world apart from the world of men and would often remark on the cultural differences between the two. On one such occasion she explained "Diana's Day," a winter solstice holiday where "we Amazons play Goddess Diana at the festival of the Returning Sun, just as you men play Santa Claus at Christmas."[7] By creating Wonder Woman, Marston introduced a character who became a powerful inspiration to many girls and boys, and later women and men, who were seeking inspiration from an alternative role model.

Marston's attitude toward comics did not dispute their low artistic merit but asserted their value as a potentially powerful moral force in the lives of people who read them. Superhero comics, according to Marston, differed from all other comics in that they were not concerned with humor or adventure but focused instead on wish-fulfillment through character identification. In an essay Marston published in *The American Scholar* (1943), he discussed his intentions in creating Wonder Woman:

> Shall we teach our children that the heroic thing, the deed for which they will attain desired kudos, is killing enemies and conquering their neighbors, *à la* Napoleon, Hitler, Genghis Khan, and others of their ilk? Or shall we make the great stunt in a child's mind the protection of the weak and the helping of humanity? . . . Wonder Woman saves her worst enemies and reforms their characters. If the incredible barrage of comic strips now assaulting American minds establishes this new definition of heroics in the thought reflexes of the rising generation, it will have been worth many times its weight in pulp paper and multicolored ink.[8]

The powerful assumption that Marston articulates here is that these role models were capable of changing the people who identified with them. Under the spell of the suggestive comics, impressionable young readers would suspend their own predilections and biases. Many critics have pointed out that Wonder Woman's magic rope, which has the power to compel people tell the truth, is based on the lie detector machine Marston helped develop. To a degree this may be true, but perhaps more accurately Wonder Woman's magic rope is actually Marston's view of comics themselves: because once ensnared in Wonder Woman's power, readers would be made better people.

In the next decade, another psychologist by the name of Fredric Wertham, using the same logic, would come to the opposite conclusion: that the role models appearing in comics—including Wonder Woman—were having a predominantly negative effect on society. Unfortunately for the comics industry, it would be Wertham's argument that eventually prevailed. The industry was an easy target for many critics from the beginning because comic books, unlike newspapers, were produced on the more nefarious margins of the publishing industry. Despite the efforts of a few publishers to elevate the educational value of comic books with classic stories and educational trivia, there was little that could be done with the broader public image.

The oft-repeated story of how early on in his career Will Eisner (1917–2005) turned down an offer to produce pornographic comics for the mob speaks to Eisner's enduring idealism in the face of the tough times that many artists confronted. Many, like Eisner, had gone into comics because they were the bottom rung of the publishing industry, an industry full of fly-by-night hucksters and con-men. Unlike many, Eisner saw himself not just as a hack working to make a buck till he could find a real job, but as an artist forging a new medium. Few artists at this early stage took up this challenge with the same drive and ambition as Eisner, and none would be as influential in defining the new ways that comic books would be made.

Eisner was eventually able to establish a toehold in the comic book industry with his work on the comic book *Wow, What a Magazine!* (1936) with publisher Jerry Iger. When that venture quickly failed, Eisner formed a partnership with Iger to become a "packager" like Harry Chester to create content for the new comic book publishers. Eisner did all of the drawing and much of the scripting himself, employing a number of pen names and using a variety of styles to help convince comic book publishers that the workshop was fully staffed to fulfill their order.

One of the early jobs Eisner and Iger undertook was commissioned by Victor Fox. Seeing the potential for growth in superhero comics, Fox came and requested a comic just like Superman for his new comic book–publishing venture, Fox Feature Syndicate. At Fox's request, Eisner created the character Wonder Man, who was, as Fox had specified, only superficially different from Superman. Soon after the comic hit the newsstands in May 1939, Detective Comics filed suit against Fox and forced him to stop all future use of the character because it infringed on their copyright of Superman.

Fox took the case to court and argued that Superman and Wonder Man were similar only because they both were inspired by Lee Falk's *Phantom*. The judge, Augustus N. Hand, did not agree, citing, "The attributes and antics of 'Superman' and 'Wonderman' are closely similar. Each at times conceals his strength beneath ordinary clothing but after removing his cloak stands revealed in full panoply in a skintight acrobatic costume. The only real difference between them is that 'Superman' wears a blue uniform and 'Wonderman' a red one.''[9] Judge Hand, who made little effort to conceal his condescension toward superheroes and comics, based his decision only on the characters in the lawsuit, as if Superman was wholly original and the second a mimic. Although there is no doubt that Wonder Man was a deliberate copy of Superman, Judge Hand's decision exaggerated the uniqueness of Superman, who was largely a pastiche of earlier pulp fiction and comic strip prototypes, and did not take into account the degree to which imitation was widely used in popular publications.

One of the commonly cited reasons that Fox lost his case was that Eisner refused to be coached on how to answer the questions put to him and told the court how Fox had instructed him to make a copy of Superman. Unfortunately, some of the stories Eisner has told over the years about this case do not square with the actual court record that reveals Eisner was entirely complicit in covering up the true origins of Wonder Man.[10] There has been a tendency to rewrite the history of comic books in America as if there were a few altruistic artists who were willing to make sacrifices to speak back to nefarious publishers and elevate the artistic merit of comics. It is hard to accept that the virtue and promise of a better world held out by the comic book superheroes themselves was not often held to by their creators who were forced to live a far more compromised existence with marginal autonomy and few economic assurances.

Emboldened by their victory, Detective Comics continued to try and quash the competition by becoming more aggressive about prosecuting any comic book publisher who created something remotely similar to Superman. This strategy, although not successful in thwarting imitators, had the effect of gradually increasing the copyright protection over comic characters and eventually led to one of the longest court battles between comic book publishers when Detective Comics sued Fawcett Publications over the company's Captain Marvel superhero. The case against Captain Marvel was much more complicated than Wonder Man in part because of the complex dealings with the copyright properties in various media. Furthermore, whereas the judge had concluded that Captain Marvel did violate Superman's copyright, the extent and degree of that violation was very difficult to establish because each appeared under various titles in numerous comics, radio series, and movie serials. Initially, Fawcett editors were eager to defend their work because for a while in the 1940s Captain Marvel was outselling Superman. By 1954, however, the Captain Marvel brand, along with all other superhero comics, was beginning to weaken; so after 12 years of legal proceedings, Fawcett settled out of court, paid Detective Comics (now called National Comics) $400,000, ended all publications of Captain Marvel, and closed down its comics division. The long-term legal ramifications of these protracted copyright battles resulted in comic characters achieving a level of legal protection that was broader than they—or any other creative work—had had before in history: they were now copyrightable as characters, independent of a plot or a particular medium. This development speaks to the incredible marketing potential these characters possessed; it is also a testament to the way these characters could effectively move between media.

While Detective Comics was battling to maintain its copyright from outside imitators, the company was at the same time battling the creators of Superman to keep control over the character. Unlike most comic characters at this time, Superman was an independent creation of Siegel and Shuster, so the character could not be considered work-for-hire; but as young artists happy to have a job doing what they loved, they allegedly sold the copyright for a meager $130, albeit with the promise of a 10-year contract with Detective Comics. As Superman soared in popularity and began to appear in four other comic books, a dedicated newspaper strip, a radio program, and a wide range of merchandise, Siegel and Shuster began to press for a cut of the profits, but they lacked the business savvy to make any headway. Eventually, they found themselves marginalized at Detective Comics as their later creations were not selling as well as Superman. Siegel and Shuster finally sued in 1947 to regain control of their copyright over Superman. They were cast out from the industry for turning on their employers and, in a twist of legal maneuvering, eventually gained a modicum of compensation for the rights to Superboy. As a result of further changes in the copyright law in 1976 and 1998, the heirs of Siegel and Shuster continue to press for the return of their copyright over Superman. Ultimately, the court settlements may become moot when Superman passes into the public domain in 2013.

American Comics and Cinema

Much has been made of the affinity of movies and comics. Today, as more and more comic superheroes have had their adventures made into live-action movies, this apparent affinity has become even more exaggerated. Akin to the relationship between animation and newspaper comics discussed earlier, movies have historically had a largely circumstantial relationship to comic books. Although both attempt to tell stories visually, the means and apparatus for reception are not equal or comparable beyond some elements of composition and narrative transitions. These are not minor aesthetic concerns, but they need to be circumscribed by the unique features of each medium.

The early comic book artists did not see themselves as movie directors or have any ambition to work in film. Most took their inspiration from radio, and if they had any further ambition, it was to become a book illustrator or newspaper comic strip artist. Film did have an indisputable influence on comic books, especially as the stories lengthened and artists sought ways to maintain continuity and narrative clarity. The most pervasive influence film had on comics was the introduction of the 180-degree rule, which stipulated that if two characters are talking, the camera should not move more than 180 degrees to maintain the basic orientation of the characters clear in the mind of the audience. Harold Foster's *Tarzan* comic regularly broke this rule, but by the late 1940s, the 180-degree rule began to appear with greater regularity in comic books.

The most striking similarities between cinema and comic books are compositional: tight framing that cropped figures, dark shadows that enveloped the scenes, and acutely angled compositions at either a bird's eye or worm's eye view. These similarities perhaps had to do with the common influence of the modern art movement of expressionism rather than just cross-fertilization between the media of film and comics. Expressionism had entered the United States from Germany through art, theater, and film and was especially influential among socialist artists. Will Eisner has said that he was inspired by the expressionist "wordless books" of American Lynd Ward an artist inspired by the expressionist publications of Frans Masereel. During the 1920s and 1930s, expressionism appeared on and off Broadway in productions by leading theater playwrights such as Eugene O'Neill (1888–1953) and directors such as Max Reinhardt (1873–1943). Also, several prominent film directors, among them Fritz Lang (1890–1976) and Robert Siodmak (1900–1973), emigrated from Germany during World War II and introduced a visual style later known as film noir. All this work in abundant circulation was fodder for pulp fiction and adventure comics.

Will Eisner was one of the early innovators who understood that the comic book was a unique art form in which—unlike in a movie or a comic strip in a newspaper—the sequential movement had to be directed by an internal compositional logic that responded to the dimensions of the page or even across two pages. Instead of lining up his panels in orderly rows as Hal Foster did in his *Tarzan* comic, Eisner experimented with odd-sized frames, or frameless panels, to break up the dominant grid and create a different sense of the rhythms and pace of action being represented inside the panel. Shifts in the style of a panel boarder were also used to convey different frames of reference in the narrative, introducing dreams and distant memories inside the narrative. One of the most enduring visual elements that Eisner created was the "splash page" that functioned in a manner similar to a monoscenic narrative where the whole page would be turned into a single large image that would grab the reader at the start of the story. Like the cover of the comic book, the splash page often illustrated some important later moment in the story, distilling the conflict, and setting the mood for what was to come.

The other narrative techniques Eisner developed expanded the kinds of transitions between panels. Instead of using the direct causal relationship between actions that comics typically relied on, Eisner experimented with combinations of panels that foreshadowed future events, or leaped from one aspect of the scene to another thematically related aspect, or switched between two different stories happening at the same time. In some instances, these ideas had equivalent techniques in the cinema or were occasionally used by some of the adventure comic strips by Milt Caniff, Alex Raymond, or Hal Foster. Eisner was distinguished from other pioneers for being more willing to push his experimentation further, expanding what was possible in a comic, and for his daring he is frequently called the Orson Welles of comic art.

Eisner achieved a unique position in the comics world in 1940 when E. M. Arnold at Quality Comics asked him to create a 16 page comic book as a Sunday insert for newspapers in the Register-Tribune Syndicate. This newspaper comic gave him a long comic book format to develop more complex stories and to try out more sophisticated themes for a much larger and broader audience than typically found in the comic book market. Contrary to most comic book production at the time, Eisner was not much interested in superheroes, and so he used this opportunity to create a solitary private detective, Denny Colt, aka the Spirit, to develop new ways a story could be told in pictures. The Spirit's single costumelike conceit, a blue mask, was really just an afterthought, urged on him by the syndicate, which was foremost concerned with establishing a marketable brand. Eisner worked against the established patterns of the trade by not creating a single-header style for the Spirit and instead made each splash page and title design follow the theme of the plot. This made it difficult for the syndicate to market the strip, but it allowed Eisner to shape all aspects of his comic pages to tell the story. The film noir–like plots and how they were rendered even trumped Eisner's development of the characters themselves, who were often an unremarkable assortment of "the usual suspects" and who were in many instances such bad ethnic stereotypes as the Spirit's Jim Crow sidekick Ebony White, who seems to have been given no serious thought.

Actual effects that are unique to cinema are relatively rare in U.S. comics. Comic artists seldom employ the kind of cinematic montage expounded by Sergei Eisenstein (1898–1948), where the sequence of images is arranged to create dissonant associations through conflicting images. More often, it is common to see effects called cinematic when the action is broken down into a close fitting sequence of panels that look like the scattered pages of a flip-book. The effect is not exactly cinematic because as the images of a character multiply, the reader is made increasingly aware of the whole sequence on the page. These effects are more akin to synoptic narratives where the repeated characters in action are framed by a single continuous scene. Just as in a synoptic narrative, once an action is parsed into incremental moments it becomes a defined repeatable gesture describing an ecapsualted moment of "being in action." Eisner was particularly effective in utilizing these design elements in his work, and it was through him that most comic artists came to employ "cinematic" effects in comics.

CHAPTER 9

Mainstream American Comics, Post–World War II

The comic book industry in the late 1930s continued to expand despite the lingering problems of the Depression economy. As the United States entered World War II, the impact of paper rationing led to a winnowing of the market of smaller publishers, but eventually those constraints would slowly fall away, too. The publisher DC Comics continued to lead with its popular superheroes who sold war bonds and appeared to charge into battles across the globe. Comics also received a lusty boost when U.S. soldiers were shipped abroad because comics served as easy, portable entertainment for the troops on the move. Whether it was for escapism or nostalgia, comics offered a brief respite from the staggering tedium and uncertain schedules of military life. Out of all the printed matter mailed to soldiers in 1942, 30 percent were comic books. As they were folded into camp gear, passed around in foxholes, and traded to locals, comics spread around the globe, inspiring new readers and a new generation of comic artists. The U.S. military not only bought thousands of comic books to entertain the troops but also employed several staff comic artists to prepare comic art for their own publications, and they used comics as an innovative means to teach soldiers about maintaining their equipment and getting along in foreign countries. Will Eisner was drafted and put to work crafting many of these publications. After the war, he would continue to make informational comics for the government and private industry.

Many young comic artists were sent to war, and their experiences abroad set the stage for a dramatic transformation in comics toward becoming an adult-oriented medium. The military comic artist Bill Mauldin (1921–2003) spent two years (1943–1945) on the Italian front in World War II as a member of the U.S. Army's 45th Infantry Division as a cartoonist and journalist who submitted six cartoons a week for the U.S. military publication *Stars and Stripes*. At first, he had to work from the front with whatever supplies he could muster, Mauldin was eventually given his own jeep as a portable studio, but the cheap printing presses he worked with forced him to draw more simply with fewer bolder lines and more clearly delineated forms. As the campaign across Europe continued, his soldiers went from being clean-shaven kids to bearded men, slouching under the strain of exhaustion. The light-hearted, fine-lined chummy humor turned into a single-frame comic with two infantry men, Willie and Joe, who summed up their dire situation with sardonic wit: "I'm beginnin' to feel like a fugitive from th' law of averages." Mauldin masterfully understated the heroics and drama of the war and found ways to communicate the absurd conditions that underscored a soldier's daily acts of courage. Across a trench, holding an enemy German soldier at bay with a pistol in his face, Joe asks casually, "Didn't we meet at Cassino?"

Soldiers appreciated Mauldin's fine attention to the essential details of their camp gear and guns, capturing the cadence and posture of the dog-faced men who made up the lowest ranks of the military. Most of all, he was willing to authenticate their struggles and recognize their daily pains and grievances against military authority. In a letter to *Stars and Stripes*, Gen. George S. Patton threatened to have Mauldin's work banned from the 3rd Division if it did not stop publishing what he called "Mauldin's scurrilous attempts to undermine military discipline."[1] Gen. Dwight D. Eisenhower, however, defended Mauldin because he believed any censorship in the publication would ultimately undermine morale. At the end of the war, Mauldin returned to the United States a wealthy celebrity and went on to become a successful editorial cartoonist; but for the rest of his life, he struggled with the guilt he felt for having profited and become famous at a time of loss and suffering.

The 1950s saw growth in the genre of war-themed comics, and though they initially focused on the Korean War (1950–1953) and anti-Communist stories, the bulk of this market gravitated toward reenvisioning World War II. Beginning in 1952, Robert Kanigher (1915–2002) wrote and edited DC Comics' five war comics titles that over time included the popular war stories *Sgt. Rock* (1959, with art by Joe Kubert) and *The Haunted Tank* (1961–1987, with art by Russ Heath). War comics were deeply indebted to the gritty realism of Bill Mauldin and carried on with the close attention to the details of army life.

Bill Mauldin, "Didn't we meet at Cassino?" ca. 1943–1945 (Copyright 1944 by Bill Mauldin. Courtesy of the Bill Mauldin Estate LLC)

Only a few stories questioned the purpose of war or the value of heroism, but they often reflected on futile gains made at a terrible sacrifice. War comics were some of the earliest mainstream adult-oriented comics; despite the violence and horror they often depicted, many titles were able to survive the later backlash against mature comics.

Romance and Horror Comics

MLJ Comics was one of the first publishers to branch out from superheroes and capitalize on a burgeoning teen culture craze with the introduction of *Archie* by Bob Montana (1920–1975). The character first appeared in *Pep Comics* #22 in December 1941 and because of his popularity was given his own comic a year later. Other artists took up drawing *Archie* comics when Bob Montana was drafted. Montana returned four years later and worked on drawing the widely circulated *Archie* newspaper comic strip; but when Dan DeCarlo (1919–2001) began to work on *Archie* in the early 1950s, the feature took on its signature style of clean outlines and shining expressive faces. Most notably, it was the understated but vivid sexuality of the girls in *Archie* that made DeCarlo's work so iconic. Given his talent for making dynamic female characters, it is not surprising DeCarlo went on to create a number of important new characters in the *Archie* franchise, including Josie and the Pussycats, and Sabrina the Teenage Witch.

From pubescent teen humor, a more serious strain of longer romance-themed comics emerged in the late 1940s with *Romantic Picture Novelettes*[2] and *Young Romance* (1949) created by Jack Kirby (1917–1994) and Joe Simon (b. 1913) and published under the auspices of Timely Comics. Sensing a new fad, comic publishers rushed into the new market, creating a flood of poor imitations and knockoffs. By 1950, Victor Fox had more than 20 titles devoted to romance, but the sudden glut of romance titles weakened the market and thinned the competition. Between 1952 and 1953, romance comics reached their peak popularity before dying out in 1955. Most notable were St. John Publications' romance comics that emphasized classy fashions and created some memorable stories willing to address such mature issues as racial prejudice. As the Korean War was heating up, St. John published a long 12-page story about a Korean couple at an American college and how their different sympathies for the two sides of the conflict tore them apart. The story is remarkable for its sensitivity and sympathetic representation of the Korean couple and the hostility they faced in the America.[3] For romance comics to be effective, they required greater attention to natural details; so the artists at St. John were in many cases provided with live models for their artwork. Artists were also able to ink their own drawings to help produce higher-quality comics. Western-themed comics, also popular after World War II, mixed freely with romance, but it was the advent of crime and horror comics that would have the most dramatic impact on the future of the industry.

Crime comics first appeared in 1942 with Lev Gleason Publications' *Crime Does Not Pay*, written and edited by Charles Biro (1911–1972) and Bob Wood. Detective stories such as *Dick Tracy* and *The Spirit* had been in circulation for some time, but the focus shifted away from canny deduction and heroic action toward deranged criminal behavior portrayed with a brutal Grand Guignol naturalism. The standard narrative device Biro and Wood developed for their stories was an omnipresent narrator with a devilish face and a top hat with his name, "Crime," emblazoned on it. The character, Crime, was a ghost-like cartoon that contrasted with the more realistic-looking criminals and environments he hovered above. Crime indulged in sarcastic comments, egging on the characters to undertake evermore sadistic actions, and was always on hand to deliver the cruel moral of the story. The evil interlocutor went on to became a signature feature of many crime —and later, horror—comics of this period.

Horror titles first appeared in 1947 with the publisher Avon, but this one-time publication did not inspire any followup by Avon. It was only the following year when American Comics Group published its long-lived *Adventures into the Unknown* series that horror comics began to appear on a regular basis. The most important player of the new horror genre, EC Comics, would not field a horror title for another year because it was in the midst of transforming itself from Educational Comics, publishing stories from classic literature and the Bible, to Entertaining Comics, where it aggressively pursued more populist pulp fiction tastes. Max Gaines, who had been instrumental in the formation of the comics industry and who had been a major editor and business partner at DC, perennially sought to uplift the content of the comics trade by introducing higher-quality educational and religiously themed comics. Gaines had helped in the creation of Wonder Woman, Flash, and Hawkman, but after a fallout with Harry Donenfeld at National Comics (DC), he sold his share in the company along with the superhero characters he had a stake in creating and started his own company, Educational Comics, featuring such titles as *Picture Stories from the Bible*. Educational Comics' wholesome titles were failing badly when Max Gaines suddenly passed away in a boating accident in 1947 and his son, William Gaines (1922–1992), inherited the business. At the start, William Gaines, a recent divorcee, had no particular interest in being a comic book publisher and continued to run the company out of familial obligation and a lack of anything better to do. Slowly, as he began to get a feel for the business, he took more interest in the publications and hired a number of younger artists, among them Al Feldstein (b. 1925), who shared William Gaines's enthusiasm for science fiction and horror. EC introduced a line of horror comics that included *Tales of the Crypt, Vault of Horror*, and *Haunt of Fear*, and although their titles were indistinguishable from dozens of other horror comics, their contents tended toward a cruel humor with heavy does of irony and creepy carnivalesque mystery.

As primary scriptwriter for the flagship EC titles, Feldstein wrote about four stories per week on top of editing seven magazines. After a morning session with Gaines, fielding ideas for stories, Feldstein would return to his drawing table and write the script directly onto illustration board, sorting out on the page how the story would be told over six to eight pages. Gaines would review the Feldstein draft pages, reading them aloud with the dramatic flourishes of a radio drama to see if the story captured the proper theatricality. Finally, as the artist filled out the page with finished drawings, Feldstein's dialogue and narrative text would be erased.

The younger Gaines was able to inspire some dedication from his artists by not enforcing a house style and allowing each one to develop his own idiosyncratic manner of telling the story. Gaines was also one of the very few publishers who included inside the publication the name of the artist who had worked on a story. There prevailed an atmosphere of competitive camaraderie among the artists at EC, and many who got their start there went on to become some of the leading comic artists of their day, representing a remarkable range of styles, including Harvey Kurtzman (1924–1993), Wally Wood (1927–1981), Graham Ingels (1915–1991), Joe Orlando (1927–1998), Will Elder (1921–2008), Bernard Krigstein (1919–1990), and Basil Wolverton (1909–1978). The diversity of styles and outrageous content gave EC a rebellious character that was well ahead of most mainstream comics, which were tacking in a different direction by trying to be accepted as legitimate publications for middle-class youths.

Although EC became best known—and later reviled—for its horror comics, EC also produced a number of serious works that ushered in a new, higher benchmark for dramatic graphic narratives, taking on mature subjects with a kind of daring that could not be found anywhere else in American popular culture. Harvey Kurtzman edited, wrote, and drew some of the best war comics from this period in *Two-Fisted Tales* (1950–1955) and *Frontline Combat* (1951–1954), which were notable for their sensitive portrayal of ordinary soldiers in war. The EC suspense genre was another exceptional series of titles that typically offered stories couched in everyday situations that inevitably spun out of control to arrive at a shocking conclusion. Gaines and Feldstein occasionally worked in social issues by way of moral tales they called "preachies" for their lofty sentiments. The stories seldom offered easy solutions and often worked against the reader's expectations to have a startling impact without actually being preachy. Themes would include stories on racism in "Blood Brothers," "The Guilty," and "Judgment Day"; drug addiction in "The Monkey"; and anti-Semitism in "Hate."[4]

Bernard Krigstein's *Master Race* published in *Impact* #1 (1955) stands out as one of EC's landmark artistic achievements. Although no one quite recalls who came up with the initial idea for the story, it remains a remarkable suspense tale that directly confronts the horrors of the Holocaust in explicit terms. Such stories were not mainstream news in the United States and were certainly not seen at all in popular publications, let alone told in comics. Initially, the story was intended to be a brief six-pager; however, Krigstein was able to get a few extra pages to try to break up the long narrative passages that make up the bulk of the story. *Master Race* follows a cowed and terrified man, Reissman, who is haunted by his recent memories of Nazi Germany as he takes a subway train. On that ride, a man dressed in black with a pinched scull-like face comes on board, and this prompts a horrified reaction from Reissman and a long flashback sequence that describes Nazi rallies, brutal killings, incarcerations, forced medical experiments, human-skin lampshades, and even the mass graves where people were buried alive. Throughout the story, the stunning visual layout has an urgency and intensity created by the tightly packed rhythms of repeated images, fragmented moments, and stark objectivity. The final twist in the story happens when we finally learn Reissman was not a victim of these crimes but, rather, someone who had orchestrated them as a camp commandant. The man dressed in black, a survivor of the Holocaust, recognizes Reissman and pursues him out of the train and down the landing of the station, where, in a tour de force of synoptic action sequencing, Reissman slips and falls on the tracks in front of an oncoming train.

Krigstein was pushing the limits of what was possible in the comics industry that was dominated by writers who scripted the stories and often left little room for more expansive visual storytelling within the panels. To circumvent this limitation, Krigstein often split his panels into many narrow strips or placed multiple and shifting representations of a character in a single panel. It is unfortunate that Krigstein was just beginning to develop this style when his career as a comic artist was cut short by the widespread collapse of the comics industry in the late 1950s.

The Anticomics Crusades

Throughout the 1940s, the number of comics in print continued to grow past 60 million to 150 million copies a month until the number peaked at an all-time high in 1954 of 250 million per month, or roughly 3 billion published that year. That less than half that number—about 1.3 billion—were actually sold in that same period was indicative of the general dysfunction that surrounded the industry. Comics had grown swiftly and haphazardly in the previous two decades with a rush of get-rich-quick speculators, so there was little long-range economic forecasting and plenty of irrational exuberance. Much of the earlier growth had been kept in check by the economic restraints of the Great Depression and the paper and ink rations of World War II, but as these conditions began to subside in the 1950s, the growth of comics exploded, which inevitably led to a dramatic and irreversible implosion. The long-term impact of this economic collapse was exacerbated by cultural changes that were occurring at the time that singled out comics as the prime suspect as the source for what ailed society.

Despite the ubiquity of comics, the comic book industry continued to face persecution from cultural critics in the Catholic Church and from zealous politicians reacting to the notion that comics inspired "juvenile delinquency." Although the statistical evidence of a connection between comics and juvenile delinquency was lacking, a number of sensational incidents of children mimicking violent comic books raised the broader public's awareness that something needed to be done. On December 20, 1948, *Time* had a story on a comic book burning in Binghamton, New York, where "students of St. Patrick's parochial school collected 2,000 objectionable comic books in a house-to-house canvass, burned them in the school yard." As this story attracted the attention of the national media, comic book burnings sprouted up all over the country, and the anticomics furor entered a new level of activism.

Fredric Wertham was instrumental in giving the loose band of anticomics crusaders a purchase in the broader cultural landscape because he argued his case against comics, not on moral grounds or for political gains, but according to his psychological research conducted with his patients at the psychiatric hospital he established in Harlem, Wertham's selfless dedication to African American mental health in poverty-stricken Harlem also gave him the veneer of an altruistic social reformer that was very difficult to ignore. Why Wertham settled on the issue of comics as the cause to champion is hard to fathom, considering the wide range of real social issues facing the Harlem community in the 1930s and 1940s. The lack of urban infrastructure, economic hardship, and insufficient social welfare were far more dominant influences in the Harlem community than were comics. Perhaps Wertham considered comics to be an issue that was more manageable, one that might resonate with the larger U.S. population, with the hope that they would see the plight of the poor in Harlem as an extension of their own struggles to contend with changing youth culture. But these outcomes did not materialize; instead, the debate over how comics were corrupting the youth of America became increasingly histrionic. Wertham scripted himself as the prophet of doom, utilizing the same kinds of excesses in his own arguments that he accused the comics industry of using to corrupt the youth of America.

Wertham first addressed the issue of the negative impact of comics in an interview in *Collier's Weekly*, "Horror in the Nursery" (1948), which was followed by his book *Seduction of the Innocent* (1954). These writings directly led to the 1954 televised Senate Subcommittee on Juvenile Delinquency hearings, commonly referred to as the Kefauver hearings. Wertham attacked comics on several fronts, including their lack of verisimilitude (superheroes defying the laws of physics); their lack of artistic merit (terrible art, poorly printed, with bad colors); their lack of decorum (suggestive sexual content with sidekicks and female characters); and most important, a celebration of violence (eye gouging and decapitation treated as humorous or sexually enticing subjects). Although the bulk of Wertham's invective was leveled at the crime and horror comics, no genre was immune from his criticism, for he also blasted the *Classics Illustrated* market, as well as funny animals and romance comics. All comics were categorically a bad influence on youth because they promoted what he saw as a culture of violence and indifference to sincere humanistic values. For this reason, Wertham was against censorship of particular genres or types of content and instead proposed the more radical solution of banning the sale of all comics to anyone under the age of 16.

The Senate subcommittee did not endorse any specific legislation, but many local ordinances and pending state laws forced the comics industry to take action and institute self-censorship in order to protect itself from future legal action, just as the movie and TV industry had done a decade before. In October 1954, the leading comic book publishers agreed to establish an independent review board that would police the industry and give out a Comics Code Authority "Seal of Approval" to all comics that passed its standards of decency. The code that the agency adopted was specifically aimed at rooting out the horror and crime genres, but it had a much broader impact on the industry because it institutionalized the idea that comics were explicitly for children and that all comics should be made suitable to that end. Gone was any use of morbid or scandalous subjects, twisted or seductive imagery, rude or crass language; but perhaps more significant was the loss of serious subject matter and the end of comics for adults.

The Comics Code was only partly to blame for the subsequent collapse of the comics industry. Only 12 of the major 34 comic book publishers joined the Comics Code. Many soon dropped out because of the expense of having their comics reviewed or, as in the case of Dell Comics that only produced comics for children, claimed their comics were already beyond reproach. Television was also an influence in the downturn because it ate into the leisure time of many Americans. Furthermore, many comics publishers, among them St. John, had rushed into the new 3-D comics market in the late 1950s hoping to become a big success in what was widely anticipated as the next fad. Theirs was a rash move because the market was contracting, and so many publishers found themselves stuck with thousands of worthless 3-D glasses. Amy Kiste Nyberg has estimated that the single-largest influence on the comics industry in the late 1950s was actually the financial instability caused by the collapse of the American News Company (ANC).[5] In 1955, ANC, which was responsible for more than half of all national comic book distribution, stopped its entire magazine distribution in response to a federal antitrust case brought against it. This service stoppage had the devastating result of forcing many publishers to rely on more expensive and smaller independent distributors, which cut further into their already narrow profit margins.

The impact of the anticomics crusade was not just limited to the United States. The crusade was carried beyond the country's borders to have an impact on other cultures as far away as the Philippines and the Soviet Union. Between 1940 and 1960, anticomics crusades took place in at least 20 countries on four continents. Some of these battles—in Germany, Canada, and Great Britain, for example—primarily concerned fears that comics were corrupting the youth and were thus directly influenced by Wertham's opinions; others, as in France and Australia, were more about the economic and cultural influences of U.S. comics flooding the market. There was a strong sentiment among many countries that U.S. comics were drowning out their own comic book publishers and that U.S. comics were keeping their children from learning their own national heritage. In the case of the Soviet Union and China, U.S. comics were seen as antithetical to their communist philosophy and were therefore completely banned. Germany followed the United States in allowing the comics industry to self-regulate its content along strict guidelines; many other countries, however, enacted legislation that restricted the import and sale of crime, horror, and sometimes superhero comics. With all the major comic book publishers hurting from this downturn and censorship, the so-called Golden Age of comics came to an end. Indeed, the industry has yet to see a revival of the same magnitude of popularity and cultural influence.

"Silver Age" Comics

Dell Comics remained profitable for much of the 1950s by focusing on obviously chaste material from Disney and by producing a number of adaptations of television shows, especially Westerns such as *Roy Rogers*, hoping to lure a few audiences back to comics. But television audiences had only a modest interest in these comics, and Dell's profitability slid into deep decline throughout the 1960s. The return to profitability in mainstream comics came only as publishers began to refocus on their most devoted constituency, teenage boys, and their most reliable genre, superheroes. In 1959, Julius "Julie" Schwartz (1915–2004) successfully resuscitated some of DC Comics' older characters, among them The Flash and Green Lantern, by removing the plot gimmicks and returning to more character-driven action. Schwartz was also instrumental in revitalizing the idea of a superhero team in 1960 with *The Justice League of America.*

Under the editorship of Stan Lee (b. 1922), Marvel Comics (first known as Timely and in the 1950s as Atlas) took the lead by producing a number of new characters and titles that would eventually dominate the market to the present day. In 1961, following the success of *The Justice League of America*, Lee, along with the artist Jack Kirby, created a team of superheroes called the Fantastic Four. The *Fantastic Four* comics featured a group of astronauts who are infected by cosmic rays that transform each of their bodies resulting in unique superpowers. The core formula of a scientist becoming infected or wounded by some cutting-edge research became the basis for a slew of new heroic characters, including Spider-Man, Hulk, Iron Man, Dr. Strange, and Thor. What made this formula so successful was that in each instance, the transformation of the ordinary person into a superhero established a wounded character who was riddled with self-doubt as the powers bestowed upon him or her were at best a mixed blessing, both elevating and alienating him or her from ordinary life. Nowhere was this theme more fully explored than in the character of Spider-Man, originally drawn by Steve Ditko (b. 1927). In this story, the icky fascination with spiders was embodied by the high school geek Peter Parker, who is able to channel his powers and intellect to become a hero by choice. Although Parker possesses superpowers, he still suffers from problems with money, girlfriends, and family; but the ordinariness of his troubles in life highlights his transformation into the "Amazing Spider-Man."

Despite the seeming topicality of a young teen superhero, there was ongoing self-censorship from the Comics Code Authority. Comics were stamped with the code's Seal of Approval throughout the 1970s and 1980s and for much of the 1990s. One of the early exceptions to the Comics Code was *The Amazing Spider-Man* #96 (May 1971), which developed an anti-drug theme at the request of the Nixon administration's Department of Health, Education, and Welfare. The code stipulated that no depiction of drugs was allowed, even when it cast drugs in a negative way. Stan Lee went ahead to publish the story without the code's approval, however, and because of the popularity of this comic, the code loosened its restrictions; two months later, DC published an antidrug-themed comic with the code

Seal of Approval starring Green Arrow with his sidekick Speedy struggling with addiction. The code continued to be altered over the years, restricting less and less but still preventing explicit sexual content and an oddly eccentric list of material that was deemed inappropriate for younger viewers: vampires were made acceptable because of their literary pedigree, but the code otherwise forbade werewolves and zombies. Regardless of the editorial inanities the code presented, it was vigorously supported by DC and Marvel for many years. By preventing smaller publishers from creating more racy material, the chief impact of the code on the market was not just the killing off of EC and a few other competitors; the code simply made it harder for upstart publishers to enter the market.

The slippery term "Silver Age" is often applied to superhero comics in this period of comic history, essentially as a way to make a distinction between pre– and post–Comics Code work. The term becomes difficult to define because it is largely an assessment of value that collectors have assigned to certain works from this period and is not a term that comic artists or publishers originally recognized or promoted. A close examination of the style of superhero comic art from the 1950s and 1970s shows very little change aside from a slightly more exaggerated musculature and sexuality. Most of the comic book publishers had rigid house styles that prevented artists from straying too far from well-heeled formulas established by their editors. Gone were the imaginative page layouts of artists like Will Eisner, and more and more of the comic panels were uniform grids of three-by-three boxes laid out evenly on the page.

One notable exception was the work of Jack Kirby, who after many years in the comics business, began in the 1960s to develop a unique style that coalesced as hyperdynamic bodies in action that broke out of their panels and stark, bold line work that appeared like reflections off chrome. The change in Kirby's style was in part attributable to an increase in the per-page rate he was given at the time, which allowed him to devote more time to his pages; but it also seems he was responding to the graphic stylization that Roy Lichtenstein (1923–1997) added to the comic panels that he was making into pop art paintings.[6] Kirby could also make these changes because he had a fair degree of autonomy in working with the scripts he was given. Stan Lee gave Kirby a basic plot outline to work from and allowed Kirby some latitude over how he chose to develop the story. Once Kirby had penciled in the page layouts, Lee wrote in the final dialogue. This system worked well when Kirby and Lee were in agreement about the plot, but it broke down often when Lee contravened Kirby's intentions and resorted to more formulaic language and action.

Despite their ambiguity, terms like Golden Age and Silver Age continue to be used because from the mid-1960s onward, collectors and dedicated fans begin to play a more visible role in defining the direction and nature of the mainstream comics business. Bernie Bubnis organized the first comic book convention, Comic-Con '64, which was held in a union meeting hall on 14th Street and Broadway, New York. This was more than merely a swap meet among fans, for it also featured a chalk talk by *Lone Ranger* artist Tom Gill on the art of drawing comics. Over the years, comic book conventions have grown to staggering proportions and proliferated all over the country. A chief feature of these forums is for comic artists, as well as other pop celebrities from within the orbit of comic culture, to bask in the glow of their most ardent fans. For comic book artists, whose names in the 1950s still seldom appeared alongside their work, comic conventions provided an important impetus toward professional recognition that slowly helped push for greater artistic recognition and eventually creator's rights.

The downside of the phenomenon of comicons is that it has further alienated comic books from mainstream culture as publishers learned over the years to direct their publications toward this self-selecting group of devoted fans. This practice has narrowed the kinds of genres appearing in comics and made it difficult for publishers to reach out to new audiences such as young girls, minorities, and gays. When such topical issues as civil rights have been broached, as in Allan Moore's rendition of *Swamp Thing* or Chris Claremont's rendition of *X-Men*, the issues are explored entirely within the confines of the fictive world of superheroes. Referencing social issues from within the coded world of superheroes gives meaning and depth to the actions of the superheroes, but it often fails to help clarify any real-world problems. The most honest way that superhero comics could address real-world issues was by acknowledging that they could not solve them. This occurred memorably in 1970 when Green Lantern was forced by an older African American to recognize his history of helping people of many alien colors except those of the color black.[7]

A prevalent theme in comics from this time was not the engagement with real-world topical issues but, rather, a growing use of metanarrative devices that called attention to the fact that the story was a comic. The popularity of the camp television show *Batman*, produced by ABC between January 1966 and March 1968, heightened the superficial characteristics of the comic action by inserting into the fight scenes such text as "Kapow!" with a trumpet flourish. These and other extra-dramatic qualities heightened the artificial nature of the comic medium and, inspired by pop art paintings of

Roy Lichtenstein, highlighted the narrative excess of the comic book style. DC bowed to the popular television parodic style by introducing brighter colors and reviving many of the more implausible villains from Batman's past that were featured in the show, such as the Riddler. During the two-year run of the show, Batman was ubiquitous across many DC titles, bringing his gimmicky "bat belt" and deadpan dialogue to many unsuspecting titles. Batman eventually returned to his established place in the DC pantheon, but his brush with camp demonstrated television's power even over the long-time comic fan base that loathed the television show. Camp parodies in comics achieved a new prominence with *Howard the Duck* (1973) written by Steve Gerber, and later with *The Sensational She-Hulk* (1989) by John Byrne. The ubiquity of self-referential camp in these comics was a sign of the growing desperation to find novel ways to add complexity to the very proscribed and predictable worlds superheroes inhabited.

Being a collector of comics increasingly became an expensive hobby as the price of comics rose from its long-standing initial price of 10 cents in 1960 to an average 50 cents in 1980. Early on, these price changes were consistent with an overall rise in inflation, but in the following decade, the price for a comic book would rise above the general rate of inflation to $1 in 1988 and $1.25 in 1992. The change in comic prices, though not as dramatic a rise as the cost of movies, corresponded with the changing character of the comics industry that was now more focused on the dedicated collector and less on the casual collector and impulse shopper. Collectors were enticed with promotional gimmicks featuring alternative covers to the same issue and mylar-wrapped issues that were designed to encourage collectors to buy one comic to read and a second one to preserve in mint condition. Collecting's impact on comic culture emphasized the idea that comics were less a source for new adventures and characters and more another variety of merchandise branded with a popular character (see box 9.1).

Direct Market Sales to Comic Shops

Phil Seuling (1934–1984), a Brooklyn schoolteacher, was at Comic-Con '64 largely to supply soda to about 100 attendees, but while there he also began to pitch the idea of a new kind of market for comics. Until the 1960s, the comics market was largely controlled by newspaper distributors who bought in bulk and returned what did not sell. Unsold comics, like yesterday's news, had no recognized market value, so they were "pulped." In this system, the onus was on the publisher not only to produce work that would sell but also

Box 9.1   Comic Character Tie-Ins

The more aggressive marketing of comic character properties in the 1980s was a phenomenon not just isolated to comic books. As the comic strip syndicates saw their revenues decline as a result of the ever-shrinking newspaper comic pages, they began to push their properties into more merchandise tie-ins. Comic creator Charles Schulz of *Peanuts* had, for example, used his characters for years in successfully promoting everything from safety programs at NASA during the *Apollo X* mission to life insurance in the 1980s, although he eventually began to cut back for fear of overexposure. The glut of marketing was nowhere more evident than in Jim Davis's *Garfield* characters that in 1989 had sold 225 million plush Garfield toys designed to suction onto car windows, as well as thousands of other items. Bill Watterson, the creator of *Calvin and Hobbes*, was one of the very few voices of dissent against this rampant marketing. Aside from reprints of his comics, Watterson refused all merchandise tie-ins and even TV and movie offers for his characters, saying they cheapened the experience of the comic strip. Watterson has expressed his views on comics marketing on a number of different occasions, but most extensively during a talk given at Ohio State University where he concluded, "I do not buy the argument that licensing can go at full throttle without affecting the strip. Licensing has become a monster. Cartoonists have not been very good at recognizing it and the syndicates don't care."[8]

to handle any returns of what did not sell. Seuling was interested in selling directly to comic fans, so he suggested that he buy at a discount directly from the publisher with no option to return unsold comics. For Seuling, this meant he had some back-copies that collectors could use to fill out their collections, and these comics might even accrue in value if the comic proved popular. For publishers, this direct market approach simplified their business and assured sales based on actual orders with no losses from later returns. Seuling's business model worked, and in 1974, he gave up teaching and began East Coast Seagate Distributors, which funneled comics to several hundred specialty comic book shops.

Seuling held comic distribution market dominance until 1979, when Marvel Comics opened up its direct sales terms, allowing a flood of new comic distributors and comic book shops to flourish. Marvel did this because it was eager to get out from under DC, which owned the company that controlled its distribution. Although this strategy worked in the short term to increase the organization's market share, it ultimately led to greater market instability. In the 1980s, 18 different distributors worked to supply more than 8,000 comic shops. DC Comics did not follow suit by opening up its distribution terms and instead decided to privilege a handful of larger and more reliable distributors with exclusive terms. This action forced the less fortunate distributors to take orders from these distributors at a less advantageous discount. The two-tier system was expedient for DC, but it left Marvel dealing with a number of unreliable accounts.

The proliferation of independent comic book stores with their expanded shelf space provided an opening for more challenging material to find an audience. An early indication of the shift in mainstream comics came with Frank Miller's cyberpunk-styled Batman, *The Dark Knight Returns* (1987), where the superhero action confronted for the first time the taboo idea of middle age. The success of *The Dark Knight Returns*—with its square binding, higher-quality artwork and printing, and a high cover price of $2.95— suggested there was a viable opening for publications directed to older audiences. The other, more ambitious project begun that same year was Alan Moore's *Watchmen* series, which introduced a nuanced plot with a cast of mentally unstable superheroes. Moore's initial plan intended to revive old Charlton Comics superheroes purchased by DC, but DC editor Dick Giordano realized that the Charlton characters would be unusable because the story arc came to an apocalyptic conclusion that would complicate any attempt at making a sequel. *Watchmen* eventually became its own parallel universe where the United States won the Vietnam War with the help of its superheroes, but this proved an empty victory that pushed the world even closer to nuclear annihilation. The design and storytelling in both *Dark Knight* and *Watchmen* were both more dense and difficult to read; they repeatedly used a nine-by-nine grid of images to methodically parse out dramatic scenes, and they also intercut several overlapping plots rendered in different styles.

Following *Dark Knight* and *Watchmen* was the artfully written and designed series *Sandman*, written by Neil Gaiman (b. 1960) and illustrated by a host of other artistic collaborators from 1989 to 1996. Moore and Gaiman were both British expatriates who brought a degree of literary complexity to their stories, layering their plots with allusions to Shakespeare, Blake, and the Bhagavad Gita, but more significantly recast the familiar superhero action with more compelling depth and meaning. Gaiman's most accomplished work was on a shorter self-contained story, *Mr. Punch* (1994), with art by his long-time collaborator Dave McKean (b. 1963), which was initially published in Britain by

Victor Gollancz. The design of the book had the decrepit and surreal style of a Jan Švankmajer animated film, intercutting between collaged photographs of Punch and Judy characters in a puppet show and artfully crude drawings of real-life characters from a run-down seaside resort.

The expansion and maturing of comic readership was an encouraging development that prompted speculators to believe that perhaps comics in America were about to enter a new age where they would be accepted on the same artistic level as comics were in Japan and in Europe. But the foundations of the comic market expansion were shaky: distribution battles escalated as a few larger companies vied for market dominance. In their race to accrue more business, the two largest comics distributors, Diamond and Capital City, lowered the bar for establishing new accounts from $3,000 to $300, giving rise to yet another 4,000 comic book shops between 1988 and 1992. By the late 1980s, the market for comics was saturated, collectors snapped up extra copies with unrealistic ambitions of getting a future return on their investment, and the industry was on the verge of its second great collapse.

The Death of Superman

The growing influence of comic collectors on the industry materialized in the pages of the comics themselves, with many qualities that continue to dominate the mainstream medium even today. Early efforts to capitalize on collectors' interests were seen in the push to create not just new characters in old magazines but also new titles that now blazoned on their front covers "#1 Collectors Item Issue!"[9] To further instill the idea that comics of a publisher were a collectable in their entirety, publishers began to create greater continuity between their various titles and began to form what would become known as the Marvel Universe or DC Universe. The interconnection with past issues was first emphasized by Stan Lee at Marvel, who interjected his commentary and later footnotes that cited references in the current issue back to events in earlier issues. Greater continuity allowed for more crossovers between titles, and it allowed popular stories to help promote other stories in the same universe. Marvel Comics took the lead in promoting this continuity in its 1982 massive character crossover *Contest of Champions*.[10] DC Comics followed suit and in 1985 realigned the continuity of its comic line with a 12–comic book series called *Crisis on Infinite Earths*.[11]

Starting in 1987, Mike Carlin (b. 1958) was the editor of the collective titles that starred Superman, and he began a tradition of having an annual meeting of the whole creative team working on these titles to plot out the major story arc for the year. Continuity between comics and their adaptations into such other media as television and film had not been much of an issue, since writers and artist were allowed to pursue a wide latitude of interpretation of characters and plots; but in 1992, as the creative team planned a wedding between Clark Kent and Lois Lane for issue #500 of the *Adventures of Superman*, they were told they had to put that plan indefinitely on hold because the television series *Lois & Clark: The New Adventures of Superman* had been approved to begin airing in 1993 and any plans for their marriage should not conflict with the story arc of the new show. Rushing back to the drawing board, the creative team came up with an alternative plan: to stage the death of Superman. The cause of death would be the climax of a massive battle with a powerful alien named Doomsday; after a brief hiatus, wherein many characters could express their shock and grief, Superman would return. The sketchy story was unremarkable and more than a little predictable, but the promoters of the special comic event gave the impression that this was going to be the last of Superman. For many fans, such an absolute end was unimaginable, and there was plenty of commentary where people voiced anger that DC could be so arrogant as to presume they had the right to kill off such an important cultural icon as Superman.

On the day that Superman would die in *Superman* #75 (January 1993), comic shops were swamped with buyers who wanted to have a memento of the last Superman comic. The general public turned out en masse for this event, many purchasing several copies as keepsakes. The entire issue was devoted to the big blowout battle with the invincible Doomsday. Superman eventually killed the villain, but he soon died from his own wounds. In Superman's final moment, he was depicted in a three-page foldout splash page showing his battered and bruised body lying in the arms of Lois Lane as if she were the Virgin Mary holding the fallen Christ in the classical pose of the pieta. The Christ analogy was borne out in later issues, where there were unconfirmed sightings of Superman, followed by several new characters that embodied different aspects of Superman, and finally his inevitable corporeal return.

The revived interest in Superman and other superhero comics was short lived, however, as the story seemed to trivialize the character rather than give him depth. The general public reacted negatively to realizing it was all a media stunt, and as the anticipated value for *Superman* #75 did not materialize, they did not return to comic shops. Comic book merchant Chuck Rozanski regards this event as the tipping point in the inflated comics market that began to contract by late 1993 and continued to shrink for more than a decade, amounting to an 80 percent decline in sales.[12] The story arc involving the death of Superman has since prompted the industry to kill off and later revive many of its major and minor characters. The seemingly revolving door between this world and the afterlife has many incredulous fans mocking stories that concern a character's death. For most of their history, superheroes were largely immune from death, but now the idea is even more a remote abstraction—similar to a death in a video game—where the character must restart after a minor disruption to the ongoing action.

CHAPTER 10

Post–World War II Manga

Low wages and rationing in Japan during and immediately after World War II allowed for very few luxuries, and rental manga was one of the few affordable forms of entertainment still available. Kiosks in market stalls rented manga (*kashihonya*) for about 10 yen for two days. Catering to older urban audiences, the rental books developed a genre of more mature stories called *gekiga*, or "dramatic pictures," a term that was coined in 1957 by the young artist Yoshihiro Tatsumi (b. 1935). The need for a new word to describe the work of the more mature adventure themes was important because at that time, the word "manga" was wholly associated with funny children's stories. By incidentally appearing alongside manga clearly intended for younger children, the adult-oriented *gekiga* attempted to distance itself from accusations that they were attempting to corrupt Japanese youth.

Post–World War II mangaka (manga artists) were more interested than their predecessors in exploring a cinematic style that captured actions and characters that were closer to urban life. Tatsumi and other mangaka were well aware of what was happening in American comics and developed a contrasting style that had a tighter integration of words and pictures. In action scenes, they would reduce the number of words and background details to allow the action to be read more quickly. Tatsumi called this approach the "synchronization of panel and time."[1] This sympathetic integration of words and pictures in manga was largely a result of the simple fact that, for the most part, mangaka both wrote and drew their works themselves. These pieces were invariably edited by a publisher, but mangaka were able to conceive of connections between words and pictures in ways that were much harder for American comic artists, who were given a script to work with and then had their work passed on to inkers and letterers.

There were several varieties of *gekiga*—murder mysteries, adventure stories, horror—and the one that achieved the pinnacle of popularity for the time was a period piece by Shirato Sanpei (b. 1932) that was an eight-volume serialized rental called *Secret Martial Arts of the Ninja* (*Ninja Bungeichō*, 1959–1962). Sanpei took the popular theme of Ninja warriors and expanded the story to include historical insight into feudal clans and their military tactics. This work gave one final boost to the rental market shortly before it expired and was replaced by monthly periodicals.

Yoshihiro Tatsumi created some of the first alternative manga stories relating mature themes and ideas that even today can appear shocking. Starting in 1969 in the biweekly young men's magazine *Gekiga Young*, Tatsumi created brief eight-page manga stories that dealt with such subjects as the urban poor, prostitution, and abortion in a frank, unsentimental manner. Taking his inspiration from local news stories and police reports, Tatsumi worked outside the typical conventions and subject matter found in manga and pioneered the whole idea of comics that reflected soberly on the human condition. *The Push Man and Other Stories* (2005) is the first of a multivolume series translating the work of Tatsumi. In the first volume of works from 1969, Tatsumi's pacing is swift, and the economical language and line drawings place the emphasis on gestures, sounds, and subtle expressions. The title story in the collection, "The Push-man," recounts the sexual fantasies and frustrations of a "push man," someone hired to squeeze people onto the public trains in Tokyo. The ordinary worker, exhausted and sweating, finds himself dreaming about work and the stimulation of the violence and sexuality of so many bodies crammed together. He rescues a woman from the shame of a torn dress in the crush of people and they have an affair; later, she invites her friends over, and they violently and sexually crush him. Back at work, the push man becomes trapped in a crowd he was pushing and is swept into the train, which rides off with him inside. In one of the final frames, we see the push man with an enigmatic expression on his face—the push man has been pushed.

Osamu Tezuka, the God of Manga

A few inexpensive manga publications were also available for purchase; these manga were called "red books" (*akabon*) for the tacky red ink they used on their covers. They were produced by small publishers looking for a niche in the market, and they were created mostly by young artists trying to break into the comics trade. Osamu Tezuka (1928–1989) began as one of these red book artists and would eventually have such a profound influence on the direction of manga that he would earn the moniker the "God of Manga." With more than 150,000 pages of manga drawings and 600 titles to his credit, Tezuka created whole new genres and challenged what was believed possible within the medium. His great ambitions were evident in his first major success in 1947, *New Treasure Island* (*Shintakarazima*). *New Treasure Island* was an adventure story originally created with more than 250 pages of drawings—defying the scope and nature of all previous red books and looking more like a storyboard for an animated movie than a comic book. Editors drastically reduced the manga to a mere 60 pages for publication and removed much of the moment-to-moment actions; nonetheless, at a time when disposable income was scarce, it proved to be a staggering success with 400,000 copies sold. The success of *New Treasure Island* was a watershed event that encouraged larger publishers to begin to take manga seriously; it also inspired a whole new generation of young artists to take up drawing comics.

What Tezuka had done, despite the drastic editing of the publishers, is create a manga that owed more to film animation than to book illustration. The first two pages had no dialogue at all, only a sequence of four large panels depicted a car racing through the countryside. Another innovation that Tezuka popularized was the use of masking, where characters are drawn in a broad, simple cartoon style and the backgrounds are given greater natural detail. This method of rendering can be seen in classic Disney animation, such as *Sleeping Beauty* (1937), which Tezuka had grown up watching at his home.

Tezuka had an upper-middle-class background and was exposed to many Western movies and comics as a child as well as the famous all-female Takarazuka theater in his hometown. By 1946, he had earned a medical degree from Osaka University to follow in his father's footsteps as a doctor; but despite parental expectations and a high demand for doctors in Japan, Tezuka saw himself quintessentially as an animator, a job that had no prospective openings in postwar Japan. Undaunted by his situation, Tezuka exploited the field of manga to suit his own ends and repeatedly experimented with visual storytelling that deemphasized words and employed gesture and composition to create vivid dramas that leaped from the page. The Tezuka signature style introduced the luminous anglo eyes that remain the notorious hallmark of manga today. In addition, despite his medical background, he eschewed natural anatomy for expressive tubular limbs that energetically gesticulated like a

Max Fleischer cartoon. Despite the big noses and cartoony hands and feet of his characters, Tezuka's drawings always moved with an animated force, which vividly conveyed power and conviction.

Following the success of *Shintakarazima*, Tezuka embarked on an even more ambitious story, which evolved into an African take on Disney's *Bambi* and Shakespeare's *Hamlet* called *Jungle Emperor* (*Jungle Taitei*, 1950–1954). *Jungle Emperor* was a sprawling epic that introduced many of Tezuka's enduring themes of heroic compassion and perseverance in the face of futile struggles. Tezuka's original inspiration for *Jungle Emperor* may have come from an American source in Ed Hunt's "Simba, King of Beasts," published in *Jungle Comics* (1947). Given the steady diet of comics U.S. soldiers were fed in the early years of the occupation of Japan, it is likely Tezuka would have seen this comic and be taken by the idea of a white lion who protects animals in the jungle against hunters, a story that bears an uncanny resemblance to the central idea in Tezuka's own work. Such similarity does not diminish Tezuka's genius in developing the story; rather, it demonstrates the complexly intertwined nature of modern comic history.

Tezuka's first opportunity to work in film would not appear until the 1960s, when he started his own film company, Mushi Pro, and started an animated version of his hit *The Mighty Atom* (*Tetsuan Atom*, 1963–1966), which later in the United States was called *Astroboy* and became the first Japanese cartoon to regularly appear on television. Television producers gave a meager budget to Tezuka's project, so he devised a striped down animated feature that exploited slowly panning still frames, repetitions of common actions, and a minimum of talking. Although largely born out of economic necessity, Tezuka's animation style also took hold and can be seen today in some of the most lavishly produced Japanese animation (*anime*). The next project his film company created was an animated version of *Jungle Emperor* for television that later became known in the United States as the animated cartoon *Kimba the White Lion* (1965). Despite Disney's insistence to the contrary, Tezuka's animated feature was the basis for their 1993 film *The Lion King*.[2]

Tezuka never entirely switched over to anime, so even while working on animation projects he continued to produce a prodigious number of manga. This was perhaps because animation afforded him a diminished amount of the artistic control that he surely enjoyed as a star mangaka. Tezuka chaffed under the conservative restraints put in place by television producers and was never satisfied with just reproducing well-known formulas. In his search to capture new audiences and new subjects, he introduced manga for girls (*shōjo manga*) in his series *Princess Knight* (*Ribon no Kishi*, 1953–1956), religious themes in his

Box 10.1   The Hyōtantsugi

One strange reoccurring character in Osamu Tezuka's work is a snout-nosed face with a bandage on its head and patches across its body, called the Hyōtantsugi. This peculiar character appears at least once in nearly all of Tezuka's stories, although it almost never speaks and never plays any role to further the plot. Its primary function is to reveal a character's heightened tension or frustration. The Hyōtantsugi's large crescent-moon eyes are hard to read, but its bestial features shatter the character, for a moment revealing a primordial exasperation. Tezuka apparently first saw this character drawn in his younger sister's notebook when they were in school, and she explained that the Hyōtantsugi was a kind of mushroom that emits a gas when disturbed but is otherwise quite tasty in soup.[3] Although the Hyōtantsugi's appearance has little meaning in the larger arc of the story, its repeated appearance rewards the many devoted readers of Tezuka's work who enjoy identifying this signature element.

longest and most ambitious work, *Buddha* (1974–1984), and recent political history in his story featuring Adolf Hitler (*Adorufu ni Tsugu*, 1983–1985). As Tezuka's work matured, he developed a style that jettisoned some of the more obvious Disneyesque features and embraced the more natural and experimental characteristics found in *gekiga*.

Within the vast array of topics, styles, and audiences, Tezuka continually reused characters in his work. To him, they had professional lives as performers independent of the particular works they appeared in; and so with eccentric attention to detail, he wrote reviews of their performances in his own manga and maintained a ledger where he recorded their salaries depending on the size and scope of the role they played in the story. Audiences familiar with Tezuka enjoyed seeing each new incarnation of their favorite character, and it established some continuity across his wide-ranging works (see box 10.1).

Today, almost two decades after his death, new movies, television series, theater productions, and other manga are continually being minted from the remains of his vast life's work. Tezuka put manga at the center of a vast media enterprise where successful manga stories were picked up for television, which were in turn spun off into movies and other merchandising schemes. Perhaps Tezuka's most remarkable accomplishment was his ability to infuse manga with greater literary sophistication without it losing its irreverent and spontaneous appeal. Nowhere is this more evident than in his unfinished epic, *Phoenix* (*Hi no Tori*), where high drama is mixed with slapstick farce, as when in the middle of a story on ancient Japanese clans General Custer's 7th Cavalry charges through the action pursued by Indians. In the last frame on the page, an Indian warrior clubs the intruding cavalry narrator saying, "This whole page is nonsense!" Rather than undermining the story, these genre mix-ups, self-referential jokes, and obvious anachronisms keep the story spontaneous and lively. At moments of high drama, Tezuka knew how to selectively employ unexpected twists and humorous reversals to keep each turn of the page a revelation.

Tezuka's multivolume *Phoenix* has a unique structure in that it begins with the dawn of Japanese civilization in the third century and then in the next volume leaps 3,000 years into the future to the end of time. The third volume is a slightly later history of ancient Japan, and the fourth again returns to the future, but at an earlier time than the second volume. In this manner, the story moves back and forth from past to future, always framing the present. What ties these far-flung adventures together is a mythic creature, the Phoenix, that appears and drives the characters toward greater ambitions and fixes their fates on achieving a higher destiny than the society of the day gives them. Despite the lofty premise, the series is propelled by gripping drama and highly innovative page layouts, which represent some of Tezuka's most provocative work. Tezuka was most likely inspired by Stanley Kubrick's movie *2001: A Space Odyssey*, which he learned about early on when he was invited by Kubrick to work on the production. Tezuka finally chose not to be involved in the ambitious film project because it would have taken him away for too long from his manga publications in Japan.

Many adult manga readers who had outgrown Tezuka's more fanciful works were avid followers of the long-running boxing story *Tomorrow's Joe* (*Ashita no Jō*, 1968–1973), by Tetsuya Chiba (b. 1939). Chiba was especially adept at sports stories, and his story of the boxer Jō Yabuki is considered a classic and has been frequently reprinted. The story, which followed the rise of a young boxer and his endless struggle to stay on top of the brutally competitive boxing world, had a rougher and far more realistic appearance with intense boxing scenes contrasted with agonizing personal struggles. The sudden end of the story came just as the hero, Joe, defeats his long-time rival, who later dies from the wounds he sustained in the ring. Audiences were terribly shaken by this bitter victory and the loss of innocence Joe experiences. A funeral was staged for the fictional character in an actual boxing ring, and more than 700 people converged to pay their respects as a Buddhist priest administered the last rites.

Death is a far more common feature in Japanese manga today because such artists as Chiba were in control of the story arc and were willing to create stories that had definite endings.

Through such publications as *Garo* and later *COM*, manga artists were able to explore more challenging themes in a more experimental manner. Kazuo Umezu (b. 1936) employed the creepy terror that comes from agonizingly twisted domestic scenarios. He is well known for his manga *The Drifting Classroom* (*Hyōryū Kyōshitsu*, 1975), a story about an elementary school that becomes trapped in a barren future world where the students and teachers descend into barbarism. Inspired by Ray Bradbury's fantasy-horror mixtures, Hideshi Hino (b. 1946) often employs bug-eyed monsters with sharp fangs as his protagonists, as in his *Hell Baby* (*Kyōfu Zigoku-shōjo*). The monster has hideous impulses, but like Frankenstein's monster, it is always driven mad by unobtainable domestic tranquility.

Perhaps the most visionary of early Japanese mangaka is Tsuge Yoshiharo (b. 1937), creator of "Screw Style," which was originally printed in *Garo* in 1968. As one of the most enigmatic manga of its day, "Screw Style" achieves its provocative and disturbing qualities for its lack of action and narrative coherence. At the center of the story is an adolescent-looking boy who wanders aimlessly through small villages looking for a doctor to mend the severed artery in his arm that he claims happened when a jellyfish bit him. Though he fears that he may bleed to death, he receives very little sympathy from the people he encounters, who either ignore him or mock his whining. The boy seems unable to leave the town he is in when a train he rides takes him back to where he began. The futility of his search for a doctor is epitomized by a whole street of blankly staring eye-doctor signs. Eventually, he meets a woman who claims to be a gynecologist. They "play doctor," and under the sheets he is mended with a tiny heart-shaped valve on the outside of his arm. Somehow, this make-shift repair has healed him, and on the last page we see the boy appear like James Bond riding in a speed boat; he says, "When I turn the screw my arm goes numb." The peculiarities of this manga spoke eloquently to the real and existential wounds that Japanese felt after the war; because of the shame of their role in the war, they often did not feel they could identify, let alone express, their pain and suffering. Tsuge brought the art of manga to new levels of complexity, being one of the first mangaka to explore themes and ideas that had only been attempted in literature before.

The extraordinary innovation that occurred in manga was partially inspired by these innovative publications, but it was also a result of going from a monthly to a weekly magazine format in the 1960s. Despite the more frequent publication schedule, magazines such as *Shōnen Jump*, published by Shueisha, have continued to swell in size from 282 pages in 1969 to more than 474 pages in 2007. Although the price of manga has also gone up, the actual cost per page has stayed about the same since 1975. Some of the economizing that permits this low price has come from printing in black and white on recycled paper and increasing the advertisements; but the low price can also be attributed to a willingness to sell the magazines almost at cost. The ever-expanding larger-sized manga magazines included as many as 40 different stories in a single issue, so commuters on their way to work or school could easily pick up a copy to catch up with their favorite stories. Although the weekly manga issues were too cumbersome and of too poor a quality to collect, they often piled up in waiting rooms and on train cars for any casual reader to browse. For devoted fans of a particular story, several months' worth of serialized episodes were eventually compiled together into small albums (*manga tankōbon*) on good-quality paper. These collectable albums were what enabled the publishers to reap real profits. This publication model allowed manga to cast a wide net across all levels of society and produce a staggering array of story genres and styles that could appeal to many different audiences. It also allowed manga to become the dominant force in the development of new franchises as manga became a proving ground for new material with far less risk if one or another story should fail to catch on. Out of the thousands of new stories and characters in circulation, only those that proved popular would subsequently be spun out to all kinds of merchandise, television serials, and animated films.

The increased workload of weekly publication quadrupled the demand for material, and many established artists created studios with a team of supporting staff to help fill out backgrounds, research story material, typeset text, and ink the finished work. Tezuka was a leader in developing the studio system by creating a special code that keyed his staff to knowing how they were to complete his drawings for him. The studio system also broadened and deepened the population of manga artists and had the long-term impact of ushering many women into the business, many of whom would eventually challenge the boy-centric culture of manga.

The Rise of Girls' Manga

In early manga directed to young women (*shōjo manga*) in the 1940s, the ideal woman defined by male authors and artists was a generic vision of tidiness and self-sufficiency that was pretty or cute (*kawaii*) but did not have the natural grace or stunning glamour that accompanied the idea of womanly beauty. Less threatening *kawaii* girls tended to feature doe-eyed expressions of innocence and acceptance and were younger and less sexually mature as characters that conveyed beauty. This conception of *shōjo* characters was constrained by what it could do, and it tended to focus on internal and emotional issues and delegated more active roles to the male characters. Osamu Tezuka was instrumental in establishing *shōjo manga* stories that had more action by introducing a more dynamic leading female character, Princess Sapphire, in his series called *Princess Knight* (*Ribon no Kishi*, 1953–1956). Tezuka was very cautious to maintain the customary gender distinctions, but he allowed Princess Sapphire a greater dramatic range by saying she was a child born with both a boy and a girl soul. Furthermore, her father raised her as a boy to ensure that she could inherit his throne, which—like the emperorship of Japan—was forbidden to women. Throughout much of Tezuka's rambling fantasy, she often disguises herself as a Zorro-like hero so she can take action against the villains.

Despite this nudge to introduce more dynamic female characters, much of the real development of *shōjo manga* and its later impact on the larger manga industry would not appear for another 10 years when women started creating the manga that girls were reading. There were a few pioneers, among them Yoshiko Nishitani (b. 1943), who broke out of the stultifying designs of most early girls' manga by giving her characters more personality. The group of women who really transformed the genre, however, became known as the "Magnificent Forty-Niners" ("*Hana no nijuunyo nen gumi*"),[4] a reference to the coincidence that they all were born about the same year, in 1949. The list of names varies to some degree, but it invariably includes the luminary artist Moto Hagio (b. 1949), along with such other notables as Riyoko Ikeda (b. 1947), Yasuko Aoike (b. 1948), Toshie Kihara (b. 1948), Ryoko Yamagishi (b. 1947), Minori Kimura (b. 1949), and Yumiko Oshima (b. 1947), among others. In the early 1970s, these women began publishing works that reflected on the tumultuous transformation of Japanese society by examining new gender roles that obscured clear delineations between men and women, explored a greater range of relationships involving sexuality and intimacy, and gave the female characters a more active role in defining their goals and determining their own fates. *Shōjo manga* also expanded the literary and visual vocabulary of manga, quoting classical Japanese poetry, and employing a distinctive visual quality that broke out of the use of evenly spaced boxes and began to use the whole page with overlapping moments in panels without borders or scenes that bled all the way to the edge of the page. Unlike boys' manga (*shōnen manga*), which often renders realistic details in complex environments, *shōjo manga* depends more on evocative designs to render the characters' interior worlds.

Riyoko Ikeda popularized the notion of gender ambiguity in her *shōjo manga* about life at the court of Marie Antoinette, *The Rose of Versailles* (*Berusaiyu no Bara*, 1972–1973). The story of the youngest daughter of François de Jarjayes being raised as a boy named Oscar was a close imitation of Osamu Tezuka's *Princess Knight*, but Ikeda added greater naturalism and historical accuracy to help elevate the sentiments. *Berubara*, as it was affectionally known by its legion of fans, straddled the transformation of *shōjo manga* from stories about girls' innocence and struggles with popularity to more daring subjects concerning budding sexuality and death. The palpable escapism of *Berubara* as a David Bowie–styled glam-rock costume drama was in the end tempered by the social issues explored though the prism of the French Revolution. The manga story was adapted for the stage by the all-female Takarazuka troupe in 1974, becoming the theater company's most popular work ever and ensconcing *Berubara* as an iconic fixture of Japanese popular culture.

Moto Hagio's work was inspired by science fiction authors such as Isaac Asimov, who questioned the nature of what it meant to be human, or alien, or robot. Adding to this list, she also explored gender roles in her manga story *They Were Eleven* (*11 nin iru*),[5] where a team of cadets in a space academy of the future face a grueling field exam that not only tests their knowledge but also makes them question the very essence of who they are. This theme is picked up right at the beginning of the exam when the team members realize there is one extra person on their 10-member team and no one knows who it is or what purpose the impostor has in joining them. Her manga stories often revolve around siblings or classmates who share an uncomfortable intimacy. In the case of her story *Hanshin: Half God*,[6] a pair of twins joined at the hip unequally share vital organs so that one thrives while the other is sickly. After an operation to separate the sisters, the sickly sister is restored to health, but at the loss of her once-healthier sister. The story starts out as a contrast between beauty and ugliness and ends with the surviving sister becoming cute, but wounded from the loss of her sister's beauty.

Moto Hagio's most influential contribution to the genre of *shōjo manga* was the development of the theme of boys' love (*shōnen-ai*), where androgynous and fashionable young men develop powerful emotional bonds. The relationships were always framed in exotic distant locales enticing readers to imagine worlds of intimacy that broke all conventional bounds. This genre developed in the 1970s in response to her early popular work *The November Gymnasium* (*Juichigatsu no Gimunajiumu*, 1971), which took place in a 19th-century German boarding school. Although the genre of boys' love has since expanded to include more explicitly erotic themes (called *yaoi*) and evolved to include works that more directly appeal to gay and lesbian readers, the initial popularity with young girls came from the idealism and intimacy found in these perfect relationships and not as a vehicle to challenge heterosexual identity.

As Moto Hagio and her fellow Magnificent Forty-Niners matured, so did their manga, introducing manga intended for older women (*josei manga*) that have expanded the market and kept readers engaged in manga well into their adult lives. The long-term impact of *shōjo manga* on boys' manga was to create an opening for more active female roles and greater experimentation with page design. Also, it was instrumental in expanding the range of subjects beyond sports, fantasy, giant robots, and horror to include a whole host of new and mixed genres. Older fans of boys' manga initially resented the intrusion of cute characters into their manga in the 1980s; but before long, technology that had been anthropomorphized as giant masculine robots became gendered as young "budding" (*moe*) female characters. *Moe* characters representing cell phones, cars, military aircraft, software, and Web sites such as Wikipe-tan, a fan-created character representing Wikipedia, have all been metamorphosed by this growing fad.

The most significant driving force for growth and diversity in manga has been the rise of self-published manga, or *doujinshi*, where fans create parodies or spin-offs of well-known work but also delve into more experimental material than do the mainstream publishers. Both male and female manga artists who self-published small editions began forming clubs, or circles; these circles first came together to trade and swap on December 21, 1975, at Comiket (Comic Market) in Tokyo. Comiket was initially established by Yoshihiro Yonezawa, Harada Teruo, and Aniwa Jun while they were college students at Meiji University in response to what they saw as the lack of opportunity to publish more experimental manga after the closure of the magazine *COM* in 1972. The first Comiket had an estimated 600 attendees and has since swelled in size to an estimated 35,000 sellers and 500,000 fans attending over three days at the gatherings held twice a year at the 60-acre Tokyo Big Sight convention center. Comiket and other smaller conventions that appear every few weeks across Japan have dramatically bolstered the visibility of the *doujinshi* market. Fans of manga will often spend as much as 30 percent of their annual manga purchases on rare *doujinshi* publications. This sizable market has consistently challenged the mainstream manga publishers to experiment with more sexy and shocking stories to remain relevant against this tide of more outrageous material. The enormously successful women's *doujinshi* circle known as CLAMP, which includes Ageha (Nanase)

Ohkawa (b. 1967) and Mokona, Tsubaki Nekoi, and Satsuki Igarashi, has since 1998 become one of the leading forces in contemporary mainstream manga in both girls' and boys' magazines and has published many of the translated popular hits in the United States, among them *Magic Knight Rayearth* (1993), *Cardcaptor Sakura* (2000), *Chobits* (2002), and *xxxHolic* (2003).

With such a wide diversity of genres, mangaka have tremendous latitude to create work that defies classification. Although their work may not appeal to a wide audience, there is still an appreciative venue for the quiet and contemplative manga by Yuko Tsuno (b. 1966), whose *Swing Shell* (2000) reveals the scattered life and escapist fantasies of a girl suffering sexual abuse from her father, who appears in her bed as a giant bear. The story has a tenuous and fleeting quality with abrupt shifts in tone, which are evocative of a life that hangs precariously on "a border against a transparent sea." The story seems to have no direction or purpose, for the violence is never seen except for the sudden appearance of bandages across the girl's face, and just as her situation becomes apparent, the story suddenly comes to an end.

Amerimanga and Scanlations

Japanese animation (*anime*) had been making inroads into American markets since the 1960s; but because of the complexities of translation, Japanese manga began to appear in the United States only in the 1980s. The first translation was a heavily abridged version of Keiji Nakazawa's autobiographical story of the bombing of Hiroshima, *I Saw It* (*Hadashi no Gen,* 1982), translated and edited by Leonard Rifas and Educomics. The challenge of manga translation required not only converting the text to English but also reordering the page layout so that the right-to-left orientation of the Japanese original made sense to the left-to-right-oriented English readers. Japanese manga also used idiomatic expressions and literary references that would be wholly lost on a foreign audience and included a wide array of onomatopoeic words that had no English equivalent. The shape and character of these onomatopoeic expressions were often so prolific and tightly integrated into the composition that it was difficult for them to be removed or ignored.

It was only with the introduction of digital publication tools in the mid-1980s that this process was efficient enough to contemplate translating the long, convoluted manga stories. Marvel Comics broke into manga with a colorized version of Katsuhiro Otomo's *Akira* (first serialized in Japan from 1982 to 1990 and published in the United States from 1988 to 1995). The coloration of the pages was done by Steve Oliff and was one of the first major coloration projects done entirely by computer. The project proved popular, but it was concluded just as the U.S. comics market was imploding. A trickle of new publications of translated manga in the late 1990s continued to question just how far manga needed to be translated. Initially, it was believed that American readers would not accept black-and-white comics, or that all the Japanese-language sound effects needed to be removed or translated, or even that the panels had to be reversed to flow from left to right. In each instance, American readers—especially young girls new to comics—proved willing and adept at accepting the strange conventions of manga.

Because of the very derivative nature of manga, the strangeness faded as readers persisted in figuring out the coded visual language of peculiar expressions, of nose bleeds, of foaming mouths, and eventually were quite comfortable reading the panels backward. Once manga fans in America adopted the visual code, many began to learn to draw the manga way, creating hybrid comics called amerimanga, and for a few, the final challenge was to learn enough Japanese to translate their own. Novice translators of Japanese manga and anime have fueled a large expansion of manga available outside Japan, and like the communities of self-made manga groups (*doujinshi*), translators have banded together and on their own assembled and shared translations with each other. All this was made possible through the Internet, where people with specialized interests could find one another and share files digitally; hence, the name for a translated digital copy is a *scanlation*. These files are created and translated without the permission of the artist or publisher, so they are pirated copies that violate the copyright of the original work. Scanlation groups are, for the most part, sensitive to limiting the access of their translation to only those manga that have not been translated by the publisher. Although they may post a file on the Internet for virtually anyone to download, they will take down the file as soon as they learn that a particular title is slated for translation and publication abroad. Publishers and artists have so far been tolerant of this practice and seem to use it as a means to judge which titles may be worth developing into published translations.[7]

CHAPTER 11

Post—World War II Art Graphic Narratives

With Europe in the grips of war, New York eclipsed Paris and became a new cultural capital that embraced the avant-guarde movements of surrealism and abstract expressionism. Socialism had originally advocated for constructivist and expressionist works in the 1920s and early 1930s, but it was now openly hostile to the avant-guard and was giving way to the Soviet socialist realism promoted by Stalin. In this shifting cultural landscape, a few artists such as Ad Reinhardt (1913–1967) remained strong advocates of avant-guarde socialist art despite the diminishing idealism of the socialist movement and the growing pull of the commercial art market.

Reinhardt worked as a cartoonist and designer throughout his school years at Columbia University, where he initially studied literature in the mid-1930s. During this time, he worked as a freelance illustrator and cartoonist on a number of socialist publications. In 1943, he began work at the popular leftist-oriented daily newspaper *PM* (Picture Magazine), where he contributed hundreds of small cartoons that fit beneath short human-interest stories. Because of the small format, Reinhardt's comic style was a loose amalgam of expressive lines that forced readers to pause to make sense of what they were seeing. In his comics, Reinhardt liberally used Dada and surrealist collage techniques to cut and paste Victorian-style illustrations into his cartoon. The smallish comics were also often bordered with elaborate decorative frames in a mock self-aggrandizing manner that further called attention to the playful squiggles that haphazardly described the characters.

Unlike other artists who explored comic art, Reinhardt kept his comic work quite separate from his elegant and minimalist abstract paintings. His comics, like his critical essays on art, became means to advance his agenda of promoting abstract art. In 1946, Reinhardt contributed a series of full-page comics for the *PM* Sunday magazine on the theme of *How to Look at Modern Art*. Each comic quoted liberally from the history of art and literature to support Reinhardt's ideas about the importance of abstract art. Inside each of these elaborate comics, Reinhardt inserted a small comic of a man laughing at an abstract painting saying, "Ha ha, what does this represent?" The painting then sprouts legs and arms and a stern face to point back at the man, "What do you represent?"[1] Some of the readers of *PM* were in support of these ideas and liked how he challenged people to think about what they saw in abstract art, but many disliked the condescending tone and rejected the elitist attitude that abstract painting was somehow going to make the world a better place. Within a year, Reinhardt left *PM* and began publishing his comics in other, more art-oriented magazines like *Art News* and *Art Bulletin*; with the change in venue, the work became increasingly abstract and oriented more to art makers and patrons.

It was through his art comics that Reinhardt hoped to engage an audience in the joys of the subversive production of art. In the comic *How to Look at a Good Idea*, he shows a picture of an elderly woman in an old-fashioned bathing suit being bitten on the toe by a crab. The lady has a label attached to her that says "painting" and the crab has a label that says "pictures." In a caption, Reinhardt explains, "All you need to make a political cartoon is a picture, some labels, and some paste." Arranged to the sides of the images are some additional labels the reader can choose, thereby inviting readers to make political comics of their own. This kind of subversive and spontaneous image making follows in the tradition of Dada art collages, but it also sets the stage for a whole new direction in graphic narratives, where pictures can be subverted by emanata.

During the war, Saul Steinberg (1914–1999), a trained architect from Romania, published reams of cartoons in *The New Yorker* magazine and other popular publications while acting as a U.S. military service member in China, North Africa, and Italy. In these loosely drawn strips early in his career, Steinberg invokes the seminal ideas and ironic detachment that would undergird his work as he parodied goose-stepping Fascists and made Nazi swastikas seem like absurd toys. Steinberg was one of the very few comic artists who was able to successfully move between popular publications and the modern art world. As early as 1947, Steinberg was included in an exhibition at the Museum of Modern Art in New York, where his work hung alongside the works of leading American painters and sculptors of the day.[2]

The curator for this exhibition, Dorothy Miller, was friends with Steinberg's wife, Hedda Sterne, who was a highly regarded abstract expressionist painter. No doubt Steinberg benefited from this relationship, but times were beginning to change; as art historians and critics reevaluated the contributions of William Hogarth and Honoré Daumier, the door opened to the possibility of including comic art. Edward Alden Jewell from the *New York Times* favorably reviewed Steinberg's work in the show; but in a separate article published earlier, Howard Devree pointedly asked, "It's Funny, But is it Art."[3]

Steinberg's work was something of a mix between the social commentary and wry humor of James Thurber (1894–1961) and the visual economy and

Saul Steinberg, "The Spiral," from New World Series published in *The New Yorker*, 1964. (© The Saul Steinberg Foundation / Artists Rights Society [ARS], New York)

irony of Paul Klee (1879–1940). Steinberg's economical use of lines were not just a means to convey a gag; they were, in essence, the gag itself. His simplicity and evocative power captivated the art critic Harold Rosenberg, who wrote, "Steinberg is the Houdini of multiple meanings: the line with which he creates his labyrinth and entangles himself in is also the string that leads him out of it."[4] In Steinberg's 1964 cartoon "The Spiral" for *The New Yorker*, he has drawn a man drawing a spiral inside which he is standing. The spiral opens outward and eventually becomes a distant landscape of rocks, trees, and clouds. W. J. T. Mitchell has described this cartoon as a metapicture, that is, "a picture about itself, a picture that refers to its own making, yet one that dissolves the boundary between inside and outside, ..."[5] Steinberg is the acknowledged master of such metapictures, making a huge body of work that continually called into question conventions of language and visual representation. The narrative strategy of metapictures in comics had been in use since the time of Gustave Doré, but it began to flourish in the 1960s and became one of the dominant themes of late-20th-century comics and art about comics.

Following World War II, the modern art world was predominantly under the influence of abstract expressionism, which mixed the formal aspects of the art of Wassily Kandinsky (1966–1944) and the emotive power of the surrealists to create abstract forms and colors with almost no concrete representation of actual things and places. Abstract expressionism was by its nature opposed to the idea of narrative as it strove for more "pure" forms of abstraction that embodied spontaneous gestures rather than concrete physical forms. Although abstract expressionism avoided mimetic representation, there was a persistent interest in how a work was experienced over time. Numbered series and deliberate sequences appeared in works by Jackson Pollock (1912–1956), but these paintings steadfastly defy narrative interpretation because they limit representation to the sensation of each moment. With only abstract forms to establish the continuity from one moment to the next, the narrative exists outside of cause and effect and becomes a string of disconnected moments only describing the here and the now. Despite the general disinterest in narrative, a whole new generation of artists was emerging that had grown up with comics in newspapers, and many of them had *cut their teeth* in art by imitating the comic pages. In this new environment, it was only a matter of time before the form and character of comics would appear in their work.

Early uses of comic forms emerged in art that was sympathetic to the work of outsider artists (*Art Brut*), who created works without academic training and often were inspired by a spiritual calling or psychological torment. Outsider artists did not always hold to the same categories and boundaries as formally trained artists and often created works with a powerful sense of intuition and struggle that made their works startling and unpredictable. In 1967, Pierre Alechinsky (b. 1927) began to use his searching, bold line work to define two kinds of spaces on his canvases: one dominant, colorful frame that commanded the center of the painting and a series of other, smaller black-and-white frames that encircled the the other, suggesting successive narrative images like a newspaper comic. The splashy line forms, done with ink and a Japanese-style brush, merge and dissolve into something like a child's imitation of a comic page, which circles around without beginning or end. Playwright and dramatist Eugène Ionesco (1909–1994) wrote of Alechinsky's style, "This is a painting that is pure and impure. It may seem impure in the sense that it is narration, pure because it is the interplay of transformation."[6] By creating frames within frames, Alechinsky evokes the idea of time moving from one moment to the next, but without the concrete sense of the purpose of time's passing. Alechinski's scrawling, impulsive comic-styled creations were similar to the work of other artists, such as Arshile Gorky (1904–1948) and early Jean Dubuffet (1901–1985), who sought to find a middle way between objectively representing the world as it is seen and wholly subjective abstract expressionist work that reduced art to its essential forms.

Comics became an important touchstone for a new generation who sought to use commonplace cultural icons in the service of a new kind of radical art that attempted to subvert those icons. At the core of this use of comics was an iconoclasm that upended high-art pretentions and created works that called attention to our distracted impulses. The Situationist International, or SI, formed in 1957, was one such group of artists and writers who were largely regarded as anti-artists, rebelling against accepted conventions of beauty and form with a mix of Marxism and surrealism. The Situationists found their unique voice when they began to focus their rebellion on the idea of spectacle in modern society. In their publications, they eschewed individual works of art, authorship, and copyright and wrote manifestos critiquing the character of modern capitalist popular culture.

One important strategy for that critique was *détournement*, which was a means of deflecting or rerouting something from its original course. *Détournement* was achieved primarily by taking one known element and putting it into a new context. This strategy was already evident in the surrealist collage works of Max Ernst and others; but Situationists saw that by quoting elements, they could subvert the intended "spectacle" of popular culture and force a more critical response to accepted ideas. The strategy of *détournement* was first applied to quoting, or what was often called "plagiarizing," existing texts with incongruous other texts. Comics proved a natural media for *détournement* experiments because they could be made of disparate words and pictures that could be forced into a new union—for example, by having such a popular cultural icon as a fashion model or comic book hero spouting Marxist ideology. The Situationist René Viénet noted the potential disjunctions that can occur when pictures are given a new and unexpected voice when he argued, "In fact, the whole of commercial advertising could be subverted simply by adding speech bubbles."[7] *Détourned* comics repeated comic panels or completely did away with narrative continuity by jumping between different comic styles, drawings, and photos. The resulting chaos embodied the freedom, anarchy, and rebellion of the Situationist agenda.

Détourned comics first began to appear in the late 1950s in Situationist publications, and then later in a few imaginative, though crudely fashioned, stand-alone publications. The most memorable of the comic publications was *The Return of the Durutti Column* (*Le Retour de la Colonne Durutti*), a four-page Situationist comic by André Bertrand, paid for by absconded student funds and given away at Strasbourg University in October 1966. The comic created quite some controversy in the local papers when it surfaced, and thereafter *détourned* comics became a more prominent feature in Situationist publications.[8] Bertrand's comic is a stunning display of provocative juxtaposition, in which characters did more than mouth Marxist propaganda; they spoke something more like real dialogue. In one panel, a pair of cowboys chat.

White hat:	"What exactly are you busy with?"
Black hat:	"Reification."
White hat:	"I see; that's a very serious job with thick books and lots of papers on a big table."
Black hat:	"No, I wander around. Mostly I wander around."[9]

Here, and elsewhere in the comic, Bertrand was mocking academics for their self-important intellectual endeavors. The word "reification" in the context of Marx refers to a distortion of consciousness where abstract relationships, such as social class, are accepted as having a tangible and fixed material form. Thus, the black-hatted cowboy—a decadent symbol of American culture—blithely describes his passive acceptance of the spectacle of capitalism. *Détourned* comics were only a small part of the Situationists total literary output, but near the end of their collaboration, Situationists counted *détourned*

... C'EST L'ARGENT EN EFFET LE MOTIF DE TOUTES LES DISCORDES, DE TOUTES LES HAINES, DE TOUTES LES AMBITIONS, C'EST EN UN MOT LE CREATEUR DE LA PROPRIÉTÉ. SI L'ON N'ÉTAIT PLUS OBLIGÉ DE DONNER QUELQUE CHOSE EN ÉCHANGE DE CE QUE NOUS AVONS BESOIN POUR NOTRE EXISTENCE, L'OR PERDRAIT SA VALEUR ET PERSONNE NE CHERCHERAIT ET NE POURRAIT S'ENRICHIR PUISQUE RIEN DE CE QU'IL AMASSERAIT NE POURRAIT SERVIR À LUI PROCURER UN BIEN ÊTRE SUPÉRIEUR À CELUI DES AUTRES. DE LÀ, PLUS BESOIN DE LOIS, PLUS BESOIN DE MAITRES
LA PRÉSIDENCE PASSE ENCORE, MAIS LA TRÉSORERIE IL N'EN ÉTAIT PAS QUESTION. ILS CONVAINQUIRENT AISÉMENT UNE PASSANTE, QUE LE HASARD AVAIT MIS SUR LEUR TROTTOIR, DE PRENDRE LE RÔLE PLUS COMPROMETTANT DE TRÉSORIÈRE.
LEUR CONNAISSANCE DE LA VIE NE DEVAIT RIEN À LEUR PRÉSENCE ÉPISODIQUE DANS L'ENCEINTE DES FACULTÉS NI AUX QUELQUES DIPLOMES QU'ILS AVAIENT ACQUIS PAR LES MOYENS LES PLUS DIVERS ET LES MOINS AVOUABLES.
DE QUOI T'OCCPES TU EXACTEMENT ?
DE LA RÉIFICATION
JE VOIS, C'EST UN TRAVAIL TRÈS SÉRIEUX, AVEC DE GROS LIVRES ET BEAUCOUP DE PAPIERS SUR UNE GRANDE TABLE.
NON, JE ME PROMÈNE. PRINCIPALEMENT JE ME PROMÈNE.
MES PRINCIPES ET MES GOÛTS FIRENT MON BONHEUR DEPUIS MON ENFANCE. ILS FURENT TOUJOURS L'UNIQUE BASE DE MA CONDUITE
PEUT-ÊTRE IRAI-JE PLUS LOIN, JE SENS QUE C'EST POSSIBLE, MAIS POUR REVENIR, NON. J'AI TROP D'HORREUR POUR LES PRÉJUGÉS DES HOMMES, JE HAIS TROP LEUR CIVILISATION, LEURS VERTUS ET LEURS DIEUX
RAVACHOL JULES, DIT KOENIGSTEIN FRANÇOIS, NÉ LE 14 OCTOBRE 1854. TAILLE 1m 666; PROFESSION: TEINTURIER RELATIONS: RÉVOLUTIONNAIRES. CAUSE DE LA DÉTENTION: DESTRUCTION D'IMMEUBLES ET DÉTENTION D'ENGINS EXPLOSIFS.
L'EXCELLENCE DE CE SAVOIR THÉORIQUE NE POUVAIT ALLER SANS UNE PRATIQUE APPROPRIÉE. ILS AVAIENT, PEU À PEU SU RECONNAÎTRE CEUX AVEC QUI LA DÉTÉRIORATION DE LA MACHINE SOCIALE SERAIT UN JEU IMPITOYABLE. C'EST AINSI QUE LES POURPARLERS AVEC L'«INTERNATIONALE OCCULTE» S'ENGAGÈRENT.

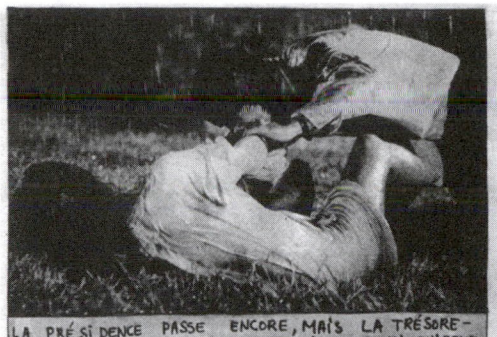

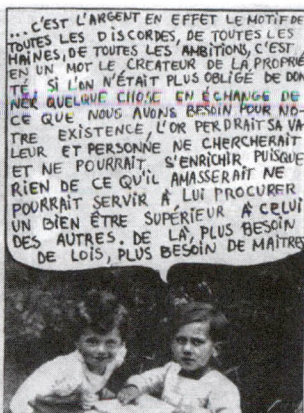

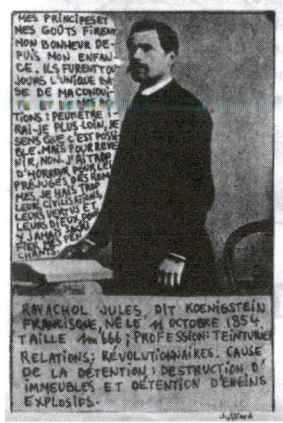

André Bertrand, *Le Retour de la colonne Durutti* (*The Return of the Durutti Column*), page 3, 1966.

comics among their few wholly original contributions to the production of revolutionary publications.[10]

Pop Art

Shortly before the Situationists, Jess Collins (1923–2004), a San Francisco–based artist, began work on a series of collages from 1953 to 1959 called *Tricky Cad* which were based on Chester Gould's *Dick Tracy* comics. Jess, as he was known professionally, cut and pasted the contents of Gould's panels and speech balloons so that they lost any sense of narrative cohesion and became surrealist dramas in the spirit of Max Ernst. In 1952, Jess had, at great expense, procured his own copy of Ernst's *A Week of Kindness* so that he could study the collage technique more closely. From Ernst's work, Jess developed what he called "Paste Ups," which were collages that densely combined visual elements that conveyed "a million paths and a million stories."[11] By utilizing contemporary comic art for his collages, Jess anticipated a major shift in art away from pure abstraction toward art that forcefully engaged modern popular culture in general and comics in particular (see, for example, box 11.1).

In Britain, comics entered the art world through the emergence of a new art movement, pop (short for "popular"), which would collapse the long-standing barriers between high and low forms of culture and bring comics into the vanguard of the elite art world. In 1956, Richard Hamilton (b. 1922) created a collage, provocatively titled, *Just what is it that makes today's homes so different, so appealing?* In this collage, Charles Atlas poses with a giant Tootsie Pop masking his groin and a burlesque dancer is ensconced on the couch with a lampshade hat, all inside a house that is replete with signs of American materialism. Hamilton, like Ernst before him, put on the walls of this house pictures that seem to expose the interior of the characters. Prominently featured on the back wall of the room, as if it were a work of art, is the actual cover of the comic book *Young Romance* #26 (1950), drawn by Jack Kirby. Here, Hamilton suggests that the psychological interior to this scene is nothing more than superficial and garish conceit, the cover for a hollow dream.

A fixed attention to the surface of the world became the hallmark of pop art, and its early and persistent interest in comic art as the quintessence of that vacuous surface can be seen in the abstract painting *Alley Oop* (1958) by Jasper Johns (b. 1930), created right on top of an actual Sunday page of the comic of the same name by Vincent T. Hamlin (1900–1993). Johns's wax encaustic layers on top of the comic reduced Hamlin's comic to a play

> **Box 11.1**   Tom Phillips's *A Humument*
>
> In 1965, inspired by William S. Borroughs's cut-ups, Tom Phillips found in a used-book shop a copy of W. H. Mallock's novel *A Human Document* (1892), which he purchased for three pence and began drawing, painting, and collaging its pages until he had created a new work derived from selected words or bits of words on each page. Given its large vocabulary and rich literary allusion, Philips has said—though it was mere happenstance that led him to Mallock's novel—he has never found a more suitable text for his artwork. Phillips has mightily transformed Mallock's mannered and occasionally anti-Semitic book into a soul-searching picture-poem of startling beauty that contains many ideas never imagined by its original author—ideas such as fascism, the atomic war, and the Bush presidency. By selecting out pieces across the linear text, a new text emerges in twisted emanatas that gives voice to Phillips's drawings, which responds to the visual shape and form of blocks of words. Phillips's altered art book *A Humument: A Treated Victorian Novel* is an ongoing work-in-progress that has seen four editions since its first complete publication in 1970. With each new edition, Phillips has rediscovered new interpretations from the pages of this book and found the means to endlessly comment on the modern world.

of colorful abstract shapes, eliminating the narrative content by obscuring the text along with the expressions and gestures of the figures. What remains is reminiscent of a comic page, but now emptied of specific purpose and context, with the intent to liberate the underlying forms by representing all comics without being any one comic in particular. The impossibility of actually reading the page or forming a coherent narrative from the shapes is Johns's way of calling attention to our preoccupation with materialism and normative meanings.

In striving to liberate comics from their common function and meaning, modern artists often exploited their unequal relationship to comics by representing the work of comic artists to a fine art audience without permission or much care about what the artists themselves were trying to communicate. This was done much the same way African art was interpreted by Picasso in his cubist paintings for the rest of Europe. For just as comic books were diversifying their content to attract older and more mature readers, pop art took and used comics as an empty sign for shallow materialism, making no reference to the ongoing passionate debates about the social dangers of comic art or any recognition of the actual efforts of comic artists to address more significant issues. The comics that were cut and pasted into Richard Hamilton's and Jasper Johns's work and later painted into the work of Andy Warhol (1928–1987), Roy Lichtenstein (1923–1997), Eduardo Paolozzi (1924–2005), Öyvind Fahlström (1928–1976), and Mel Ramos (b. 1935) was presented as an authorless, generic idea of mass culture. According to the pop artists and their handlers, if comics represented anything at all, they represented absurd pretensions and callow ambitions. Several of the artists within the pop art movement went on to defend comics as an art, but the larger art world's reaction and commentary on their work continued to emphasize the absurdity and banality of the content and paid no attention to the original comic artists. A few of the pop artists would be charged with plagiarism, but nothing would come of these accusations; instead, the contemporary art world embraced pop art, and little effort was made to identify or understand the sources of their work.

Roy Lichtenstein, who made his career sampling panels from army and romance comic pages, was an immediate and long-lived success, selling his paintings at prices that surpassed what most comic artists struggled to earn in a year. It is important to note that Lichtenstein was careful not to mechanically reproduce comic pages verbatim but actually based his paintings on drawings he made of specific panels. It was always his own drawings that he then projected onto a canvas to reproduce in paint. Changes that Lichtenstein made to the comic panels included flattening out the image by removing subtle modeling from the original and introducing stronger, more contrasting graphic elements so that hair and bodies appeared more rigid and facial expressions were more flaccid. Words in speech bubbles also tended to appear taller and thinner than the original lettering, creating a more shrill and hollow impression. The most striking change Lichtenstein made was in the exaggeration of the benday dot patterns, which he made larger and with more obvious contrasting colors so they no longer functioned to create natural halftones. These and other changes, when executed on the dramatic scale of a canvas typically six feet wide, created a garish riot of color and form—an image that demanded one's attention, yet offered little meaning in exchange. Taken from its context, the narrative content in the individual panels became a kind of nonsense riddle without an answer, calling attention to the impossibility of sense and meaning from the now awkward conventions of zip lines and emanata.

Pop art used comics as a way to quote iconic elements of distinct cartoon characters and rearrange them so they lost their narrative continuity and projected only their visual power. This strategy is similar to what Jess had employed earlier on his *Tricky Cad* series, and it was also later utilized by Öyvind Fahlström in his work based on *Krazy Kat* (1962), as well as by Gudmundur Gudmundsson (aka Erró, b. 1932), who used this approach in his vibrant and grand painting *Comicscape* (1972).

Pop artists also rearranged such distinct formal elements in comics as the graphic quality of a line describing comic-esque anatomy, so the forms are disassociated from specific comic icons and become more distinct abstract elements. This strategy is evident in the work of Elizabeth Murray (1940–2007), Sue Williams (b. 1954), Polly Apfelbaum (b. 1955), Arturo Herrera (b. 1959), and Julie Mehretu (b. 1970). Their work utilizes the striking graphic quality of cartoons to arrive at painterly abstractions that hover just outside full recognition. Another prominent direction pop art took was to employ such comic narrative forms as panel-framed images in sequences, with more subtly subversive content. This approach can be seen in the near-minimalist line work of Ida Applebroog (b. 1929), as well as Alexander Roob (b. 1956). Each of these artists is a master of understatement and of-ten employs sequences of keenly depicted mundane events to heighten the perception of stasis and nuanced change. (See also box 11.2.)

The political and cultural upheaval of the mid-1960s began to rattle the for-mal and "pure" approaches to art. One of the most dramatic departures from abstract expressionism was the late work of Philip Guston (1913–1980), who in 1970, after a long and celebrated career of pure abstraction, presented an ex-hibition of new work featuring vaguely threatening Ku Klux Klan caricatures in lurid pink. Guston's change was not a sudden and impulsive revolt; rather, it was a two-year process of artistic investigation and soul-searching, which even-tually had disastrous consequences for his relationships with artists, critics, and galleries in New York. The shock and cries of betrayal underscored how fer-vently the art world had come to loathe figuration, allegory, and narrative. Stung by the acrimony of the critics, especially *New York Times* critic Hilton Kramer, the exasperated Guston defended his new work by saying, "I got sick and tired of all that purity! I wanted to tell stories!"[12] In this new work, Guston relied on a limited number of visual elements—books, paint brushs, shoes, light bulbs, bottles painted to look like a scratchy drawing in a comic strip—repeating them over and over, recalling the hermetic character of Bud Fisher's *Mutt and Jeff* and especially George Herriman's *Krazy Kat*. One of the repeated themes was of a large head made only of one large, searching eye in profile, a small ear, a furrowed brow, and a stubbly chin.[13] The head encapsulated iden-tity like a cartoon character, presenting a shorthand sketch of a complete per-son, but it still retained the raw, undiluted intensity of a complex personality.

> **Box 11.2**   Comics and Modern Art
>
> Comic artists were not indifferent to the changing modern art world and would sometimes insert or play off cubism, surrealism, or abstract expressionism for a laugh. Often, the modern art appeared menacing or was used to convey some kind of alien presence or evil power that induced nightmares. On November 2, 1930, Frank King used the Sunday full-page comic of *Gasoline Alley* to ruminate on the anxiety produced by modern art. The strip began with Skeezix and Uncle Walt at an art museum looking at a painting that is vaguely expressionist. Walt says, "Modernism is a bit beyond me, I would hate to live in the place where that picture is painted." To this, the young Skeezix asks to explore the painting, and the two of them set off on a journey through the abstract landscape. Their comments along the way reflect their growing discomfort in this world, and they eventually get lost in the abstraction. Walt asks directions of a "native," who, frowning and looking vaguely ape-like with twisted limbs, tells them bleakly, "There is no way out." Suddenly, they do find a way back into the sunshine, and Skeezix asks, "That was an awful dream, Uncle Walt, or was it a dream?" The veiled hostility to modern art was not unique to Frank King but something indicative of the cultural void that separated comics from art.

Guston moved out of New York and settled in Woodstock, where he befriended a number of writers who would influence his new work and with whom he would collaborate on a number of projects. Philip Roth (b. 1933) was particularly close to Guston, for they shared a common taste in literature and politics and together they regaled each other with jokes about the absurd pretentions of the current president, Richard Nixon (1913–1994). Roth went on to write the political satire *Our Gang* (1971), and in the same year, Guston responded in turn with a series of 80 drawings initially entitled the *Phlebitis Series* (after a physical ailment President Nixon suffered), which was only published posthumously under the title *Poor Richard*.[14] The number of drawings and the care with which Guston arranged them to tell the story of Nixon indicates that Guston was quite serious about this work and for several years seemed intent on publishing it. His failure to do so stems in part from the polemical character of the work, but it also comes from Guston's ambivalence about facing hostile critics again. *Poor Richard* depicts a decrepit and self-loathing yet self-loving Nixon with a distended phallic nose. He is surrounded by his cohorts, Spiro Agnew and Henry Kissinger, who on occasion disguise themselves as Ku Klux Klansmen. The story focuses on the craven and self-congratulatory events in Nixon's biography, especially toward the end with his trip to China. There are also possibly some personal grudges that Guston is expressing in his damning portrait of Nixon. Guston was particularly embittered by Hilton Kramer's comments on his new work and on occasion referred to the critic as having a great "schnozola," not unlike the caricature of Nixon he created. Guston never returned to update the series even after Nixon's shameful departure from office under threat of impeachment. It must have seemed to Guston already complete enough to speak back to the arrogance and stupidity of authority.

Imagined Worlds

In Guston's cartoonlike shorthand, his paintings assumed the plastic qualities of a hermetic world sustained only by the continuity of the line. Early comic artists developed this technique as a means to fill out a scene without getting bogged down in realistic details but also as a way to expand the playful and vivid nature of the characters into their surroundings. Masters of this technique, such as Herriman with his comic strip *Krazy Kat*, were able to evoke a powerful sense of wonder at the way ordinary objects were rendered in novel ways, inviting the viewer to enter into this world and accept its peculiar pidgen language, history, and physics. Many modern artists have taken this idea of an interior world to great lengths, creating fantastically vast alternative universes which are engaged in epic struggles.

The most famous of these imagined worlds is found in the work of Henry Darger (1892–1973), whose secret passion as a self-taught artist and writer was discovered only after his death, when it was revealed he had typed more than 15,000 pages and created hundreds of mural-sized drawings concerning a story he called "In the Realms of the Unreal."[15] The title indicates that Darger was aware of the fictive nature of his story; at the same time, his obsessive-compulsive work on the project over several decades demonstrates his fervent devotion to the themes and ideas. The story followed the adventures of seven morally pure little girls, collectively named the Vivian Sisters. Darger began this work as an homage to *The Wizard of Oz*, but he soon invested it with notions of martyrdom from his devout Catholic faith and darker themes of capture, torture, and mutilation as he delved deeper into his personal demons.

In 1911, Darger was just a teenager as he began to write and illustrate his story. For this task, Darger relied on copious examples from children's readers, coloring books, and comics such as the Orphan Annie knockoff *Little Annie Roonie* by Brandon Walsh and Darrell McClure. Most of what he used for his paintings was salvaged from garbage cans in the Chicago neighborhood where he lived by himself. Over the years, he developed complex methods for manipulating the found images, including slide projection, which allowed him to reproduce, scale, and flip his favorite images again and again. Darger occasionally put collage elements into his paintings, but mostly he augmented, mixed, and manipulated found images by adding ram's horns, butterfly wings, and dragon tails to create fantastic creatures from pictures of little girls. As an amateur meteorologist, Darger also brought his keen observations in atmospheric phenomena to bear on his epic murals to create a sense of cataclysmic action that sweeps everything before it.

Darger kept his works hidden away for his own personal pleasure, so their meaning is clouded except by what we can adduce from the pictures themselves and from the copious notes he made in his journal. Given that Darger was a reclusive man, it will always remain unclear whether it was out of ignorance or some symbolic design that the girls, who often appear naked in his stories, have the genitals of young boys. Aside from the disturbing iconography, what makes these works interesting as narrative art is the excess of information that illustrates the story. Each picture is accompanied by a brief narrative description in Darger's distinctive prose style that has the clipped urgency of a newsreel or a Mary Pickford cliffhanger. The images themselves are fanciful and threatening with the kind of intimacy and intensity of a child's game and bringing to bear a powerful mix of innocence, danger, vulnerability, and courage.

Inspired by Darger, other artists have also pursued the idea of a copiously inventive parallel world, commonly as a means to evoke the self-absorption

Henry Darger, "6 Episode 3 Place not mentioned. Escape during violent storm, still fighting though persed for long distance," [*sic*]. (Henry Darger [1892–1973], ca. 1950–1970, Chicago, Collection of the American Folk Art Museum, New York. Gift of Nathan and Kiyoko Lerner. © Kiyoko Lerner. 1995.23.1A. Photographed by Gavin Ashworth, New York)

of popular culture. Among these artists are Keith Haring (1958–1990) and Takashi Murakami (b. 1963), but also Twins Seven Seven (b. 1944) and Heri Dono (b. 1960), whose work embodies the ongoing invention that occurs in the clash between traditional and modern cultures. Trenton Doyle Hancock (b. 1974) has gone the farthest to develop the cosmology of his alternative universe, a place populated with sentient "Mounds," which are lumpy black-and-white-striped heaps with childlike expressions. In the series of etchings on the "Life and Death of Number One," animals of the jungle take turns eulogizing the first Mound of them all, who was born from a masturbating ape-man in a field of flowers 50,000 years ago. Each etching employs twisting emanata that characterize the convoluted nature of the animal's speech. Hancock, like many of his contemporaries, prepares elaborate installations of his works to allow audiences to become immersed in the narrative and help envision the vast nature of this imagined world.

Art Comics

In the early 1980s, graffiti and other forms of urban street art started to appear in art galleries in New York, introducing a new generation of artists who unabashedly embraced the idiom of comics. Jean-Michel Basquiat (1960–1988) produced large paintings in an eclectic ironic style that had the defiance and inscrutable character of an outsider artist. His brief international fame prompted the recognition of other underground artists, such as Raymond Pettibon (b. 1957) who had worked in obscurity for years in the fringe culture of the Los Angeles punk rock scene doing album art and self-published works. Pettibon creates scattered installations made of drawings he has traced from pop cultural icons from the 1950s and 1960s—Gumby, atomic explosions, cowboys, and surfers—that he conjoins with quotes from literary texts that, in a Situationist manner, divert the received meaning of these icons. The messages are not resolute statements rather than equivocal questions that read more like the entry of a journal. The resulting alienated humor has a searching quality laced with irony. In a scratchy ink painting of a steam engine, the text captures the rush of a revelation that does not understand its whole significance, "I have, I confess, truly to jerk myself with violence from memories and images, stages and phases and branching arms, that catch and hold me as I pass them."[16]

Some of the more recent artists to engage in graphic narratives, among them Maria Kalman (b. 1949) and Renée French (b. 1963), do so with little or no interest in reproducing classic comic icons or mimicking formal elements of well-known comic artists; rather, they seem drawn to the idea of creatively telling stories with pictures. Kalman, who began her career as a children's book illustrator, has begun working on digital blogs for the *New York Times*, incorporating photos and gouaches of photos. Her work was collected into a memoir of eclectic observations of fleeting experiences and other ephemera that were published together in *The Principles of Uncertainty* (2007). It has the disarming intimacy of a scrapbook annotated with an artful scrawl; out of the mundane and awkward paintings, revelations about beauty and life abound.

Anke Feuchtenberger (b. 1963) was a trained fine artist in East Germany who began making narrative drawings shortly after the fall of the Berlin Wall (1989). Her work possesses the allegorical and surrealist qualities of Max Ernst, with compelling images that lie just outside full comprehension, but the actions are more clearly linked together, allowing one moment to flow into another. Feuchtenberger's stories do not share Ernst's cool intellectual mysticism; rather, the darkly rendered images convey the primal human experiences of birth and death, in a manner more akin to the expressionist work of Kathe Kollwitz (1867–1945). In *The Whore Makes Her Tracks* (2000), done in collaboration with the author Katrin de Vries, Feuchtenberger creates a poetic world where a young girl, the "whore," searches through a strangely threatening dreamscape wearing a white dress, which gets progressively soiled. The words and actions do not make sense enough to be paraphrased in any other language; but despite this abstraction, there remain subtle feelings of elation, exposure, and degradation. Feuchtenberger skillfully demonstrates a kind of daring to present the human condition in a way that profoundly challenges what has so far been deemed possible with words and pictures.

Comic Art Exhibitions

Seeing original comic pages as "art" was never the intent of most comic artists in the 20th century, and therefore few comic artists pursued having their original work put on display in museums. Some artists, Charles Schulz and Osamu Tezuka among them, even actively discouraged such ideas during their lifetimes. Aside from a few retrospectives of such supremely popular artists as Winsor McCay and Georges Remi, exhibitions of comic art in museums have occurred with relative infrequency. One of the earliest displays of comic art was an exhibition in 1963 celebrating the historic development of comics, called Cartooning from Gillray to Goldberg, which was put on by the San Francisco Art Museum. In 1967, an exhibition entitled Bande Dessinée et Figuration Narrative was displayed by Musée des Arts Décoratifs at the Louvre, which for the first time began to examine the impact of comic art on modern artists, but the exhibition focused largely on European work. This theme with a decidedly American pop art focus was picked up again in The Comic Art Show at the downtown gallery at Federal Hall of the Whitney Museum in New York in 1983. This show, curated by John Carlin, was hugely successful and, despite the smallish venue, gave ample room for original drawings by 25 early comic artists like Outcault and Dirks, shown alongside paintings and prints of such gallery artists as Jasper Johns, Andy Warhol, Stuart Davis, and Peter Saul. Carlin addressed the issue of comic appropriation by high art by redirecting the debate to say this show is "art about art."

A far more controversial show in 1990 was held at the Museum of Modern Art in New York called High and Low: Modern Art and Popular Culture, curated by Kirk Varnedoe and Adam Gopnik. The show was savaged both by art critics, who argued that comics had no place in an art museum, and by such comic critics as Art Spiegelman, who critiqued the show in the form of a comic where he wrote, "High & Low is a question of class and economics, not aesthetics."[17] Spiegelman went on to publish many articles in print and comic form that attempted to raise people's awareness of comics as an art form. Spiegelman was also instrumental in promoting the idea of a much more ambitious exhibition that would feature comic art exclusively.

Spiegelman's support instigated a very ambitious exhibition called Masters of American Comics, curated by John Carlin and Brian Walker and mounted in two large Los Angeles venues, the Hammer Museum and the Museum of Contemporary Art, and later toured to Milwaukee and New York. The 15 artists included in the exhibition were among some of the most popular of American comic artists, including not only Chester Gould's *Dick Tracy* and Charles Schulz's *Peanuts* but also some less well-known work by Lyonel Feininger and Gary Panter. The show ably demonstrated the wide range of expression found in American comic art, but there seemed no common aesthetic ideas that were identified to justify why these particular 15 artists were included but many others left out. Most awkward was the lack of women and minorities included in the exhibition; indeed, in the effort to canonize a handful of artists of comic art, the collaborative aspects of the business were lost.

In the first decade of the 21st century, the relationship between art and comics has increasingly become more symbiotic than parasitic as artists move more freely between mainstream and art publications, and comic artists are actively selling their original artwork and putting it on display in galleries and art museums. The gulf between the elite and popular arts is still very significant in many respects, but narrative is no longer a taboo area for exploration in fine art, and comics are no longer regarded as an undifferentiated entity outside of artistic concerns.

The current interest in original comic art pages for exhibition has changed the nature of the comics page, which was commonly seen more as a means to an end rather than as an object of intrinsic value. Audiences of original page art are now able to see the editing process in comics, for they can see changes the artist made to a work that lie beneath the threshold of what is visible in mechanical reproduction. There may also be blue-pencil notes that identify technical issues but also may indicate questions or alternative ideas that were not included in the final product. This unveiling of the processes has the potential to educate audiences to new ways of seeing comic art and appreciating the work behind the finished product. As artists now prepare their original artwork with an awareness that it may be put on exhibition, the nature of the comic page will undoubtedly continue to explore means to communicate within this new context.

CHAPTER 12

The Return of Graphic Narratives for Adults

In the 1950s, the comic book industry in the United States gained a modicum of cultural sanction through appearing to bow to the Comics Code. Becoming a respectable medium suitable for children had come at a considerable cost to the kinds of lurid, manic, and preposterous qualities that had made comics rebellious and seductive. Though comics were banished from the mainstream, these aspects of early comics would eventually resurface in a new growing market for the cynical youth culture. The comic book *MAD* from EC was one of the first to identify this audience, and although there were many imitators, few were able to copy its successful mix of audacity and irreverence. The next wave of comics innovation, the underground movement, would take hold a decade later when the means of comics production would become widespread and cheap enough for the young fans of *MAD* to make their own.

MAD, from Comic to Magazine

In 1956, the fallout from the Comics Code was swift and brutal for EC Comics, which had built a lucrative business in horror comics that were now all essentially banned from further distribution. Hoping to distance himself from comics while still appealing to older readers with more mature stories, William Gaines pursued a last-ditch strategy of marketing his comics as "picto-fiction." These publications had all the same cynical horror and terror of the earlier crime stories but were sold in a magazine format with high-quality illustrations to accompany larger blocks of text. The illustrations were dramatic, but they lacked the swift movement of the comics, and the lurid graphics had been toned down. Picto-fiction titles failed to sell, and all the titles were collectively shut down after a few issues; at that point, Gaines had only one publication left, a humor magazine called *MAD*. Fortunately for Gaines, this last eccentric venture proved to be a transformative publication that ushered in a whole new era of comic art.

Four years earlier, Harvey Kurtzman, an editor and contributing artist to EC's excellent war comics, had been given the assignment to develop a humor comic. *MAD* originally set out to parody EC horror and crime titles, and the first few issues relied mostly on pratfall antics with heavy-handed puns. Despite the magazine's slow initial sales, Gaines let Kurtzman continue, and in April 1953, *MAD* #4 included a parody of Superman, "Superduperman,"[1] which originated a new formula that would significantly raise the popularity of the new magazine. Instead of broadly lampooning a genre of comics, Superduperman leveled its sights on a specific and recognizable comic character. National Comics (DC), the owners of Superman, did not hesitate to threaten a suit against EC for publishing Superduperman; although Gaines was not eager to get into a legal battle, Kurtzman did some research to discover that parody was a protected form of speech and was not to be legally constrained by copyright. This legal cover established the basis for Kurtzman's new editorial direction and became the bedrock of *MAD*'s humor ever since. But as Kurtzman and Gaines both learned, the protection for parody was far from clear-cut, for it relied on a nebulous area of the copyright law called "fair use." A company that wanted to protect its brand from ridicule could hire lawyers to argue copyright infringement in an attempt to shut them down. Kurtzman later lost one such a suit to Archie Comics in 1960, but Gaines won his suit for the right to parody popular songs in 1964.

Through Wally Wood's obsessively detailed renderings, "Superduperman" had layers of visual and verbal humor, called "eyeball kicks" or what Kurtzman called "tchotchkes," that expanded on the plot and made it fun to pour over each panel to pick up on all the incidental gags.[2] Wood also injected a buxom sexiness to the work that would make any teen's eyes pop out. What made this piece particularly interesting is how the absurd story not only parodies the basic plots of most Superman heroics but also provides some winking and nodding for comics insiders, as when Superduperman does battle with Captain Marbles (a parody of Captain Marvel). Captain Marbles proves invincible to Superduperman, but Captain Marbles is eventually destroyed when Superduperman ducks and Marbles accidentally punches himself in the face. This implausible action is actually making fun of the long-running *Fawcett vs. National* legal battle over copyright infringement that was finally concluded that year. Just as the *MAD* comic implies, Captain Marvel was a serious competitor to Superman until Fawcett settled the suit out of court by "killing off" Captain Marvel.

From early on, Kurtzman was willing to let *MAD* be more outrageous and unpredictable in its format; examples include printing its cover so that it looked like an English composition book (thus making the comic easier to hide from teachers at school) or printing the cover upside down so that people reading it would look like fools. *MAD* went further with the EC tradition of letting artists use different styles. Style became the subject and the means for telling jokes, as when *MAD* parodied George McManus's comic *Bringing Up Father,* the pages alternated the lighthearted, delicate drawings with comic violence in the style of McManus with Bernard Krigstein's gritty depictions of the same comic, but now with realistic wounds where Jiggs was hit with a plate by his wife, Maggie.

Krigstein had only a few pieces in *MAD*, one of which, a satire on the movie *From Here To Eternity,*[3] had the earliest use of collage in a *MAD* comic. Krigstein used a crude black-and-white photograph for the iconic image of Burt Lancaster and Deborah Kerr kissing on the beach and had that pasted into the otherwise-color pages of the comic, highlighting the strangeness of the image and subverting its iconicity. The incongruous pasted-in image appears four times in the story, each time in the upper-left-hand corner of the page, captioned with the word "meanwhile," and each time the image reappears, the photograph appears to be progressively more inundated by the tide. Krigstein used collage to quote the movie to make fun of the way the advertising for the film was constructed around this one iconic moment.

Soon after Krigstein's use of collage, it became quite common in the pages of *MAD* to use collaged images for humor. This practice reached a peak with the "Special Art Issue" (*MAD* #22, 1955), which had on the cover Picasso's painting *Girl Before a Mirror* (1932), with the collaged face of the *MAD* artist Will Elder pasted over her reflection. The pages inside are a departure from the usual eclectic mix of comic features and instead offer an extended visual essay that tells the fictional life story of the artist, Will "Chicken-Fat" Elder, which parodies the 1949 *LIFE* magazine photo essay on Jackson Pollock.[4] Inside the "Special Art Issue," many black-and-white reproductions of well-known works of art by Picasso, Rodin, Vermeer, and Leonardo da Vinci were all claimed to have been made by Will "Chicken-Fat" Elder, along with his new "abstractions," which included electronic diagrams, weather maps, playing

---

Box 12.1 *MAD* Words

In the Polish-language section of instructions for the use of aspirin, *MAD* magazine's Harvey Kurtzman found the word "*potrzebie*." The word first appeared in a parody of a suspense thriller, "Murder the Story" (May 1954), with art by Jack Davis, where all the character dialogues were mixed up as non sequiturs. The meaning of *potrzebie*, a variant of the Polish word for "need," was incidental to Kurtzman's interest in the odd spelling and pronunciation of the word, which he pasted into all manner of stories to become one of the many long-running gags in *MAD* magazine. Other invented words Kurtzman used in *MAD* were Yiddishisms or other odd-sounding words: "axolotl," "hoohah," "furshlugginer," "ganef," "halavah," "Moxie," and "veeblefetzer." The idea of employing an invented language can also be found in the early comic strips of Dirks, Outcault, and Dorgan, and demonstrates Kurtzman's appreciation of classic comic strategies.

---

cards, anatomical drawings, and hula dancers. By blurring the boundaries between high and low art, *MAD* presaged the idea of pop art a decade later and the subversive collages of the Situationists in their comics that employed an ironic strategy they called *détournement*. (See also box 12.1.)

MAD comics, like all comics of the day, had the typical spread of inducements to buy telescoping glasses, camping gear, or Charles Atlas body-building courses. By March 1955, fake advertising began to crop up in its pages, making fun of the way advertising comics, newspapers, or upscale magazines manipulated language and distorted reality with unrealistic expectations. This new kind of humor proved very effective at maintaining the kind of unrepentant anarchy of the comic, but it was difficult to maintain as long as there were real advertisers, who were very upset by the prospect of being skewered right beside a space they were paying for. In July 1955 (*MAD* #24), the comic was transformed into a longer-format magazine, and thereafter no real advertisements appeared in the publication. Gaines *ultimately* decided there was not much money in the advertising to begin with, and he enjoyed the liberty to parody whatever he wanted without repercussions.

The decision to make *MAD* into a magazine was partially motivated by Kurtzman's ambition to work in a format that provided an opportunity for longer and higher-quality material. It also provided some legal cover for their off-beat humor because as a magazine, they were not obligated to work under the imprimatur of the Comics Code. With *MAD* magazine's continued success, Kurtzman's ambition soon got him into trouble with Gaines when he asked for a 40 percent cut of the profits. Gaines refused, and Kurtzman left *MAD* along with some of the top artists, including Wally Wood, Jack Davis, and Will Elder. Gaines replaced Kurtzman with Al Feldstein, who had been a staff artist during EC's heyday as a horror comic publisher. Feldstein was able to rebuild *MAD,* despite the sudden departure of all the senior talent, by enlisting a score of new artists who went on to define the character of *MAD* for decades to come. Kurtzman left *MAD* well before it would reach its peak popularity a decade later, but even though he was never able to recreate the success he had with *MAD,* to his credit he had been seminal in establishing the formulas that defined *MAD* magazine long into its future.

Kurtzman did go on to create several other humor magazines aiming for an elusive adult audience, including *Trump,* which lasted only two issues; followed by *Humbug* (1958); and finally—with some obvious desperation—*Help!* (1960 to 1965). The magazine *Help!* introduced a Candide-like character, Goodman Beaver, who was a perennially upbeat boy despite the brutal hostility and cynicism he found in the world. Kurtzman put Goodman Beaver into situations where he would be the straightman up against a caricature of a popular icon of the day. The most controversial of these pieces was *Goodman Beaver Goes Playboy,* where Goodman spends some time reminiscing with Archie (called Archer) and his gang, only to find they have become hedonists espousing the *Playboy* magazine worldview. Archer, who apparently sold his soul to fund his extravagant and decadent lifestyle, is seen in the end trapped in a small bottle held by a dapper-looking stranger. As the gang realizes Archer's fate, there is a sudden press for them all to get in line to sell their souls and enjoy the Playboy lifestyle. Standing behind the characters of Joghead (Jughead) and Roggie (Reggie) are a whole host of other idealistic comic characters eager to sign up and sell out. Archie Comics sued Kurtzman when the feature first appeared in 1960 over the use of their characters and eventually won the legal battle, forcing Kurtzman to pay $1,000 in damages and hand over the copyright of the episode to Archie Comics.[5]

Although the character Goodman Beaver died along with the magazine *Help!,* Kurtzman and Elder went on to create a female version of Goodman in their long-running feature in *Playboy,* "Little Annie Fanny" (1962–1988, with a brief revival in 1998). Here, Kurtzman developed what he was ultimately trying to achieve all along in lavishly published comics that were in equal measure cynical and sexy. "Little Annie Fanny" improved upon the Goodman formula because the character Annie was now the soul of virtue, but with a buxom body and a ditzy bouffant hairstyle that seduced people to reveal their essentially perverse and selfish ways. The underlying theme of the comic was not the pleasures of the decadent *Playboy* lifestyle but actually a subtle critique of of that lifestyle; characters who proclaimed lofty goals and ambitions were suddenly willing to throw everything away for a chance to have sex with Annie. Annie, for her part, seems unable to comprehend what is making everyone act so crazy and maintains her ideals despite the unraveling of any pretext that would give those virtues meaning.

The Underground Press

Key to the development of underground comics was the expansion of an alternative press that appeared in the mid-1960s in and around major urban areas with such papers as the *LA Free Press* (1964–1970), *Berkeley Barb* (1965–1980), *San Francisco Oracle* (1966–1968), *East Village Other* (1965–1972), and *Oz Magazine* (1967–1973). Each embraced the emerging hippy culture and appealed to youth audiences that were alienated from mainstream politics and culture. The visual language of this movement encouraged an anarchic style that willfully flauted middle-class virtues. Hippy culture generated a pastiche of older elements from such artists as Gustave Klimt, Aubrey Beardsley, and Alphonse Mucha, exploring sensual and hallucinogenic visual qualities without looking too deeply into their historical context. There was a broad focus on protest against the war in Vietnam and support for civil rights, but the visual style resisted easy reading. By incorporating psychedelic abstractions, the words and images were distorted in ways that suggested an occult language intended only for the initiated.

An important part of the allure of the new underground comic art was the way it emerged from a handful of homespun projects that inspired many people to try their hand at comics for the first time. Much of this revolution in self-publishing was attributable to the first photocopy machines by Xerox that became widely available in the early 1960s, allowing for substantially better-quality and less expensive printing in small quantities. Modern printing presses were only cost-effective in large quantities, and prior to the photocopy machine, the only alternative for a small-scale project was a mimeograph, which required special carbon paper and produced only a bluish print. Photocopy machines encouraged a number of small-format comics and fan magazines, or *zines*, to go into larger and broader production. The crude character of these early self-published works was part of the rebellious image that these artists cultivated, resisting the clean, formal appearance of the mainstream or "straight" press and were content to remain crude to avoid the stigma of looking as if they had "sold out."

Despite the aversion to professionalism, a number of quality artists emerged at this time. Under the pen name Foolbert Sturgeon, Frank Stack (b. 1937) first sold and distributed to friends his photocopied comic *The Adventures of Jesus* at the University of Texas at Austin in 1964. Later that year in Austin, Jack Jackson, under the pen name Jaxton, would also produce 1,000 copies of a self-published comic called *God Nose*, which quickly sold out. Both of these publications were surreptitiously printed and then compiled and bound by friends, so the profits were large and perhaps unrealistically encouraging. Stack's and Jackson's publications were also well received at the University of Texas because it was home to the alternative paper *The Texas Ranger*, which had included underground comics as early as 1962 under the editorship of Gilbert Sheldon (b. 1940), who also occasionally contributed adventures of his own superhero parody, *Wonder Wart-Hog*. Sheldon's Wonder Wart-Hog was featured in Kurtzman's *Help!* and was eventually given its own reoccurring feature in various college humor magazines and finally a stand-alone comic book in 1967. *Wonder Wart-Hog* was surpassed in popularity only by Sheldon's *Fabulous Furry Freak Brothers* (1968): Phineas Freakears, Freewheelin' Franklin, Fat Freddy, and his cat, who distilled the hippy experience into an ongoing slapstick struggle to procure food, indulge in drugs, and defy authority.

Underground comic books wildly flauted the restrictions of the Comics Code, so they had no access to such typical venues for comics as drug stores and newsstands; they were rescued from obscurity by latching onto a new marketing niche, the head shop, where hippies congregated to buy drug paraphernalia and other psychedelic music and toys. The first head shop appeared in 1966 in the Haight-Ashbury neighborhood of San Francisco, which was a nexus for the hippy culture and the location of one of the seminal moments in the awakening of underground comics in February 1968, when Robert Crumb (b. 1943) sold his self-published comic *Zap* from a baby pram he pushed down the street. *Zap* electrified the underground comics movement in part because it had a higher level of professional production than most self-published zines had at the time, but also because Crumb's drawings and characters were accessible, even nostalgic, reminders of how crazy and irreverent comics could be.

Crumb had been making comics with his older brother, Charles, since he was very young and was deeply inspired by the cynical irreverence he found in Kurtzman's *MAD*. Crumb cultivated a style that was a mix of Max Fleischer funny animals and Basil Wolverton monstrosities, creating the cute-scary formula that would become a signature characteristic of all future underground and independent comics for decades to come. His most notable creations were Mr. Natural, the opportunistic self-help guru; Fritz the Cat, the morally bankrupt playboy; and White Man, a sexually depraved middle-class businessman. In 1972, his character Fritz the Cat was made into an animated film by Ralph Bakshi that was the most successful independent film at that time, grossing more than $100 million worldwide. That year, frustrations with making the film and a penchant to kill off anything that smacked of commercial success prompted Crumb to unsentimentally kill off the character with a jilted psychopathic lover putting an ice pick into his head.[6]

As in the work of other underground comic artists, there was a strong propensity in Crumb's comics to shock and disgust, especially with sexual themes that explored disturbing fantasies involving racism, incest, and sexual violence. His comics were also often targeted by feminists for their apparent misogyny as Crumb graphically represented his obsessions with wide-hipped women whom he could dominate. Taken at face value, the images show a level of cruelty and dehumanization that is obviously disturbing, but underneath the glaring stereotypes is a tone of self-mockery and social criticism that upends readers' voyeurism by exposing the hypocrisy of their moral standards against their deep-seated desires. As Crumb's drawing has matured over the years, he has been able to give his characters greater physical presence and psychological depth. Although his later work does not have the same shocking social commentary, it has a more nuanced irony and emotional intensity. This maturity is especially evident in his ambitious comic rendition *Book of Genesis* (2009). Here, he has demonstrated far greater restraint in portraying the physical features of the biblical world and has let his commentary appear only in the drawings he has used to represent the text. (See also box 12.2.)

The Air Pirates and Disney

Five months after the death of Walt Disney in December 1966, the magazine *The Realist*, edited by Paul Krassner, published a scathing critique of Disney coupled with pornographic illustration of Disney's animated characters drawn by the one-time *MAD* comic artist Wally Wood. At first Disney ignored the copyright infringement in order to avoid giving Krassner any free publicity, but after the print was also sold as a color poster through head shops, Disney lawyers went to the extraordinary length of opening their own fake head shop in Glendale, California, in order to capture and close down the publisher.[7] This was one of the first of many legal volleys that would define the American

> **Box 12.2** *Détournement* in Alternative Comic Art
>
> During the late 1960s, translations of comics by the French Situationist Internationale (SI) began to appear in the alternative press in the United States. These comics demonstrated for British and American readers the *détournement* strategy, where polemical statements about resisting the machinations of "late capitalism" were set inside speech balloons attached to icons of popular culture. The cover of *the Berkeley Barb* in May 1969 presented a translation of a French Situationist poster, and before long, the ironic strategy was broadly disseminated to the alternative press and became a means for quickly producing captivating protest images for a whole host of causes, including the one used to shore up support for a wildcat strike of cable-car drivers in nearby San Francisco (1971). Such alternative comic artists as Bill Griffith (b. 1944), Art Spiegelman (b. 1948), Peter Kuper (b. 1958), and Robert Sikoryak (b. 1964) have used the strategy in slightly different ways. Instead of relying on collage to create the alienating discontinuity, they began mixing and matching disjointed text and art styles within their own drawings. Bill Griffith's "Situation Comedy" (in *Mondo Snarfu*, 1978) switches between different art genres from panel to panel while the dialogue maintains the mundane patter of a typical family over breakfast. Griffith has one of the longest-running alternative daily comics, *Zippy the Pinhead*, which began in the *Berkeley Barb* in 1976 and is currently distributed by King Features Syndicate. Over the years, Griffith has maintained the playful irreverence and ironic association that lies at the heart of the *détournement* strategy.

counterculture for decades to come. As a high-profile company that had actively voiced a very conservative cultural and political agenda, Disney was a ripe target for such an attack. One of the crusaders who took up the anti-Disney cause was Dan O'Neill (b. 1942), who at age 21 had been one of the youngest artists ever to have a syndicated comic strip, *Odd Bodkins* (1964–1970).

O'Neill's work in *Odd Bodkins* had brought some of the underground rebelliousness to the otherwise conservative world of syndicated comics. In the comic strip's brief run, it introduced a sketchy, surreal whimsy with an eclectic cast of characters: Hugh, Fred the Bird, $5 Bill O'Brady (Abraham Lincoln), a "Werechicken," John Barleycorn, and the Bat-winged Hamburger Snatcher. To the dismay of the Hearst Syndicate, the comic strip also from time to time included Disney's Mickey Mouse and dog Pluto as minions of hell. Disney complained of this abuse of its copyright, and the syndicate eventually dropped the strip in 1970 after O'Neill repeatedly failed to maintain the syndicate standards.

With no legal strategy or money, O'Neill was determined to directly target Disney, one of the largest media corporations in the world that had by 1970s already fought more than 1,700 copyright cases worldwide. O'Neill surrounded himself with a number of young comic artists—Bobby London, Ted Richards, Shary Flenniken, and Gary Hallgren—who each had an individual interest in comic artists of the past and set to work publishing a comic book called the *Air Pirates Funnies* (July 1971). O'Neill convinced the group to take on Disney as a battle for free speech and parodist's rights. Disney brought a suit against all the artists (except Flenniken), which evolved into a long-running legal battle that *Air Pirates* lost at the district court level in 1972. *Air Pirates* lost again at the Ninth Circuit Court of Appeals in 1978 and were then turned away from appeal by the Supreme Court in 1979. Throughout it all, O'Neill remained defiant and refused to pay the fines levied against him. Furthermore, he continued to draw Disney parodies, which he sold at comic conventions under his new banner, "The Mouse Liberation Front." He claimed the proceeds of those sales were intended to pay his court costs and fines, but they also worked to increase the visibility of his cause. In 1980, faced with a growing public relations disaster, Disney dropped the $200,000 fines in an agreement with O'Neill that he would cease drawing and selling Disney characters. O'Neill firmly believed he had won the case because he had avoided jail time, but the unfortunate truth of the matter, as the legal scholar Edward Samuels concluded based on the legal precedents that were established in the case, is otherwise. Samuels said, "They set parody back twenty years." Still, Samuels concurred with the ruling, saying, "They made damn good comics, and reading them gave you a thrill of being a co-conspirator; but did they go too far, yeah."[8]

Bande Dessinée Albums for Adults

Following World War II, the francophone press consolidated its lead in Europe by producing some of the highest-quality and most widely circulated comics (*bande dessinée*, or BD) in the world. The pattern for publication was similar to what emerged later in Japan, where brief episodes were first circulated in the Belgian magazines *Spirou* (1938–present) and *Tintin*

(1946–1988) and in the French *Pilote* (1959–1989) and later republished in 46-page hardbound books called albums. The significant difference between the francophone and Japanese publications was that French and Belgian publishers were willing to take up to a whole year to create 46 pages, whereas most manga artists by the 1960s were producing that many pages every month. The BD albums featured a complete story arc with beautifully rendered scenes in rich and varied colors printed on high-quality paper. They were designed to be read over and over, with the result that the most popular stories of *Tintin* and *Asterix* have each sold hundreds of millions of copies.

In a supplement to the Belgian newspaper *Le Vingtième Siècle*, Georges Remi (1907–1983), under the pen name Hergé, began the adventures of a boy reporter, Tintin (January 10, 1929). Although Tintin never demonstrated much of a work ethic toward his profession as a reporter, his character was unimpeachable and his loyalty and dedication to friends was unsurpassed. This Boy Scout optimism in the face of peril was the reoccurring theme of each adventure, but it was the exceptional pacing of the drama, the exciting turns of fate, and the touches of slapstick humor that have inspired a legion of devoted followers in Europe and elsewhere across the globe. The 23 Tintin books have sold more than 200 million copies in 40 different languages, making Tintin one of the most widely read comics in the 20th century.

The signature style Hergé became renowned for was called *ligne claire* (French for "clear line"), where every line of the drawing was given exceptional clarity with a minimum of shadow. Before creating Tintin, Remi worked as a graphic designer and illustrator. His work was heavily influenced by the cool geometry of art deco; this gave his comic art an economy, clarity, and precision that was especially effective in the researched and elaborately rendered backdrops to the Tintin adventures. The series was appealing in its boyish obsession over the detailing of the cars, trains, boats, airplanes, and rocket ships. Tintin and his dog, Snowy, had a more elemental design, with mere dots for eyes, which made them stand out against exotic locales that ranged from the surface of the Moon (*Destination Moon*, 1950–1953, and *Explorers on the Moon,* 1950–1954) to remote Himalayan mountains (*Tintin in Tibet*, 1960). This masking technique, where the main characters appear more cartoonish than their environment, has proven to be very effective in many adventure comics in Europe and Japan, but it is seldom seen in the United States, where characters and backgrounds tend to have a more unified character and style.

During World War II in Nazi-occupied Belgium, Tintin was published in a right-wing magazine, and Remi neither endorsed nor condemned the pro-Nazi propaganda. His disturbing neutrality at this time of crisis has compromised the otherwise glowing legacy of Remi and his virtuous boy hero. The early work also contained some crude caricatures of Russians, Africans, and Jews. Many of these renditions would later be edited out as Remi's style and content became more developed, and his work began to be published and translated outside of French-speaking Europe. Today, Tintin represents a model European citizen; with his past errors smoothed over, he acts in the world with circumscribed goals and ambitions. He is, in short, as an adventure hero with "rationalized impotence."[9]

As the editor and lead writer of *Pilote*, René Goscinny (1926–1977) was one of the key talents who helped shape the direction of the magazine by contributing his own best-selling story, *Asterix*, with artwork by Albert Uderzo (b. 1927), and by helping to nurture many new talents, including Jean Giraud (b. 1938), Marcel Gotlib (b. 1934), Claire Bretécher (b. 1940), and Philippe Druillet (1944). During the 1960s, with more secure financial backing under George Dargaud (1911–1990), *Pilote* emerged as the leading BD magazine in Europe and continued to expanded its readership with more mature stories that moved away from slapstick farces and into more ironic and rebellious stories.

The shift was partially inspired by *MAD* magazine and later the American underground comics but also by a sharp rise in political activism in Europe, which reached a breaking point in the Paris riots of May 1968. The riots were a watershed event for left-wing radicals who channeled the dissatisfaction of a broad swath of society. Inspiring some of the ideology of this moment were the Situationists, who, as noted earlier, found ways to articulate this dissatisfaction with such rebellious visual strategies as *détournement*. As editor at *Pilote*, Goscinny was at first open to more adult-themed comics but soon found himself struggling with several artists as he attempted to rein in their work. Fed up with Goscinny's editorship, the artists Bretécher, Gotlib, and Nikita Mandryka (b. 1940) left and created their more adult-oriented BD magazine *L'Echo des Savannes* in 1969.

From the late 1960s and throughout the 1970s, adult-themed BD magazines grew in stature and sophistication, especially as artists in other European countries—Hugo Pratt (1927–1995) and Guido Crepax (1933–2003) in Italy, for example—began to introduce works that were comparable to a novel for their narrative sophistication and character development. Pratt was an early leader in this with his publication of *Ballad of the Salt Sea*

(*Una ballata del mare salato*, 1967), featuring the independent adventurer Corto Maltese battling Pacific island pirates during World War I. *Ballad of the Salt Sea* was compiled into a book only nine years later in 1976, so much of its early innovation was not as significant an influence until much later. Crepax, on the other hand, was widely known for his erotic and psychedelic style that employed fragmented panels that lingered in extreme close-up over the anatomical details of his slim protagonist Valentina. These and other works from this time decisively drove out the notion that comics were a medium only for children. Also, the long-standing quality of most BD albums had helped to achieve some legitimacy and wider cultural recognition for their work.

The adult-themed BD magazine *Metal Hurlant* (*Screaming Metal*, 1975–1987) had a lasting international impact. Published by Philippe Druillet, Jean Giraud, and Jean-Pierre Dionnet (b. 1947), the magazine delved deep into science fiction and fantasy with a heavy dose of Crepax-inspired eroticism. Giraud was one of the more accomplished artists who had begun his career at *Pilote* with a gritty cowboy Western, *Lieutenant Blueberry*, and who worked under the pen name Moebius to experiment with lavishly detailed fantasy worlds in the spirit of Frank Herbert's science fiction novel *Dune* (1965). In his most memorable work for *Metal Hurlant*, Giraud created four short BD stories without any dialogue called *Arzach*, which involved an ancient and futuristic warrior who rode a pterodactyl-like creature. *Metal Hurlant* was soon picked up by *National Lampoon* publisher Leonard Mogel and translated and republished in the United States as *Heavy Metal* starting in April 1977. This publication was not the first opportunity for an American audience to see adult-themed comics from Europe, for Jean-Claude Forest's *Barbarella* was translated in the literary journal *The Evergreen Review* in 1967, but *Heavy Metal* was the first time it was possible to make a direct comparison with American mainstream comics. *Heavy Metal* was impressive not only for its higher-quality production but also in its greater range of styles by artists who were promoted by name in the publication.

Funny Animals and Creator's Rights

As American mainstream comics continued to slide into irrelevance in the mid-1970s, Marvel Comics suddenly achieved something wholly unexpected. In the middle of a sword-and-sorcery adventure, the hero, Korrek, lamented his fate: "At this point I welcome death. What else is there—for one whose life has become an absurdity," and at that moment a cigar-chomping duck in a blue coat and pork-pie hat appeared out of nowhere with the pithy rejoinder, "Aw, clam up, bud! You don't even know the meaning of the word! Finding yourself in a world of talking hairless apes—now that's absurdity!"[10] The duck tagged along in the adventure for a short while until he accidentally tripped and fell into an endless void. Stephen "Steve" Gerber (1947–2008) was writer for a few Marvel Comics titles when he came up with the incongruous plot twist of putting a Carl Barks–styled animal character into an adventure comic. Aside from providing a little comic relief, Gerber seemed to have no great plans for the character, since he did not even bother to give the duck a name, but fans soon clamored for more. A few years later in 1976, graced with the name Howard, the duck was given his own comic, set in Cleveland, Ohio, where he was "trapped in a world he never made."[11] The camp and social satire of Gerber's thinly disguised caricatures of Anita Bryant and the Rev. Sun Myung Moon proved hugely popular and was soon spun off into a daily newspaper strip (1978–1979) and a radio program. As *Howard the Duck* grew in popularity, Gerber tried to negotiate with Marvel over the ownership of the character, but Marvel was obstinate, citing a long history where creators had no rights over the characters they created while working under contract. Gerber was fired from the company in 1978 for supposedly unrelated matters, and he later filed suit against Marvel, which was settled out of court for an undisclosed sum in 1981. Without Gerber writing the stories, the comic faded in popularity and was dropped in 1979.

In December 1977, Dave Sim began work on his own self-published funny-animal adventure series, *Cerebus the Aardvark*, that ran for an unprecedented 300 monthly issues, the last appearing in March 2004. At its peak circulation of 36,000 copies, it defied all bounds of what was then thought possible with black-and-white self-published comics. The critical acclaim and success of this independent venture spawned many subsequent funny-animal-styled adventures, but Sim's *Cerebus* was superseded in popularity by only one other, *Teenage Mutant Ninja Turtles* (May 1984) by Kevin Eastman (b. 1962) and Peter Laird (b. 1954). Unlike Steve Gerber, Sim, Eastman, and Laird were able to maintain artistic control over their creations and successfully push back against the dominant position of publishers and distributors. Sim, Eastman, and Laird became strong advocates of creator's rights and worked with a few other comic artists to develop what they first called a "Creative Manifesto" to define their objectives. Hoping to solidify their gains and establish a firmer set of business principles, 18 comic artists[12] came together in Northampton, Massachusetts, in 1988, to discuss a Creator's Bill of Rights. Scott McCloud had penned the first draft, which began with a preamble: "For the survival and health of comics, we recognize that no single system of commerce and no single type of agreement between creator and publisher can or should be instituted. However, the rights and dignity of creators everywhere are equally vital."

The rest of the text outlined in broad terms the rights of comic creators to "full ownership of what they create" and from that premise established that creators should have "approval" over reproduction, distribution, and promotion. Although the draft was recognized by the participants as lofty and idealistic, it was intended to establish that when creators negotiate with publishers, they are negotiating on the basis of these given rights. Publishers did not comment publicly on the document, and it is unclear what precedent it set for future negotiations. It is a clear sign that some progress on these issues has been made when some of the seemingly radical ideas at the time—"the right to prompt and complete return of our artwork in its original condition," for example—have since become the standard practice in publishing.

The long-standing publisher-dictated policies by Marvel and DC were put in check by the rise of Image Comics in 1992. Many leading artists and writers abruptly left Marvel Comics the year before when their demands for more equitable benefits and royalties from merchandising were not met. Image Comics was founded by Todd McFarlane, Jim Lee, Rob Liefeld, Marc Silvestri, Erik Larsen, Jim Valentino, and Whilce Portacio on the principles of creator's rights. With the initial administrative, publishing, and distribution help of the independent comic book publisher Malibu, Image Comics owned no creative properties it published, but it facilitated artist studios publishing their own work. The star power of the creators involved in Image Comics and the invention of the popular *Spawn* series by McFarlane allowed the company to quickly snap up 10 percent of the market and in a few years establish its own publishing and distribution systems independent of Malibu. The ongoing challenge to Image and many other independent comic book publishers has been maintaining the demanding schedules of regular monthly comic production without strict editorial oversight.

Autobiographical Comics

Last Gasp Comics in Berkeley, California, published a number of sensational and voyeuristic comics that explored violent alternative fashions as seen in the *Checkered Demon* comics by S. Clay Wilson (b. 1941) and *Tales from the Leather Nun* (1973) by Dave Sheridan (1944–1982). These disturbing comics set a benchmark for perversity that has seldom been surpassed and have carved out a territory that has defined many of the heterosexual underground comics to the present day. Although homoerotic content was exploited for its shock value, it was not until women comic artists began making underground comics that homosexual themes were explored with any conviction or understanding. Lee Marrs (b. 1945) was one of the early women comics creators who demonstrated that there was real drama and fun to be found in believable gay relationships. Marrs worked on the first feminist comic, *It Ain't Me Babe* (1970), and was a part of the collective that went on to publish *Wimmen's Comix* (1972–1992), both of which were distributed through Last Gasp. *Wimmen's Comix* often parodied the fantasies set out in the 1950s romance comics, but it also had a penchant for generating honest autobiographical comics that gave real depth to women's sexual experiences and desires. Other women who participated in this publication, among them Trina Robbins (b. 1938), Aline Kominsky (b. 1945), and Roberta Gregory (b. 1953), went on not only to redefine the way women were represented in comics but also to challenge the male-dominated production of comics.

Last Gasp publisher Ron Turner agreed to pay Justin Green's rent and grocery money so long as he worked to finish his comic, *Binky Brown Meets the Holy Virgin Mary* (1972). Green was suffering a serious neurosis complicated by the animosity and guilt he felt from renouncing his Catholic upbringing. The resulting comic is a tortuous and funny story about how he learned to gain control over "rays" that shone out from every member of his body. Green uses the comic medium to diagram his obsessions, dreams, and fantasies; through his careful rendering of these situations, the reader begins to understand and even laugh at the pain, confusion, and eventual catharsis that Green experienced. Binky Brown reappeared in a number of later comics that inspired other underground comic artists to experiment with the idea of autobiographical comics.

Harvey Pekar (1939–2010) was an amateur music critic and file clerk at the Veterans Administration in Cleveland when he began framing his everyday experiences into comics. Robert Crumb, a long-time friend of Harvey's, drew up the comics and helped him self-publish the first *American Splendor* (1976). Appearing at infrequent intervals and drawn by a whole host of underground comic artists, Pekar's *American Splendor* has slowly gained a cult following at comic conventions, and he has since become something of a minor celebrity. The style and skill of each story varies depending on the artist involved, but Pekar is the master of understatement and has never wallowed in cheap sentiment, although he has enjoyed projecting the image of a working-class intellectual.

RAW Magazine and the Rise of Alternative Comics

Just prior to the publication of *Heavy Metal*, Art Spiegelman and Bill Griffith had worked together to edit a larger-format quality comic magazine, *Arcade: The Comics Revue* (1975–1976), in order to promote more experimental adult–themed comics. *Arcade* struggled to find an audience and lasted only seven issues. It was not until Spiegelman began work on *RAW* (1980) with his companion and art editor Françoise Mouly (b. 1955) that he was able to create an impressive venue for adult–themed experimental comics. The original format was 11 × 17 inches in order to make itself comparable in scale to Andy Warhol's art magazine, *Interview*. At its heart, *RAW* was Spiegelman's homage to Kurtzman's *MAD* with its all-capital three-letter name and similarly cheeky bylines, "The Graphix Magazine That Overestimates the Taste of the American Public." It included not only many of the leading comic artists of the 1960s underground but also a wide swath of experimental European comic artists as well as graphic narratives from Japan by Yoshiharu Tsuge and from the Democratic Republic of the Congo by Cheri Samba.

RAW introduced a new generation of experimental comic artists in a wide array of styles: from the scratchy and expressive punk rock–styled comic *Jimbo* by Gary Panter (b. 1950), to the delicate ink washes found in Ben Katchor's (b. 1951) *Julius Knipl Real Estate Photographer*, which delved into the sentimental attachments people have to the ephemera of urban life. Several of the next-generation comic artists had much higher-quality work, and like the *Air Pirates'* artists who parodied Disney, demonstrated a deep appreciation for classic comic art styles. Notable among them was Charles Burns (b. 1955), who created film noir–inspired surreal horror stories drenched in heavy black in the manner of Chester Gould's *Dick Tracy*, and Chris Ware (b. 1967), who distilled the classic elements of comic art into an exquisite geometry.

Anchoring *RAW* was Spiegelman's own serialized comic, *Maus I & II* (1980–1991). Nowhere has the power of autobiographical comics been better demonstrated than in Spiegelman's *Maus*. It belongs to a large body of literature known as a "survivor's tale," for it chronicles the life of Spiegelman's father and mother as they narrowly escaped death during the Holocaust. *Maus* is original in that it embodies the funny-animal tradition of comics, where the Jews are represented as mice, Germans as cats, Poles as pigs, Americans as dogs, French as frogs, and so on. Although even the premise of making a comic about the Holocaust is shocking—the words "Holocaust" and "comic" seem at best oxymoronic and at worst a gross parody of the magnitude of the events—here

Spiegelman found a way through the story that is at once disarming for its immediacy, and richly evocative of the terrors and hardships, but also indicative of the complex moral landscape. He accomplishes this not by attempting to redeem the premise that people are animals (as George Orwell did with his novel *Animal Farm*) but by questioning it. Almost two centuries earlier, J. J. Grandville created his human-animal caricatures with a self-evident power by playing on the cultural proclivities of the time and suggesting that his irrational mix-ups were ordinary and natural. Spiegelman, by contrast, repeatedly calls attention to the artificial idea that people have become animals by convention, or by choice, or under duress, and is able to employ simple visual cues, as when the characters put on masks of the other animals when they are in disguise. The conventions move us away from directly seeing the real complexity of the actual history. By doing this, they give the reader the job of interpreting the actions as they move the story to a realm where we can contemplate the possibility of the events without losing sight of the distance they have to the real history. Although *Maus* does not attempt to become "the" defining narrative of the Holocaust, it very clearly and evocatively conveys the power of the experiences in a manner that makes those experiences no longer horrific beyond imagining.

In 1992, *Maus* was awarded a Pulitzer Prize in a special category because the Pulitzer board members had found the work "hard to classify."[13] Just as *Maus* did not sit easily in any of the existing 21 categories for a Pulitzer Prize, it also was unclear where it belonged in bookstores and libraries, for it seemed out of place in history or even biography, and especially in the humor section, where the other comic titles were kept. The publisher, Pantheon, promoted the book as a "graphic novel." Yet, though Spiegelman acknowledged that *Maus* had novelistic qualities, he was ambivalent about describing all long-format comics as graphic novels because the term seemed more an effort to validate the form than to actually describe the contents of the work.[14]

The problem stemmed from the fact that the term "comic book" was already in use for material that was less substantial than a magazine, so there was no accepted term for describing comics when they were actually compiled into book form. This issue had been around for some time: a number of long-format comics from after World War II had called themselves variously a picture novel, novel in pictures, illustrated novel, comic novel, graphic album, and graphic story. Although not the first to employ the term, Will Eisner gave the term "graphic novel" greater circulation and stature with his 1978 collection of four stories on urban Jewish life in the 1930s entitled *A Contract with God and Other Tenement Stories: A Graphic Novel.* The success of *Maus* along with the compilations of serialized stories by Frank Miller (*Dark Knight*) and Alan Moore (*Watchmen*) suggested that the new category of the graphic novel would soon expand to include many new works, but there were few immediate successors, and it would take more than a decade before any such work could match the wide circulation and critical acceptance of *Maus*.

Autobiography detailing an artist's difficult childhood and budding sexuality has become one of the common genres within graphic novels. Chester Brown's poignant memories of his childhood are distilled in shaky frames that are loosely scattered on the pages of his comics *The Playboy* (1992) and *I Never Liked You* (1994), published by Drawn and Quarterly. Artful explorations of personal struggles also include Craig Thompson's *Blankets* (2003), David Beauchard's *Epileptic* (2005), Alison Bechdel's *Fun Home* (2006), and Marjane Satrapi's *Persepolis* (2007). *Persepolis* returned to something closer to Spiegelman's *Maus* by describing the social unrest surrounding the Shiite Islamic Revolution in Iran. Satrapi couples this compelling story with her own rebellions as a child and young adult.

Nonfiction Comics

Comic artist Eduardo del Rio (b. 1934), under the pen name Rius, inserted his own caricatures into collaged bits of wood engravings, maps, and distorted photocopies to create *Cuba for Beginners* (*Cuba para principantes*, 1969) in honor of the 10th anniversary of Fidel Castro's rise to power. The comic employed the irreverent and iconoclastic style of Situationist *détournement*; in this instance, the icon being *détourned* was the American version of its history with Cuba leading up to the Cuban Revolution. Rius's comic reads like an extended editorial cartoon conveyed in a vivid and distilled fashion, where he argues that the small island nation of Cuba was the victim of U.S. belligerence. Rius's playful lines shifted the tenor of the story to emphasize the positive accomplishments of the revolution and subdued some of the more serious aspects of the story, with the result that the Cuban Missile Crisis (1962) appeared like a petty squabble on a school playground. Once translated, the comic proved widely popular on college campuses and inspired other histories to be rewritten in the comic format. Rius went on to create *Marx for Beginners* (1977), and the publisher Pantheon picked up this title and developed a whole series of books in this style. The first few titles in this series on capitalism and Darwin were illustrated by the British artist Borin van Loon, and they all have remained in print for over two decades.

Inspired by Rius, Larry Gonick (b. 1946) a graduate student in mathematics at Harvard, created a cartoon history of the American Revolution serialized in the *Boston Globe* (*Yankee Almanac*, 1977–1978) and a comic book about tax reform (*Blood from a Stone*, 1977). Later that same year, with the help of Gilbert Sheldon, Gonick began publishing a series of 48-page comic books covering the whole history of the universe. Gonick had these compiled and published together as a book in 1990; he then went on to publish a number of cartoon guides to subjects in science and mathematics, finally returning in 2009 to complete the cartoon history of the universe that in its entirety consists of more than 1,500 comic pages in five volumes. Unlike Rius, Gonick does not use collaged elements to quote period elements; rather, he creates a continuous cartoon world that includes vividly drawn characters along with exhaustively researched maps, charts, and diagrams that all have the drama and fun of a comic by Walt Kelly. Gonick does employ Rius's ironic humor by exposing the foibles and failings of historical figures, but Gonick is far more nuanced in his approach. While discussing the history of Islam, for example, Gonick is critical of its violent past steeped in anti-Semitism and "holy war" (*jihad*), but he refrains from representing Muhammad as a person. In this manner, he keeps a respectful distance to the long-standing Muslim prohibition against representing the Prophet, all the while maintaining his ongoing critical commentary on human hypocrisy and cruelty.

With the support of Eastman and Laird and their newly formed Tundra Press, the independent comic artist Scott McCloud produced his widely influential *Understanding Comics* (1993) on the history and perception of comic art. As one of the first comics to attempt to explain how comics work, it effectively puts forth its main argument that any topic can be made into a comic. McCloud's own comic avatar, a checker-suited version of himself wearing a shirt with lightning emblazoned on the front, acts as our guide to comic art, conveniently morphing into ready examples of his ideas. *Understanding Comics* follows in the style of Rius in the way McCloud quotes a huge array of styles and artwork within his comic, commenting on the variety of expressive forms that different artists have achieved in comics.

Since the debut of *Understanding Comics*, McCloud has been faulted for his grandiose theories of art and his sweeping generalizations. Early on, he uses the word "comics" to indiscriminately describe neolithic cave art, ancient Egyptian hieroglyphs, and Mixtec codices when what he is really describing is a much more limited form of graphic narrative art that appears only after Rodolphe Töpffer in the 19th century. In this respect, *Understanding Comics*

Larry Gonick, *The Cartoon History of the Universe*, Book 1, *From the Big Bang to Alexander the Great*, 1997. (© Larry Gonick. All rights reserved.)

is more akin to a manifesto than a history or an essay on theory, since McCloud's stated objective is to upend old associations of the word "comics" as badly drawn and poorly composed pulp fiction and inspire artists and audiences to be open to new communicative possibilities in comics.

Following McCloud's success with *Understanding Comics*, the genre of nonfiction comics has expanded significantly. Moving away from the polemical strategies of Rius, there have appeared several ambitious biographies of famous events and people, but this time with far less subjective-narrator intrusion. Chester Brown's *Louis Riel: A Comic Strip Biography* (1999) demonstrates remarkable restraint even while exploiting the comic medium to communicate the story through caricature and the innovative use of emanata. The extent to which nonfiction comics have become an accepted genre can be seen in *The 9/11 Report: A Graphic Adaptation* (2006) by Sid Jacobson and Ernie Colón. At the beginning of the book, the complex events of the day are spread out along a continuous timeline allowing each of the individual hijackings to be seen simultaneously in relation to each other. The powerful effect of this organization is the unmistakable perception of a total breakdown in communication.

New vigor can be seen in the substantially longer and higher-quality graphic novels and manga that have begun to appear in large numbers in bookstores. In the first decade of the 21st century, these types of publications have expanded faster than any other area in publishing. Unlike earlier growth, this time the expansion is not attributable to collectors or a devoted fan base; rather, graphic novels and manga have found a significant number of new readers who have demonstrated an interest for a broad array of genres. The growing number of literary awards that graphic novels have won in competition against other books[15] coupled with an increasing number of book reviews that no longer marvel at the idea that a comic can tell significant stories has demonstrated there is an audience that is willing to give serious critical evaluation to graphic novels. Although the advance of graphic novels has never before seemed more assured, it comes at a time when publishing itself is undergoing an unprecedented transformation with the advent of digital books distributed over the Internet. How graphic novels will be defined by the changes brought on by digital media is not yet known, but what is certain is that they will now have to compete inside an ever wider, deeper, and swifter stream of popular entertainment.

Chapter 13

Digital Comics

The growth of personal computers linked together by means of the Internet has, over the past two decades, instigated a vast systemic change in the way information and entertainment are created and distributed. The full impact of the digital media revolution on publishing in general and comics in particular has yet to fully materialize, but its contours are becoming more evident as the means of digital creation, distribution, and sales have become standardized and accepted as a viable alternative to print media. Digital publications viewed on computers, cell phones, or other digital readers may never wholly supplant print publications, but the dramatic growth of digital publishing from $1.6 million in 2002 to $37.5 million in 2008 suggests that the comics industry will need to find a way to exist predominantly in digital form if it has any hope of remaining a viable presence in the 21st century.

Digital Tools

Peter Gillis wrote the digitally generated comic *Shatter* in 1985 and had it laboriously illustrated on a first-generation Apple Macintosh computer by Mike Saenz.[1] The effort pushed the boundaries of what was deemed possible at the time, but ultimately the result proved difficult to read, the figurative drawing awkward with very evident pixilation of the modeling, and little impact aside from its novelty. Five years later, with significantly improved technology, DC Comics went to considerable effort to develop Pepe Moreno's stand-alone story *Batman: Digital Justice*, which employed computer-generated 3-D modeling techniques to expand backgrounds and create more complex environments. Like *Shatter, Digital Justice* was valued more for the sake of novelty, and it would be several more years before any sustained use of digital tools made their way into comic production. The experimental graphic novel *Mr. Punch* (1995) by Neil Gaiman and Dave McKean was more successful in using technology to produce images that did not obviously appear digitally constructed due to higher resolution graphics and a more seamless integration of drawing and photography. Even when successful, the chief problem with many early digital experiments was that they increased the visual complexity of the comic at the expense of the quality of the reading experience.

Digital tools for enhancing comics have been in use since 1992, when publishers began switching to digitally applied color and digital lettering. Digital lettering was initially explored by Richard Starkings, who went on to become the industry leader in developing fonts that mimicked the style of well-known comic letterers. Before the use of digital technology, both coloring and lettering were time consuming and done by contracted labor near the very end of the production when deadlines were tight and mistakes difficult to correct. Coloring and lettering were also at the bottom rung of the artistic hierarchy of comics production in which writers were at the top, followed by pencilers and inkers, so digital production did not substantially change the appearance of comics right away. Over time, digital technology most noticeably changed the character of comics by adding a wider range of color in finer gradations, thereby allowing artists to model forms through color rather than through cross-hatching in black. The largest significant improvement with digital production of comics has been the way it is now possible to digitally move and adjust speech bubbles. This capability has significantly enhanced the reading quality of digital comics and become extremely useful in translating comics because the size of the emanata can be changed to suit the needs of the language. Such flexibility has greatly reduced the cost of producing translations and dramatically expanded the diversity of titles in different languages.

Digitized Comics

Digital versions of print comics began to appear on CD-ROM with *The Complete Maus* published by the multimedia company Voyager in 1994. *The Compete Maus* included, along with the original pages, links to interviews, sound recordings, and video clips that offered up some of Spiegelman's process and original research in making the graphic novel. Evident in this multimedia package were some of the persistent failings of early digital comics. The landscape orientation and resolution of most computer screens prohibits reading a full page or two pages at a time. Reading the work involves a great deal of scrolling down each page to catch the last portion off the screen. Early computer-processing power also placed significant limits on the speed with which an image could be loaded and would often stall the reading speed with pauses between each page turn. Some of the problems of adapting comics to the technology of CD-ROMs would diminish as the technology improved over the years, but key issues remained about how to take this technology beyond translating existing published works to creating works specifically designed to exploit the possibilities of the digital media.

Eagle One Media has since 2001 published a number of digital comics on CD-ROM that employed motion graphics, spoken dialogue, music, and sound effects to create a multimedia experience that approached the experience of seeing an animated film. Instead of using actual frame-by-frame animation, these titles rely on slow pans across the comic frame and on smaller manipulated elements within the frame to suggest movement. The effect is similar to a mock-up of an animated film based on a storyboard. The artwork is much more consistently finished than a storyboard, but there is a lingering sense that the digital comic is only an approximation of its intended result rather than a work demonstrating a unique sensibility.

The difficulty in appreciating digital comics in this format is the way the reader is forced to proceed through the comic at a predetermined pace. It is too slow a pace for all but the slowest readers and can seem like riding an escalator where long before one arrives the destination is a forgone conclusion. So far, the multimedia approach in these digital comics has functioned to forestall or eliminate reading rather than enhance the reading experience. Audiences for these quasi-animated digital comics have been slow to materialize, but they do seem to be growing, especially with the introduction of digitized versions of such popular characters as Spider Woman and the comic series *Watchmen*. Multimedia digital comics of well-known characters have so far remained ancillary to the central media product and have functioned like music videos that are not intended to replace the original music but are one more way to expand a synergistic market strategy.

Starting in 2004, manga publishers and cell phone companies in Japan began cooperating to offer manga to cell phone customers. Within a year, Sony Corporation jumped on board with plans to more than double the number of titles available to more than 300. Cell phone manga has continued to grow at a staggering rate; in 2009, thousands of titles were available and revenue had grown

42 percent from the previous year.[2] Although cell phone manga still represents only a small fraction of print manga sales, industry analysts speculate it may soon become the industry standard. Just as in the United States, one of the chief obstacles to wider digital circulation is the publishers themselves, who are wary to change a business model that has worked for more than 50 years. So far, publishers have not issued many new works digitally but instead have offered a selection of well-established, already published works. Male readers have also been slower to take up cell phone manga reading. Although women represent only a minority of print manga readers, they constitute more than 70 percent of the readers of cell phone manga. Surveys have shown that many older women like the anonymity of the small screen on cell phones because it allows them the privacy to read adult-oriented manga while riding public transportation.

One of the chief reasons publishers have been reticent to enter the digital market is the widespread piracy of digital works. Digital copies are often indistinguishable from originals and can quickly be disseminated over the Internet, severely compromising the value of a legitimate copy being sold. In similar fashion, the music industry faced several years of contracting sales, which they blamed on the impact of widespread illegal downloading of music. Independent studies suggested the problem was the result of not just piracy but also the new competition from DVDs and video games.[3] To combat the problem of piracy, the music industry resorted to litigation against big and small offenders and introduced "digital rights management" (DRM) software to complicate illegal downloading. This DRM software compromised consumer relations, becoming more a liability to manage than acting as an effective deterrent to piracy. In January 2007, EMI was the first studio to end DRM, and within a year, all major labels had ended the practice.

The music industry was able to return to profitability only when an easy alternative to illegal downloading appeared with online music stores that offered the convenience of a large selection at a reasonable price. Apple Computer launched the first successful music player, the iPod (2001), as well as its online music store, iTunes (2001), which has proven that there is a viable market for music despite the easy and ubiquitous piracy of digital files. The comics industry, much like the music industry, has struggled to develop a digital media business model that will provide sustainable profits. The problems facing digital comics are quite similar to those facing digital music, but because of the larger file sizes and higher technical requirements for reading digital comics, the developments have come more slowly.

The online bookstore Amazon.com successfully launched the first e-book reader, the Kindle, in 2007, and the entire initial stock sold out in five hours. Despite the technical limitations, there was clearly an avid audience for electronic books once the proper conditions for ease of use, variety, and cost were met. With its black-and-white screen, the Kindle was easy to read in daylight, but it reproduced graphics poorly and proved wholly unsuitable for digital comics. The Kindle generated new hope for the market of e-book publishing, but the vehicle that will successfully carry digital comics will need to be something with more robust color graphics.

In 2008, Apple created new versions of its popular iPod with a large touch screen and an ability to purchase independently produced applications (apps). It is through this rather smallish hand-held device that a number of apps have vied to develop a comics catalogue and reader similar in design to the Apple iTunes. The iTunes model can be seen in the design of the program Comic-BookLover by Bitcartel Software which allows for easy cataloging of large collections of digital comics in a number of formats. The chief feature it lacks is the ability to easily browse, sample, and buy comics through an online store. The program Comixology has managed the browsing and shopping function with excellent controls for reading a comic on a small screen. Over two dozen publishers sell digital versions of their comics at a reduced cost and often offer the first issue of a series free with the hopes of enticing more readers. All these developments come on the heels of a new digital book reader from Apple, the iPad, with a 10-inch, color, touch-sensitive viewing screen that was made available to the public in April 2010. One of the early popular applications on the iPad was a Marvel Comics app that began to circulate 500 of its backlist comic titles for $1.99 per download. Marvel has also offered dozens of free samples to entice readers into the new format, but many complain about the price—although cheaper than a printed comic that can be as high as $3.99, it is still too high for an impulse purchase.

By June, DC comics joined Marvel by presenting its own app and by August many major U.S. comic book publishers (Dark Horse, Top Cow, IDW, and Archie) had entered the digital market alongside a host of other publishers that provide Japanese manga, European comics, and even the Hindu classics by *Amar Chitra Katha* from India. If the iPad's continued success is anything like that of its predecessor, the iPod, the comics industry will finally have a vehicle to establish a substantial digital market. Publishers still fear this could have a negative impact on the "bricks and mortar" comics retailers, but early evidence suggests that the benefit of enticing new audiences may outweigh the loss of sales.[4] Critics of Apple's iPad say the company is too concerned with controlling content by enforcing a strict ban on what it deems pornographic. This has made some independent comics publishers hesitant to join, especially if it requires them to censor themselves with the uncertain possibility of their content being banned.[5] The iPad platform does have many ways for users to download digital comic files of their own to circumvent the restrictions placed on publishers. Time will tell if this opening is sufficient to make an even greater range of material available.

Do-It-Yourself Comics

A Web site maintained by Greg Galcik, Dysfunctional Family Circus (1995–1999), posted reprints of Bil Keane's syndicated comic *Family Circus*, but without the the original captions, and invited readers to submit their own. Galcik and a few friends sorted though more than 1,000 entries each week to choose a few dozen of the most memorable alternatives. The result was a collection of scatological and crude parodies of the originally chaste material, but there were also many jokes about the agelessness of the family and the rudimentary drawing style of Keane. At its peak, Galcik's Web site had about 70,000 views per day. Then, just prior to posting the 500th comic to his site, Galcik received a letter to cease and desist from King Features, which owned the copyright. Galcik has said he was willing to defend his Web page based on fair use regarding parody, but he received a phone call from Keane and, after a lengthy discussion with the artist, decided he would pull the plug on the project and no longer post new comics or solicit new captions.[6] The content that Galcik generated has been picked up by a number of different Web pages and is still widely available on the Web, underscoring the new challenges that copyright holders have in defending their brands in the digital world.

Established publications have lately gotten behind this do-it-yourself (DIY) participation that the Internet has fostered. Since April 2005, the *New Yorker* magazine has had a very successful run of inviting readers to contribute captions to cartoons drawn by its stable of regular cartoon contributors. Editors sort through about 7,000 entries a week, which they say include only about 50 that are worthy of consideration.[7] All the entries are winnowed down to what the editors consider the three best, and then readers can vote on which one they like the most. This weekly feature was made into a popular board game and has spawned an unaffiliated Web site similar to Galcik's *Dysfunctional Family Circus*, where there is far less editorial restraint and readers can see many more shocking entries. More recently, The *New Yorker* has also hosted online competitions where readers can assemble their own comics from various characters and scenes created by *New Yorker* cartoon artists and graced with their own caption.

Many similar comic generators exist that offer novice cartoonists with minimal artistic skill an opportunity to assemble a comic. Such special software programs as *Comic Life, Comic Book Creator*, and a host of other online applications have made it easier for amateurs to generate comics with any manner of digital images and provide filters that make it possible to "comicify" photographs so they can approximate the garish colors and outsized benday dots of a Lichtenstein painting. A common feature of many new online services is to allow members to generate comics from a store of malleable figures, objects, landscapes, and other emanata. These services are popular because they provide mild creative competition between users who post their work online and vie for more popular ratings. Although nonartists and beginners enjoy the scope of artistic possibilities, the actual work is very limited in style and design, and end-user agreements give the service provider the option to delete any material they deem offensive or obscene.

Comics have long inspired readers to imagine what it would be like to have superhuman powers, and many comic book characters seemed to be ready-made for video games. Games that allowed players act as their favorite superhero and to go on missions have been a persistent feature of video gaming from the very beginning. Lucas Arts had great success with the *Sam and Max Hit the Road* (1993) video game based on Steve Purcell's independent funny-animal comic. But more established characters have had marginal success, and some have even been regarded as the worst video games ever made.[8]

In 2004, a new massively multiplayer online role-playing game (MMORPG) *City of Heroes* by Cryptic Studios and NCsoft proved remarkably popular by allowing a player to design and play his or her own superhero with a distinctive set of powers. As an MMORPG, thousands of players interact as characters of their own eccentric design in a virtual world where they speak to each other through speech bubbles to form superhero groups to fight crime as a team. The game took its comic book origins seriously and was promoted to early subscribers with its own comic book that expanded on the back-story to the gaming world. Later, in November of the same year that *City of Heroes* launched, Marvel Comics brought suit against both software companies alleging copyright infringement. They claimed in their suit that the online game knowingly allowed players to copy such well-known superheroes as Hulk, Wolverine, and Captain America. This was the first time a software company had been accused of copyright infringement because of the actions of its players. Although it seemed that a dangerous precedent might be set if such a suit was successful, the copyright-infringing players turned out to be legal assistants to Marvel Comics, and so the suit was quickly settled out of court. The challenge that Marvel and all the other publishers of comics now face is that the DIY movement gives ordinary players easy tools to engage in virtual superheroics of their own design; with that new-found power, players have usurped the long-standing role of comics as a vehicle for self-reinvention.

Web Comics

The most significant development in the 1990s was a new breed of comics in digital format that were accessible exclusively on the Internet. Web comics had appeared in some of the early manifestations of the Web, but they only really began to take off with the development of more intuitive graphical user inter-faces beginning with Mosaic in 1993, followed by Netscape the following year. Early digital comics were not limited by page size and color-reproduction costs, but they were significantly limited by the narrow bandwidth that fun-neled the digital files from one computer to the next. Although color, sound, and animation were possible, they often remained impractical and were too time consuming, especially when what it seems most readers enjoyed were short, regular installments of comics like those found in the newspapers. Even now as bandwidth restrictions recede, very few online comics have been cre-ated in the long format or in any other format that changes the basic orienta-tion of a comic on a printed page.

In 2000, Scott McCloud came out with his second nonfiction comic about comics called *Reinventing Comics*, in which he examined the prevailing trends and issues confronting digital comics. Here, he advocated for an eventual shift away from the basic orientation of a comic on a page and offered innovative possibilities new comics could explore now that digital comics opened up an "infinite canvas." Despite the possibility of an infinite canvas, most digital comics today employ a comic strip format that fits inside a typical computer screen. That Web comic artists did not broadly embrace the new dynamic flex-ibility of the Internet was in part because of technical limitations that made scrolling through long material tedious, but also because readers were often wary of entering into reading a long Web comic when there was no clear end in sight. Also, the innovative visual effects too often superseded the basic story and undermined the essential invisibility of the mechanisms that made immer-sive reading of the comic possible.

Bill Holbrook was a professional comic strip artist who began circulating a new strip, *Keven and Kell*, in 1995 exclusively on the Internet and through regular postings was able to build up over 3 million views per month. Among the most common advantages that such Web comics offer is instant access to an archive of past material, making it possible to guide readers through more complicated plots. They also allow readers to interact, post comments about the strip, and recognize each other as belonging to the reading community of the strip. The biggest ongoing problem Web comics continues to face is how to harness the casual Web-browsing audience into a reliable source of income. Even with millions of viewers, only a tiny fraction of that number will follow an advertising link, and even fewer have demonstrated a willingness to donate or subscribe to see the content when so much is free. One common way that digital comics has attempted to pay for themselves is through publishing anthologies of past comics; but unlike manga, where the original serialized comic is crudely published, it is much harder to add value to a digital comic in print because the quality of the original is nearly identical to the print and because the Web page already offers an archive of past material, so it is unlikely a reader has missed a past episode. Another option is for an artist to use the characters in the digital comic to generate branded merchandise. Doing so requires much more work and a close relationship with other business partners to function effectively and even then has not proven to be an assured business model with dependable results.

Chris Onstad (b. 1975), through his Web comic, *Achewood* (2001), is among the most successful of online Web comic artists and has exploited every one of the aforementioned strategies to create a dynamic Web presence. Onstad has a large cast of funny-animal characters based on stuffed animals that have distinctive and in some cases disturbing personalities. All the lead characters have their own blogs, where they regularly comment on their various exploits outside the strip. Onstad has also generated short stories, cookbooks, several issues of a zine, and a collection of "greeting cards for men," all fictionally generated by the characters in *Achewood*. Computer technology is the source for a great deal of humor in *Achewood* and many other online comics, but Onstad is far more preposterous and shocking in his scenarios, where he regularly demonstrates his willingness to bend his characters until they very nearly break. The drawing in *Achewood*, as in many Web comics, is rendered with computer-graphic tools and does not have the expressiveness or nuance of a hand drawing. The awkward shorthand Onstad uses often hinders dramatic action, but it does succeed in making the characters appear more outrageous in their far-fetched schemes.

Digital comics are often dependent on the art of quotation, and some of the most innovative digital comics employ simple clip art, snapshots, toys, or screen captures for novel effects. *Get Your War On* by David Rees began shortly after the devastating attacks of September 11, 2001, but it soon branched out to voice humorous and sarcastic commentary on the events of the day, employing a cast of generic clip-art office workers conversing on the phone. Even more reductive to the level of absurdity is Ryan North's *Dinosaur Comics*, which changes only the dialogue between the dinosaurs and has continued to use the exact same images in the same panel layout since 2003. The result is something akin to a Samuel Beckett play, where novel events are forced to occupy a very narrow time, order, and location. The greatest innovation in Web comics has been this kind of minimalism that dares to reduce the comic to the barest abstract relationships as seen in the humorous charts drawn on index cards in Jessica Hagy's *Indexed*. Hagy applies her graphic analysis to the relationships between such ideas as the Tooth Fairy, Santa Claus, and the Easter Bunny, which overlap as a Venn diagram to form a territory marked "Religious Doubt."[9]

Changes to Reading Cultures

In 1995, David Kurlander developed at Microsoft a new variety of online communication called Comic Chat, which allowed members to communicate with each other as if they were characters in an unfolding comic page. Kurlander employed independent comic artist Jim Woodring to take an ordinary chat-room dialogue and turn it into a comic. Kurlander and the other programmers then "reverse engineered" Woodring's comic so that depending on the words and phrases that chat participants used, a suitable comic page would appear looking just like something Woodring could have devised. The word balloons, backgrounds, and body language changed automatically, but the program also provided easy tools for participants to change expressions and gestures as they wanted. Initially, Comic Chat gave participants the option of choosing their online appearance within a range of possibilities created by Woodring; however, as the service grew popular and millions of users entered, thousands of Comic Chat players were given the tools to make their own designs.

In 2001, Microsoft changed its online service and dramatically reduced the availability of Comic Chat. Chat rooms, and now Twitter and texting from cell phones, have continued to flourish with simpler and more direct mechanisms as participants now seem less concerned about maintaining a visual presence while they converse. The demise of Comic Chat raises the question of whether there is a real future for comics in the digital world. Comic Chat itself was not important to the larger comics industry, but the visual structures that informed Comic Chat were the foundation of graphic narrative communication. These structures have developed over the centuries as a means for communicating within the confines of two-dimensional print media. Although there is a logic to these structures in communicating ideas visually that may translate into any new media, there is a real possibility that against video games, 3-D television, virtual reality, and a dozen other yet-undreamed-of technologies, comics as we know them may no longer be necessary.

The great proliferation of Web comics and DIY comics have vastly scattered readers who can communicate within their own specialized interests and using vocabulary, gestures, and images which they find appealing. Such diversity has fragmented the comics audience and made it difficult for critics to make meaningful assessments about comics as fewer and fewer artists find the kind of broad popular support Charles Schulz or Bill Watterson enjoyed. With the diffused and uncertain markets that comics now circulate in, it is also hard to imagine that any artist will ever be able to gain the same kind of reward and international fame as the leaders in the field a century ago were able to achieve.

A few years before his death in 1989, Osamu Tezuka famously warned, "We are now in the condition of manga as air." Tezuka recognized the achievement of the comics medium demonstrated by its ubiquity at the time, but he was wary of assuming that such popularity would inevitably carry forward into the future. For the greatest threat to comics today is not from antipathy but from indifference. Whereas a century ago comics sold newspapers, today it seems unlikely that any future device will be bought simply because it provides access to reading comics. More likely, comics will continue to exist as one type of entertainment among many, but with the potential to still serve as a powerful and exciting engine for generating new ideas.

The language of graphic narratives has already become ubiquitous in the formation of storyboards for all manner of time-based arts such as film, video games, and motion graphics, and now there are new ways that comics are being developed to communicate ideas. Andrew Park, Dan Roam, Austin Kleon, Mike Rohde, Sunni Brown, and Dave Gray, among others, have begun to promote a new kind of visual notetaking called "scribing" or "sketchnoting" that employs the graphic vocabulary of comics to generate a visual record of a lecture or panel discussion. Scribing, when it is done well, does more than illustrate an outline of the presentation; it has a way of drawing out important themes and suggesting new directions. Many of these artists employ scribing in a manner similar to the way that vaudeville chalk-talk performers were a hundred years ago by having the scribing visible to the audience as it unfolds, thereby providing a striking visual process that reinforces the proceedings of an event. The resulting gestalt of the scribing creates a tangible artifact that has a satisfactory feeling of accomplishment and its unique hand-drawn character gives it a sense of spontaneity wholly lacking from most PowerPoint presentations.

It is encouraging to see that over the centuries graphic narratives have continued to evolve into a hybrid word-image language that is well suited to express complex ideas across a variety of print and digital platforms. With its ever-increasing exposure, the vocabulary of possible ideas only grows in complexity as readers become more proficient in understanding old conventions and become more open to developing new ones.

Notes

Introduction

1. David Kunzle mentions the term "graphic narrative" in the second volume of the history of the comic strip, but he does not define or delimit the term except to imply that it refers broadly to everything included in his book *History of the Comic Strip, Volume 2: The Nineteenth Century* (Berkeley: University of California Press, 1990).
2. Wolfgang Kemp, "Narrative" in *Critical Terms for Art History*, ed. Robert S. Nelson and Richard Shiff (Chicago: University of Chicago Press, 2003), 62.
3. Lera Boroditsky, "How Does Language Shape the Way We Think," *Edge* (2009), www.edge.org (accessed July 22, 2010).
4. David Kunzle, *The Early Comic Strip: Narrative Strips and Picture Stories in the European Broadsheet from c. 1450 to 1825* in *History of the Comic Strip, Volume 1* (Berkeley: University of California Press, 1973), 3.
5. Peter Brooks, *The Melodramatic Imagination: Balzac, Henry James, Melodrama, and the Mode of Excess* (New Haven, CT: Yale University Press, 1976), 206.
6. Rodolphe Töpffer, *Enter: The Comics*, trans. and ed. Ellen Wiese (Lincoln: University of Nebraska Press, 1965), 11.
7. Scott McCloud, *Understanding Comics: The Invisible Art*, Harper Perennial ed. (New York: HarperCollins, 1994), 34–37.
8. The term "path" is similar to the term "vector," used extensively in Gunther Kress and Theo van Leeuwen, *Reading Images: The Grammar of Visual Design*, 2nd ed. (New York: Routledge, 2006).
9. The term "emanata" was coined by Mort Walker in his *Lexicon of Comicana* (Port Chester, NY: Comicana, 1980), though for a slightly different purpose. The term has been used to describe any visual manifestations of a character's interior thoughts. The term is used here more generically to cover all those

expressions as well as expressions enclosed in scrolls, balloons, bubbles, explosions, and clouds to represent speech or thought.

10. This particular *Nancy* comic strip is examined in further detail by Mark Newgarden and Paul Karasik in their insightful essay "How to Read Nancy" (1988). This essay was further expanded into a book of the same name from Fantagraphics Press (Seattle, WA, 2010).

11. Boris Breiger, "The Use of the W-B Picture Arrangement Subtest as a Projective Technique." *Journal of Consulting Psychology* 20, no. 2 (1956): 132.

Chapter 1

1. Christopher Anderson and Françoise Dussart, "Dreamings in Acrylic: Western Desert Art," in *Dreamings: The Art of Aboriginal Australia*, ed. Peter Sutton, 89–141 (New York: G. Braziller in association with Asia Society Galleries, 1988).

2. Candace S. Greene, "Structure and Meaning in Cheyenne Ledger Art," in *Plains Indian Drawings, 1865–1935: Pages from a Visual History*, ed. Janet Catherine Berlo (New York: Abrams, 1996), p. 26.

3. Meyer Schapiro, *Words and Pictures. On the Literal and the Symbolic in the Illustration of a Text, Approaches to Semiotics*. Paperback series, 11. (The Hague: Mouton, 1973), 18–35.

4. There is much confusion between scholars about the specific terms related to narrative art, especially regarding the distinction between synoptic and continuous narrative. For the purpose of consistency and clarity, this book has adopted the definitions established by Vidya Dehejia, which differ from those of A. M. Snodgrass in that Dehejia considers multiple representations of a character within a single-frame to be a synoptic narrative, distinguishing them from the longer continuous narratives that cannot be taken in all at once.

5. Jocelyn Penny Small, "Time in Space: Narrative in Classical Art," *Art Bulletin* 81 (1999): 562–75.

6. Victor H. Mair, *Painting and Performance: Chinese Picture Recitation and Its Indian Genesis* (Honolulu: University of Hawaii Press, 1988).

7. This *patua* performance was commissioned for the bicentennial of the French Revolution under the patronage of the director of Alliance Française de Calcutta, Michael Carriere.

8. Frank J Korom, *Village of Painters: Narrative Scrolls from West Bengal* (Santa Fe: Museum of New Mexico Press, 2006).

9. Julia K. Murray, "Buddhism and Early Narrative Illustration in China." *Archives of Asian Art* 48 (1995): 17–31.

Chapter 2

1. The more common usage of "phylactery" is an amulet that is worn for protection against evil spirits. The amulet derives its power from a small scroll on

which scripture or magical passages are written. The word phylactery comes from the Greek verb *phykatti*, meaning "to protect." The Rosetta Stone mentions a golden phylakteria worn by Egyptian kings to protect them from malign influences. The practice is maintained by orthodox practitioners of the Jewish faith, and similar amulets are still worn by the Berber and Tuareg peoples in North Africa. For more on the origin and development of phylacteries, see Robert Petersen, "Metamorphosis of the Phylactery: Changes in Emanata from the Medieval Times through the 18th Century," *International Journal of Comic Art* 10, no. 1 (2008): 226–247.

2. Laura Kendrick, *Animating the Letter: The Figurative Embodiment of Writing from Late Antiquity to the Renaissance* (Columbus: Ohio State University Press, 1999).

3. David Kunzle, *The Early Comic Strip: Narrative Strips and Picture Stories in the European Broadsheet from c. 1450 to 1825* in *History of the Comic Strip, Volume 1* (Berkeley: University of California Press, 1973), 20.

4. Prices were seldom printed on broadsheets before the 18th century, so it is difficult to ascertain the precise cost of these items. Kunzle, *The Early Comic Strip*, 426.

5. Translated in Kunzle, *The Early Comic Strip*, 176.

6. David Bland, *A History of Book Illustration: The Illuminated Manuscript and the Printed Book*, 2nd rev. ed. (Berkeley: University of California Press, 1969), 104.

7. Translated in Kunzle, *The Early Comic Strip*, 29.

8. David Carrier, *The Aesthetics of Comics* (University Park: Pennsylvania State University Press, 2000), 41.

9. Amelia F. Rauser, *Caricature Unmasked: Irony, Authenticity, and Individualism in Eighteenth-Century English Prints*, University of Delaware Press Studies in Seventeenth- and Eighteenth-Century Art and Culture (Newark: University of Delaware Press, 2008), 26.

Chapter 3

1. Virginia Skord Waters, "Sex, Lies, and the Illustrated Scroll: The Dojoji Engi Emaki." *Monumenta Nipponica* 52, no. 1 (Spring, 1997): 59–84.

2. *Giga* is also used to describe any casual or humorous drawing, but this has largely been supplanted by the more commonly used term "manga."

3. One of the earliest known uses of the word comes from Jin Nong (1687–1763), a Chinese scholar who described his casual sketches (*manhua*) of plums in a self-effacing literati manner.

4. Adam L. Kern. *Manga from the Floating World: Comicbook Culture and the Kibyoshi of Edo Japan*, Harvard East Asian Monographs 279 (Cambridge, MA: Harvard University Asia Center, Harvard University Press, 2006).

5. The complete title of the production was "The Harlot's Progress; or the Ridotto al Fresco: a Grotesque Pantomime Entertainment." Quoted in Martin Meisel, *Realizations: Narrative, Pictorial, and Theatrical Arts in Nineteenth Century England* (Princeton, NJ: Princeton University Press, 1983), 99.

6. Algernon Graves, "Old Prints and Their Engravers, and Coloured Books," in *The Collector*, Vol. 3, ed. Ethel Deane (London: Horace Cox, 1907), 252.

7. Second ed., p. 51. Reprinted in Kunzle, *The History of the Comic Strip*, 198.

8. Kunzle, *The Early Comic Strip*, 29.

9. David Kunzle, "Goethe and Caricature: From Hogarth to Töpffer," *Journal of the Warburg and Courtauld Institutes* 48 (1985), 164–188.

Chapter 4

1. The Roman philosopher Horace famously wrote, "*Ut pictura poesis*" ("As is poetry so is painting"), which was understood to mean that painting and poetry sprung from a common source; but following the collapse of the tower of Babel and the subsequent scattering of all human languages, it was believed, painting remained a more primal form of communication, which could communicate more directly and universally to all people.

2. David Kunzle, *The Early Comic Strip: Narrative Strips and Picture Stories in the European Broadsheet from c. 1450 to 1825* in *History of the Comic Strip, Volume 1* (Berkeley: University of California Press, 1973), 419–422.

3. Janis A. Tomlinson, *Francisco Goya: The Tapestry Cartoons and Early Career at the Court of Madrid* (Cambridge: Cambridge University Press, 1989), 220–223.

4. Douglas W. Druick and Peter Kort Zegers, "Odilon Redon: The Image and the Text," in *Odillon Redon: The Prince of Dreams, 1840–1916*, ed. Douglas W. Druick (New York: H. N. Abrams, 1994), 137.

5. Fred Leeman, "Changing Directions, 1890–1900: Redon and the Transformation of the Symbolist Aesthetic," in *Odillon Redon: The Prince of Dreams, 1840–1916*, ed. Douglas W Druick (New York: H. N. Abrams, 1994), 180.

6. Wassily Kandinsky, *Sounds*, trans. Elizabeth R. Napier (New Haven, CT: Yale University Press, 1981), 17.

7. David Kunzle, "Voices of Silence," in *The Language of Comics: Word and Image*, ed. Robin Varnum and Christine T. Gibbons (Jackson: University Press of Mississippi, 2001), 3–18.

8. Lothar Lang, *Expressionist Book Illustration in Germany, 1907–1927*, trans. Janet Seligman (Boston: New York Graphic Society, 1976), 69–70.

9. Later sources of the woodcut attempted to claim that the image was medieval in origin, but all evidence suggests that it was commissioned for Camille Flammarion's *L'Atmosphere: Météorologie Populaire* (Paris, 1888), 163.

10. Thomas Mann, Introduction to Masereel's *Passionate Journey*, reprinted in Jeet Heer and Kent Worcester, *Arguing Comics: Literary Masters on a Popular Medium* (Jackson: University Press of Mississippi, 2004).

11. Samantha Kavky suggests that Loplop, who appears in many paintings and collages in Ernst's work at this time, is an alter-ego of Ernst himself. Loplop functions in the same manner as Freud's father or totem as a way of asserting Ernst's creative rebellion from the conventional role of an artist. Samantha Kavky, "Authorship and Identity in Max Ernst's Loplop," *Art History* 28, no. 3 (2005): 357–385.

12. Charlotte Stokes, "Collage as Jokework: Freud's Theories of Wit as the Foundation for the Collages of Max Ernst." *Leonardo* 15, no. 3 (1982): 199–204.

13. M. E. Warlick, "Max Ernst's Alchemical Novel: 'Une semaine de bonté.'" *Art Journal* 46, no. 1 (Spring, 1987): 61–73.

14. *A Week of Kindness* (*Une semain de bonté*) was created during a three-week stay in Italy in 1933 and was created from a number of Victorian sources, including some of Gustave Doré's illustrations.

15. "Pablo Picasso: Dream and Lie of Franco (1986.1224.1[2])," in *Timeline of Art History* (New York: Metropolitan Museum of Art, 2000).

16. Wolfsohn published his theories about voice and art in his book *Orpheus, or the Way to a Mask* (*Orpheus oder der Weg zu einer Maske*) (Berlin 1938).

17. Charlotte Salomon, *Life? or Theatre?* trans. Leila Vennewitz (Zwolle, Neth.: Wanders Publishers, 1998), 20.

18. Salomon, 819.

19. Salomon, 820.

Chapter 5

1. Carlos Franciscato, "Journalism and Change in Experience of Time in Western Societies," *Brazilian Journalism Research* 1, no. 1 (2005): 167.

2. David Kunzle, *History of the Comic Strip, Volume 2: The Nineteenth Century* (Berkeley: University of California Press, 1990), 348–349.

3. Napoleon Bonaparte instituted the law of preliminary authorization in 1800. The law was abolished in 1814 and reinstated between 1820 and 1830, only to be abolished for the next five years and reinstated once again in 1835 until 1848. The law was reinstated once more during the Second Empire of Napoleon III and was not finally abolished until 1881. See Paul Jobling and David Crowley, *Graphic Design: Reproduction and Representation since 1800*, Studies in Design and Material Culture (New York: St. Martin's Press, 1996), 43–44.

4. Robert J. Goldstein, "Fighting French Censorship, 1815–1881," *The French Review* 71, no. 5 (1998): 785–796.

5. Alexander Roob, "Against Daumier: A Revision of Early French Caricature and Social Graphics" (abridged version) Melton Prior Institut (May 2010).

Available online at http://www.meltonpriorinstitut.org/pages/textarchive.php5 ?view=text&ID=74&language=English.

6. Translation from the French by Clive F. Getty "Max Ernst and J. J. Grand-ville" in *Twenty-First-Century Perspectives on Nineteenth-Century Art: Essays in Honor of Gabriel P. Weisberg*, ed. Laurinda S. Dixon and Petra ten-Doesschate Chu (Newark: University of Delaware Press, 2008) 121.

7. Grandville's iconography was not entirely without literary precedent. He and several of the other caricaturists who worked for Philipon were inspired by the utopian fantasies of Charles Fourier (1772–1837).

8. *Punch, or The London Charivari* 5 (1843): 23.

9. R. C. Harvey, "Comedy at the Juncture of Word and Image," in *Language of Comics: Word and Image*. ed. Robin Varnum and Christina T. Gibbons (Jackson: University Press of Mississippi, 2007), 77.

10. Thomas Gretton, ed. *Murders and Moralities: English Catchpenny Prints, 1800–1860* (London: British Museum Publications, 1980), 20.

11. Roland Barthes, "The World of Wrestling," in *Mythologies* (New York: Noonday Press, 1957), 18–19.

12. Kunzle, *History of the Comic Strip, Volume 2*, 258.

13. Roger Sabin, "Ally Sloper: The First Comics Superstar?" reprinted in *Comics Studies Reader*, ed. Jeet Heer and Kent Worchester (Jackson: University Press of Mississippi, 2008), 177–189.

14. J. L. Thompson, *Northcliffe: Press Baron in Politics, 1865–1922* (London: John Murray, 2000), 18.

15. Cited in Brian Walker, *The Comics: Before 1945*, ed. Brian Slovak (New York: Harry N. Abrams, 2004), 9.

16. Wayne Morgan, "Palmer Cox, the Brownie Craze and the Brownie Camera" (Paper presented at the Photographic Historical Society of Canada, March 21, 2007). Available online at www.phsc.ca/Brownie2007.html.

Chapter 6

1. Walter Ong, *Orality and Literacy: The Technologizing of the Word* (New York: Routledge, 1988).

2. H. L. Mencken, *The American Language: A Preliminary Inquiry into the Development of English in the United States* (New York: A. A. Knopf, 1919).

3. Harlan Tarbell, *How to Chalk Talk* (Minneapolis: T. S. Denison and Co., 1924), 20–23.

4. Mark Winchester, "Litigation and Early Comic Strips: The Lawsuits of Outcault, Dirks and Fisher," *Inks* 2, no. 2 (May 1995): 16–25.

5. In an interview in the *Atlanta Constitution*, June 11, 1911, McCay discussed the way he makes "mind sketches," by making a detailed mental sketch. He stated, "Simply because I have studied these things with my eyes; I have put

them up in my cranium, and they will be there till I need them." Reprinted in *The Complete Dream of the Rarebit Fiend (1904–1913) by Winsor McCay 'Silas'*, ed. Ulrich Merkl (Marienberg, Germany: Beduinenzelt, 2007), 135.

6. Roy L. McCardell, "Opper, Outcault & Company," *Everybody's Magazine* 12 (June 1905), 766.

7. Clare Briggs in his book *How to Draw Comics* (Chicago: Frederick J. Drake, 1937, 23) advises comic artists working for a syndicate, "It is imperative that you confine yourself to general ideas."

8. The National Cartoonists Society (founded in 1946) under the suggestion of Al Capp considered taking action as a trade union to secure better contracts for its members and eliminate the work-for-hire status. This idea foundered when the group recognized it had no power against the hegemony of the comics syndicates. Only the most popular comic artists, among them Milt Caniff, Al Capp, and Walt Kelly, were eventually able to wrest control of their work from the syndicates. See Brian Walker, *The Comics: Before 1945*, ed. Brian Slovak (New York: Harry N. Abrams, 2004), 358.

9. Frank King, *Gasoline Alley*.

10. Chic Young, *Blondie*.

11. George McManus, *Bringing Up Father*.

12. Herriman had tried out a few other funny-animal strips prior to *Krazy Kat*. In 1909, with the World Color Printing Company, Herriman created *Alexander Cat* and *Daniel and Pansy*, which appeared briefly before *Gooseberry Spring*. By late January 1910, *Gooseberry Spring* had ended and Herriman soon began work on *The Dingbat Family*.

13. George Herriman, Patrick McDonnell, Karen O'Connell, and Georgia Riley De Havenon, *Krazy Kat: The Comic Art of George Herriman* (New York: H. N. Abrams, 1986), 54.

14. Gilbert Seldes, "The Krazy Kat That Walks by Himself" in *The Seven Lively Arts* (New York: Sagamore Press, 1957), 245.

15. *Krazy Kat*, September 13, 1940.

16. Herriman also showed great deference for Navaho custom, art, and design in his strip, responding to the bold geometry of Navaho rugs and silverwork in the patterns that filled out the comic panels. Furthermore, there is a mystical reverence for nature in *Krazy Kat*. See Herriman et al., *Krazy Kat*, 73–76.

17. Donald Crafton, *Before Mickey: The Animated Film, 1898–1928* (Chicago: University of Chicago Press, 1993), 81–84.

Chapter 7

1. Most of the people hired to clerical status were Hindus of the Kshatriya caste. They were not from the highest caste, Brahman, nor were they from the lower castes, Vaishya or Sudra.

2. Aruna Rao, "From Self-Knowledge to Super Heroes: The Story of Indian Comics" in *Illustrating Asia: Comics, Humor Magazines, and Picture Books*, ed. John A. Lent (Honolulu: University of Hawaii Press, 2001), 41–42.

3. Although 38 languages is quite an accomplishment in publishing a single title, it must be put in the context of India, where there are 22 national languages, public schools teach 58 languages, and newspapers are printed in 87 different languages.

4. As James A. Flath observed of these prints, "While an expansion of print capitalism could be used to promote new freedoms for women, it could also objectify women in new and entirely novel ways." From *The Cult of Happiness: Nianhua, Art, and History in Rural North China*. Contemporary Chinese Studies (Vancouver: UBC Press, 2004), 132.

5. Jin Nong (1687–1763), in a self-effacing manner, used the word "*manhua*" to describe his casual sketches of plums.

6. Jean Chesneaux, *The People's Comic Book, Red Women's Detachment, Hot on the Trail and Other Chinese Comics,* intro. Gino Nebiolo, trans. Frances Frenaye (Garden City, NY: Anchor Press, 1973), 5.

7. Translated in *Rosetta 2: A Comics Anthology,* ed. Ng Suat Tong (Gainesville, FL: Alternative Comics, 2004), 90.

8. Seth Faison, "Beijing Journal; If It's a Comic Book, Why Is Nobody Laughing?" *New York Times* (August 17, 1999).

Chapter 8

1. Hugo Gernsback preferred the term "scientifiction," which was coined to describe a type of fiction based more on scientific fact than fantasy. His magazine was actually a broad mix of fiction that included generous portions of both science and fantasy.

2. Bill Blackbeard, "Artist of the Absurd," in *Tarzan in Color*, Vol. 1, 1931–1932 (New York: Flying Buttress Classics Library).

3. *Comic Book Marketplace* #121 (Gemstone Publishing, May 2005), 12.

4. Jules Feiffer, *The Great Comic Book Heroes* (New York: Dial Press, ca. 1965), 39.

5. Umberto Eco, "The Myth of Superman," originally published as "Il mito di Superman e la dissolozione del tempo" (1962), trans. Natalie Chilton for *Diacritics* 2, no. 1 (1972).

6. *Detective Comics* #38 (1940).

7. *Wonder Woman* #3 (February–March 1942), 3.

8. William Moulton Marston, "Why 100,000,000 Americans Read Comics," *The American Scholar* 13, no. 1 (1943–44), 41.

9. *Detective Comics, Inc. v. Bruns Publications, Inc., et al.*, April 29, 1940.

10. Ken Quattro posted the entire court record on his blog, *The Comics Detective* "DC VS VICTOR FOX: The Testimony of Will Eisner" (Thursday, July 1, 2010), thecomicsdetective.blogspot.com.

Chapter 9

1. *Stars and Stripes,* 1945.
2. There is no publication information that provides a date for *Romantic Picture Novelettes*, but best estimates suggest that it appeared sometime after 1946.
3. Interview with Ric Estrada by John Benson, *Published in Confessions, Romances, Secrets, and Temptations: Archer St. John and the St. John Romance Comics* (Seattle: Fantagraphics Books, 2007), 55–61.
4. "Judgement Day," *Weird Fantasy* #18 (Joe Orlando); "The Guilty," *Shock and Suspense* #3 (Wally Wood); "The Monkey," *Shock and Suspense* #12 (Joe Orlando); and "Hate," *Shock and Suspense* #5 (Wally Wood).
5. Amy Kiste Nyberg, *Seal of Approval: The History of the Comics Code*, Studies in Popular Culture (Jackson: University Press of Mississippi, 1998), 125–126.
6. Andrei Molotiu, "Kirby after Lichtenstein" presented at the national College Art Association Conference in Chicago, Feburary 13, 2010.
7. *Green Lantern/Green Arrow* #76 (May 1970), story by Denny O'Neil, pencils by Neil Adams, and inks by Dick Giordano.
8. Bill Watterson 1989, quoted in Michael G. Rhode, "The Commercialization of Comics: A Broad Historic Overview," *International Journal of Comic Art* 1, no. 2 (Fall 1999): 149.
9. *The Savage She-Hulk* #1 (1979).
10. The Marvel series *Contest of Champions* was published from June to August 1982 and was written by Mark Gruenwald with art by John Romita Jr. and Bob Layton.
11. The DC series *Crisis on Infinite Earths* was written by Marv Wolfman with art by George Pérez, Mike DeCarlo, Dick Giordano, and Jerry Ordway.
12. Chuck Rozanski, "Death of Superman" Promotion of 1992, *Tales from the Database*, blog posted July 2004.

Chapter 10

1. Yoshihiro Tatsumi, *A Drifting Life* (Montreal: Drawn and Quarterly Press, 2009), 625.
2. Fred Patten has chronicled much of the debate on whether Disney copied Tezuka in his essay "Simba versus Kimba: The Pride of Lions," republished in his anthology of collected essays, *Watching Anime, Reading Manga* (Berkeley, CA: Stone Bridge Press, 2004). Although Patten stops short of indicting

Disney for copyright infringement, the case for close imitation is strong. Disney, and especially the directors of *The Lion King*, are remiss in not acknowledging their debt to Tezuka.

3. Natsu Onoda Power, *Osamu Tezuka: God of Comics and the Creation of Post–World War II Manga* (Jackson: University Press of Mississippi, 2009), 78.

4. The literal translation of "*Hana no nijuunyo nen gumi*" refers to the 24th year of the Showa era in the Japanese calendar, which corresponds to 1949 in the Western Gregorian calendar.

5. *Bessatsu Shoujo Comic*, September to November 1975 (Shogakukan Publishing).

6. "Hanshin: Half God" first published in *Petit Flower*, January 1984 (Shogakukan Publishing).

7. Hye-Kyung Lee, "Between Fan Culture and Copyright Infringement: Manga Scanlation," *Media Culture & Society* 31 (2009): 1019.

Chapter 11

1. This quote Reinhardt later attributed to the painter Wolfgang Paalen (1907–1959).

2. "Fourteen Americans," curated by Dorthy C. Miller at the Museum of Modern Art, New York, 1946.

3. *New York Times*, September 8, 1946.

4. Harold Rosenberg, "The Labyrinth of Saul Steinberg," in *The Anxious Object and Its Audience* (New York: Horizon Press, 1966).

5. W. J. T. Mitchell, *Picture Theory* (Chicago: University of Chicago Press, 1994), 42.

6. Eugène Ionesco, Introduction to *Pierre Alechinsky* (New York: Abrams, 1977), 16.

7. René Viénet, "The Situationists and the New Forms of Struggle against Politics and Art," trans. and ed. Christopher Gray, in *Leaving the Twentieth Century* (London: Rebel Press, 1998). Prior to these comments, there is no other discussion of the practice of creating *détourned* comics.

8. "The Beginning of an Era," part 2, "Le commencement d'une époque," *Internationale Situationniste* #12 (Paris, September 1969), translated by Ken Knabb in the *Situationist International Anthology*, revised and expanded edition (Berkeley, CA: Bureau of Public Secrets, 2006).

9. This dialogue is actually a quote from Michèle Bernstein's 1960 novel *All the King's Horses*.

10. "The Beginning of an Era," part 2.

11. Michael Auping, *Jess, a Grand Collage, 1951–1993* (Buffalo, NY: Albright-Knox Art Gallery, 1993).

12. John T. Spike, "Switch Hitter," *Art & Antiques* 27 (2004): 96.

13. A version of this peculiar character would appear on the front and back covers of *Weirdo* #7 (1983) by Robert Crumb as a tribute to Guston. Some critics have speculated that Crumb influenced Guston's new style, when in fact it seems they arrived at their own styles about the same time and independent of each other.

14. Debra Bricker Balken, *Philip Guston's Poor Richard* (Chicago: University of Chicago Press, 2001).

15. The full title of Darger's work was "The Story of the Vivian Girls, in What Is Known as the Realms of the Unreal, of the Glandeco-Angelinnian War Storm, Caused by the Child Slave Rebellion."

16. Michael Kimmelman, "The Underbelly Artist," *New York Times Magazine*, October 9, 2005.

17. Art Spiegelman, "High Art Lowdown," *Artforum* #29, December, 1990.

Chapter 12

1. "Superduperman" was scripted by Kurtzman with art by Wally Wood.

2. Mark James Estren, *A History of Underground Comics* (San Francisco: Straight Arrow Books; distributed by Quick Fox, 1974), 38.

3. "From Eternity Back to Here," *MAD* #12, 1954.

4. "Jackson Pollock: Is He the Greatest Living Painter in the United States?" *LIFE*, August 8, 1949, 42–45.

5. Gary Groth discovered that the copyright to the story *Goodman Beaver Goes Playboy* had not been renewed by Archie Comics, so it now resides in the public domain. *Comics Journal*, May 2008, http://www.tcj.com/.

6. "Fritz the Cat Superstar," from *Police Comics*, 1972.

7. Bob Levin, *The Pirates and the Mouse: Disney's War against the Counter Culture* (Seattle: Fantagraphic Books, 2003), 80.

8. Levin, 226.

9. "Tintin: A Very European Hero," *The Economist*, December 18, 2008.

10. *Adventures into Fear* #19, Man-Thing, December 1973.

11. *Howard the Duck* #1, written by Steve Gerber and illustrated by John Buscema.

12. Participants at the meeting on the Creator's Bill of Rights included Scott McCloud, Dave Sim, Gerhard, Steve Bissette, Rick Veitch, Larry Marder, Kevin Eastman, Peter Laird, Mark Martin, Steve Murphy, Michael Zulli, Eric Talbot, Ken Mitchroney, Michael Dooney, Steve Lavigne, Craig Farley, Jim Lawson, and Ryan Brown.

13. Alessandra Stanley, " 'Thousand Acres' Wins Fiction as 21 Pulitzer Prizes Are Given," *New York Times*, April 8, 1992.

14. Interview with Andrea Juno, 1997, published in *Art Spiegelman: Conversations*, ed. Joseph Witek (Jackson: University Press of Mississippi, 2007), 185.

15. Neil Gaiman's *Sandman* #19 won the World Fantasy Award in 1991, Chris Ware's *Jimmy Corrigan, the Smartest Kid on Earth* won the American Book Award and the Guardian First Award in 2001, and Gene Luen Yang's *American Born Chinese* was a finalist for the National Book Award in 2006.

Chapter 13

1. *Shatter* was first published in the British computer publication *Big K* #12 (March 1985) and then published as a comic by First Comics, based in Evanston, Illinois.

2. Miki Tanikawa, "Mobile Gives Manga a Lift," *New York Times*, Technology Section, August 3, 2009.

3. John Borland, "Music Industry: Piracy Is Choking Sales," *CNET News*, April 9, 2003.

4. Henry Hanks, "iPad Boosts Appeal of Digital Comics," CNN online, August 12, 2010.

5. The actual terms that Apple dictates to publishers are shrouded in secrecy due to a nondisclosure clause that all developers of iPad apps must sign. Cory Doctorow, "Why I Won't Buy an iPad (and Think You Shouldn't, Either)" BoingBoing.com, April 2, 2010.

6. James Glave, "Family Circus Parody Folds Tent," *Wired Magazine*, September 1999.

7. Ramin Setoodeh, "Behind the Scenes: At the Caption Contest," *Newsweek*, December 11, 2006.

8. Superman for the Nintendo 64 game system was the lowest-rated superhero game featured in the *Guinness World Records Gamer's Edition 2009* (New York: Time Home Entertainment, 2009).

9. Jessica Hagy, "How Tenuous, That Imaginary Friendship," *Indexed*, August 9, 2006.

Glossary

bande dessinée: Comic book, from French meaning "drawings in a row."

banderole: Flag-shaped form that encapsulates text used for indicating the voice of a character. See also *phylactery*, and *emanata*.

benday dots: A printing technique used for rendering halftones and color mixing by laying down uniform tiny dot patterns.

caricature: To distort the features of an individual's portrait as a way of exaggerating personality characteristics.

chiaroscuro: Strong contrasts in light and dark that often help define the volume of an object.

collage: Using pieces of found drawings or photographs to assemble a new picture.

conflation: When a single event is expanded to include later or earlier actions allowing for more to happen within a single frame without any repetition of characters.

continuous narrative: Technique of showing consecutive episodes side-by-side against an apparently continuous background.

cyclic narrative: Multiple-frame narrative art that connects various scenes in a thematic way. Often cyclic narratives will have a clear beginning and ending, but the intermediate sequences are more arbitrary. There is no sense of causality between the separate frames, and it is very difficult to understand a cyclic narrative just by looking at the pictures. Cyclic narratives often depend on literature or an interlocutor to explain the story.

détournement: French, meaning "to turn aside," a technique used by the Situationists as a way to subvert popular culture by inserting new text into speech bubbles or adding speech bubbles and new political texts to images.

diachronic: Something that happens over time such as a sequence of events.

digital comic: Comic that has been digitized and read by means of an electronic device, such as a computer or cell phone.

dramatic sequential narrative: Multiframe narrative where the frames or panels are linked together in closely related actions.

emanata: Visual elements that describe such invisible phenomena as voices, sounds, explosions, and motion.

engraving: Print process that uses a sharp metal tool, a burin, to cut fine lines into a metal surface. Ink is applied to the plate so that it fills the cut grooves, and when paper is pressed hard against the plate, it lifts some of the ink from the cut groove.

epic sequential narrative: Series of pictures that are causally linked together though the amount of time between one picture and another is nonspecific and may suggest that days, weeks, months, or even years have passed.

frame: The border surrounding an image that encapsulates an image or a portion of an image.

gekiga: Japanese term used to distinguish adult-oriented comics from children's manga.

graphic narrative: Static image that tells a story both synchronically and diachronically.

graphic novel: Longer-format comic book. Sometimes this is an original work or often it can be a compilation of smaller volues published earlier.

kamishibai: A Japanese picture-recitation tradition that flourished early in the 20th century when paper was scarce because of rationing during World War II.

lianhuanhua: Form of sequential narrative developed in China in the late 19th century. Typically appeared as a small pocket-sized book with a picture on each page and a caption above or below describing the action and dialogue.

ligne claire: French, meaning "clear line," when all the lines in a drawing are given equal weight with a minimum of shading.

lithography: Form of printmaking that was developed from printing oil-based inks on wet sandstone slabs.

manga: Comic book, from Japanese term based on the Chinese word manhua.

manhua: Comic book, from Chinese, meaning "impromptu sketches."

miscellany: A collection of images on a page that can form a panoramic narrative mode where there is no repetition of characters or a synoptic narrative where one character is depicted many times. Popular in Victorian England, the miscellany was an early advertising strategy that gave the impression of abundance.

monoscenic narrative: Single-frame narrative image that has no repetition of characters, actions, or scenes. A monoscenic narrative often encapsulates a climactic or crucial moment in a longer story.

montage: A sequence of images that collectively communicate an idea due to their selection, order, and design.

narrative: A representation of a story or an event.

oral culture: Culture that does not have literacy.

panel: Discernible area that contains a moment in the story, a distinct visual encapsulation of a moment, similar to visual loci or frame.

panoramic narrative: Large composition that depicts several events all happening about the same time.

path: Line or direction that is either explicit or implied in a composition. Paths may or may not imply narrative, but all narrative depends on the existence of paths so that there is a clear progression in the sequence of the narrative.

phylactery: Scroll-like shape encapsulating a passage of text that is meant to represent a voice. Phylacteries emanate from the mouth or hand of one figure and often arc toward the person being spoken to.

picture recitation: Performance where a storyteller uses a picture as an aid to telling a story.

progressive narrative: Story that is told along a wide picture, where the story unfolds in one direction like a parade of individual characters who are not repeated.

register: A line that demarcates one portion of a page from another to aid in defining a narrative path. Similar to lines on a page that are used to order rows of text.

scanlation: Digitally scanned comic that has been translated. Typically, scanlations are Japanese-language manga that have been scanned and translated without the original artist's or publisher's consent.

sequential narrative: Story made of several linked images that represent a deliberate order of actions that lead from one to the other. Cumulatively, a sequential narrative evokes the idea of a montage.

serial narrative: Short sequences that appear independently that slowly make up a longer story.

simultaneous narrative: Two or more overlapping stories within a single frame. Often found as a graphic narrative mode in oral cultures.

speech balloons or **speech bubbles**: Ways to represent speech using round forms that are often placed above the character's head with a tail pointing downward to the figure speaking.

splash page: Full-page or large picture that introduces the story or indicates a dramatic event. A splash page functions in a similar way as a monoscenic narrative.

split panel: Large single image broken up into smaller panels or frames.

synchronic: Something that appears all at once or is seen all at one time.

synoptic narrative: Composition that has a single background but several representations of a character or several characters that are in motion.

visual loci: Point or area of visual focus, framed or unframed, often defined by converging paths.

Web comic: Comic that appears on the World Wide Web and is accessible through the Internet by means of a computer.

woodcut: Print process where a relief print is made from a woodblock. A woodcut is one of the oldest-known forms of printing.

wood engraving: Print process where engraved lines are cut into end-grain woodblocks.

Index

About the Author

ROBERT S. PETERSEN is an associate professor of art at Eastern Illinois University in Charleston. Previous essays include research on the role of sound in Japanese manga and the evolution of the speech bubble in British satirical prints from the 16th to the 17th century. Dr. Petersen was a Fulbright Scholar to Indonesia and has also written extensively on traditional dramatic art of Java and India.